SHIPS AND SEALING WAX
AND MANY THINGS

SS Ohio Wheel and Bell

To Brian,
With all best wishes and
"Many Happy Returns"!
from Roger Paine.
June 2018.

SHIPS AND SEALING WAX
AND MANY THINGS

by

ROGER PAINE

WWW.PENMOREPRESS.COM

i

All ship photographs are from the National Museum of the Royal Navy.
Thanks to the Honourable Company of Master Mariners for the image of the SS *Ohio* Wheel and Bell.

ISBN-13:-978-1-946409-17-1 (e-book)
ISBN-13:-978-1-946409-16-4 (Paperback)

BISAC Subject Headings:
FIC014000FICTION / Historical
FIC032000FICTION / War & Military

Copy Edit: Lauren McElroy

Cover Illustration by Christine Horner   .

Address all correspondence to:

Penmore Press LLC
920 N Javelina Pl
Tucson, AZ 85748

AUTHOR'S INTRODUCTION

The room where I write, with exposed timber beams—some of which may have come from broken-up wooden sailing ships —and surrounded by shelves overflowing with books, paintings, photographs and memorabilia accumulated from around the world during many years in the Royal Navy, might seem an idyllic place for a writer. In some ways it is.

But the historic ambience of my surroundings in a cottage, one of six built some 250 years ago inside the boundary of an ancient churchyard and a short walk from the medieval church, can sometimes distract. Looking out through the lattice windows onto a historic churchyard, last used for burials in the nineteenth century, lighting an open log fire in the inglenook fireplace in winter, or watching butterflies clinging to the buddleia which overgrows the path past my front door in summer, has a tendency to divert one's thought processes.

When this happens, I am reminded of the Victorian novelist and poet Lewis Carroll and the surrealist world he often depicted, typified in his poem "The Walrus and the Carpenter":

> "The time has come," the Walrus said,
> "To talk of many things:
> "Of shoes—and ships—and sealing wax—
> Of cabbages—and kings—
> Any why the sea is boiling hot—
> And whether pigs have wings."

"Ships", in the title of this book, is self-explanatory; "Sealing Wax" represents the diversity of historic English parish churches; and "Many Things" is just that: poets and their seasonal poems, some of my own verses, plus diversions to Gibraltar, Bexhill-on-Sea and the America of Thomas Paine.

CONTENTS

SHIPS

SEALING WAX

MANY THINGS

Chapter 1

A SHIP NAMED OHIO

In 1942 the war against Germany was going badly. During the first six months of that year U-boats had sunk over three million tons of Allied shipping in the Atlantic. The German Army under Rommel had rolled across North Africa to within 35 miles of Alexandria. The struggle for control of the Mediterranean was at its peak. The island of Malta was under prolonged siege and its airfield was of vital strategic importance. But essential supplies for the island had to get past the full force of the German Luftwaffe and the entire Italian fleet.

In August it was decided there should be one final all-out attempt to supply Malta before it was forced to capitulate. Previous desperate attempts, from both eastern and western ends of the Mediterranean, had ended in failure. The supplies were to be carried in a convoy of fourteen merchant ships from Gibraltar. It was to be escorted by two battleships, four aircraft carriers, seven cruisers and thirty-four destroyers. This huge combined force represented the most powerful fleet of warships ever gathered together for

Ships and Sealing Wax

any single operation of the war. It was named Operation Pedestal.

Britain then had the largest merchant fleet in the world but no fast oil tankers. Oil in this convoy would be carried by the SS *Ohio*—9,264 gross tons, specially registered and chartered from the United States only a few months before. Thirty-nine-year-old Captain Dudley Mason was appointed in command. The chief engineer was James Wyld. Her crew, who joined forty-eight hours after *Ohio* had been transferred to British registry, numbered seventy-seven and included twenty-four naval ratings and soldiers for the specially fitted Oerlikon and Bofors anti-aircraft guns.

Built in 1940 and capable of 16 knots, *Ohio* was loaded with 11,500 tons of diesel fuel and kerosene. In a previous convoy, her sister ship SS Kentucky, also specially chartered, had been sunk on a convoy to Malta when the force of explosions had fractured her steam pipes. The Admiralty was determined this should not happen again. To reduce the effects of shock *Ohio*'s engines were specially mounted on rubber bearings and all steam-pipes were supported with steel springs and baulks of timber.

On 10th August 1942, with instructions to "get through at all costs", the convoy sailed from Gibraltar. Almost immediately it came under sustained attack. On 11th August the aircraft carrier HMS *Eagle*, one of the largest ships, was sunk by a German U-boat, although the aircraft carrier HMS *Furious* managed to launch her thirty-six Spitfires, which flew to Malta to help defend the island.

The following day the convoy was attacked by squadrons of German and Italian aircraft. In the evening the Italian submarine Axum fired four torpedoes which sank the cruiser

HMS *Cairo* and severely damaged *Ohio*. Hit amidships, a huge pillar of flame soared high into the air, lighted kerosene bubbled up from the fractured tanks and shoots of flame spattered the deck to a distance of thirty yards from the blaze. Captain Mason ordered the engines to be shut down and with all hands fighting the fire it was eventually extinguished and the ship managed to get underway. The blast also destroyed the ship's gyro and knocked the magnetic compass off its bearings. The steering gear was put out of action, forcing the crew to steer with the emergency gear from aft. But *Ohio*'s ordeal was not yet over.

Throughout the night of 12th/13th August, the convoy crept southwards, hugging the Tunisian coastline. It was now the turn of the German E-boats to attack. Racing at high speed through the convoy, they sank four merchantmen and the cruiser HMS *Manchester*. At dawn the German bombers arrived again and *Ohio* was subjected to wave after wave of relentless attacks, receiving two more direct hits, one in the same area as the torpedo. A hole, 24 feet by 27 feet, had been torn in the port side of the midships pump room. The explosion had also blown another hole in the starboard side, flooding the compartment. There were jagged tears in the bulkheads, and kerosene from adjoining tanks was seeping through the holes in the hull. The deck had been broken open so that it was possible to look down into the ship.

Another sixty dive-bombers then attacked the convoy, focusing on *Ohio*. Bombs threw spray over the decks of the tanker, with one near miss buckling the ship's plates and filling the forward tank with water. She was then hit by a German bomber as it crashed into the sea. By superhuman efforts the crew somehow kept the engines going although

Ships and Sealing Wax

fires continued to break out, often terrifyingly close to the lethal cargo. With oil in the water pipes the ship was making alternate black and white smoke and slowly beginning to lose way, eventually coming to a stop. The crew was ordered to abandon ship and boarded the destroyer HMS *Penn* which had come to *Ohio*'s aid.

She was taken in tow by the destroyer but the tow kept parting and, although abandoned by her crew, all then volunteered to return on-board. With the towline once again in place, Penn moved ahead, straining its engines to the limit, but *Ohio* continued to list to port. The two ships were not making any progress, even drifting backwards due to the easterly wind. Both were now sitting ducks as yet another concerted attack developed, and the destroyer had to go at full speed to part the tow. A German bomber dived on the tanker and was shot down by the ships' gunners, but just before it crashed a bomb hit the tanker where the initial torpedo had struck, effectively breaking her back. With darkness falling, the order was again given to abandon ship.

The following day Penn was joined by the minesweeper HMS *Rye*. The two ships towed the tanker and succeeded in making five knots whilst overcoming the swing to port. However, another attack strafed the ships, snapping the towlines and immobilizing *Ohio*'s rudder. The two ships around the tanker were then joined by the destroyers HMS *Bramham* and HMS *Ledbury*. Meanwhile HMS *Rye* had again begun to tow *Ohio*, with the newly arrived Ledbury acting as a stern tug or rudder. But steering like this proved too difficult and a stabilizing factor was needed, so Penn moved to the starboard side and *Ohio*, with her crew once again back on board, slowly got under way. Another combined enemy air attack began just as the group of ships started moving. To save her from sinking, the two destroyers then lashed themselves alongside, one on her port beam, the other on her starboard. With this "sandwich" of five ships, and still under constant attack, *Ohio* slowly sailed the last painful miles to Malta.

On 15th August, with gaping holes in her sides and forecastle awash, *Ohio* made a dramatic sight as she inched into Grand Harbour, to be greeted by cheering crowds on the ramparts and a brass band playing "Rule Britannia". Although *Ohio*'s crew and those of her escorts were exhausted, her precious cargo of fuel was intact. Pipes were hauled aboard and emergency salvage pumps began to discharge the kerosene. At the same time, a fleet auxiliary began to pump the 10,000 tons of fuel oil into her own tanks. As the oil flowed out, *Ohio* sank lower and lower in the water until her keel settled on the bottom of the harbour. Thanks to her survival, the Mediterranean had been secured for the Allies. After three long years, the tide of war had turned. For his outstanding bravery and seamanship, Captain Mason was awarded the George Cross, the same honour as bestowed upon the island of Malta earlier the same year. *Ohio*'s ship's bell and wheel are now treasured possessions of the Honourable Company of Master Mariners on board their headquarters ship permanently moored alongside London's Embankment.

Chapter 2

"A GRAND YET AT THE SAME TIME AWFUL SIGHT!"

At a time when the centenary of the First World War is being commemorated in every conceivable shape and form, it is especially poignant that ninety-three-year-old José Loosemore, who has lived in the East Sussex village of Chiddingly for nearly forty years, is able to personally recall the part played by her father, Albion Percy Smith, who served in the light cruiser HMS *Caroline* at the Battle of Jutland on 31st May/1st June 1916.

The battle, between the British Grand Fleet and the German High Seas Fleet, was the first major sea battle for the Royal Navy since Nelson triumphed at the Battle of Trafalgar over a century earlier. It was also the last time that major warships of both countries would ever confront each other in battle at sea. Two hundred and fifty warships of the two most powerful fleets in the world clashed in an encounter in the North Sea near Denmark, which might have reshaped forever the political map of Europe and the world. In the event, although one in ten of the ships involved was sunk and 9,000 men lost their lives, the Grand Fleet, which lost more warships that its German opponent, enjoyed the strategic advantage of a victorious fleet and continued to do so for the next half century.

Such thoughts, however, would have been furthest from the mind of twenty-seven-year-old Albion (a patriotic name meaning "England", popular with his mother's family) when he wrote a long letter describing the battle to his brother and sister-in-law in Rotherfield. His graphic account was published in *The Crowborough and Uckfield Weekly* on 23rd June 1916. Albion was born one of eight children on 16th June 1889 at his home, Longcroft, in Rotherfield. His father had died when he was two years old, and he was educated at the village school before being apprenticed to a local harness-maker—it is an extraordinary eye-witness description of an historic battle.

From an early age Albion was befriended by the lady of the manor, Miss Catherine Pullen, who took an interest in him and secured a post for him in a merchant ship as an assistant steward in 1912, and in 1915 he joined the Royal Navy. Probably in light of his merchant service experience, he was rated Leading Steward, and on joining HMS *Caroline* —affectionately known as the "*Carrie*"—became the personal steward and valet to the ship's captain, Captain (later Admiral Sir) Henry Ralph Crooke. They were to stay in touch for the rest of their lives.

"Albie", as he was called by his family, wrote his letter, which accurately reflects the excitement and adrenalin rush which he and so many other brave men experienced in action and afterwards wanted to write and share their experiences,

Ships and Sealing Wax

while still fresh in the mind, with their nearest and dearest at home.

No doubt you are anxious to know how I fared and what I saw during the big naval fight. Well, I will do my best to give a slight description, but the first thing to impress on you is that it was the *Caroline's* first time in a really big action, and the same applies to most of the ship's company, with very few exceptions. During the time that I have been in the *Carrie*, my action station has been up on the open bridge in charge of the range finder which enables me to help the guns to get a more precise range. Many times during the two winters I've passed in the North Sea (when it's been bitter cold) I've wished for a warmer station down below inside the ship, but now I'm glad I've stuck an outside number for so long, because I had the chance of seeing the most terrible sea fight ever known.

On the morning of the never-to-be-forgotten 31st May we were out at sea with Sir John Jellicoe's Fleet. In the early part of the afternoon we had the news by signal that Sir David Beatty was also out with a squadron, and he had run across some of the enemy and engaged them at once. This news excited us a bit as we wondered if we would get a look in. Some of the men were hard to convince we would most probably be in action in a few hours, and they even went so far as to say it was only a "buzz" (i.e. Navy slang for rumour) while one chap offered to bet me 10 shillings that the *Carrie* would never see action; we would not have luck enough. It was a pity I didn't accept the wager, for I should now be 10 shillings better off. The sea was dead calm, with only a slight wind and occasional gleams of sunshine, the temperature being slightly chilly, with a haze hanging around the horizon. We knew that Norway was somewhere near.

About 4 p.m. we heard the sound of distant guns. Imagine our excitement and joy when we knew that after months of dreary watching and waiting we were soon to "have a go" at the Germ-huns. Soon after, our ships arrived on the scene and then the enemy, knowing that their huge force was equalled, turned and made steam to get away. This commenced a running fight which continued for hours. From the moment we got within range the sights and sounds which met our view were too varied to be fully described. It was a grand yet at the same time an awful sight. We were ahead of most of our fleet, this owing to our high speed and purpose for which our ship was built. Then the huge guns of our battleships opened fire. Added to this was the din of the fight already taking place. Guns were hurling 15" shells into the opposing fleet with roars and flashes as if scores of thunderstorms had met and got angry.

The sea, which before had been calm, became churned into waves and foam, this being caused by the speed and movement of scores of ships of all sizes. The falling of the enemy shells around us caused huge columns of water, rising many feet high. It was indeed hell let loose and the screams and sobs of the shells as they flew over and around defies description. Some German shells as they burst gave one the impression of blood bursting in billowy clouds in broad daylight. The effect at night is more awful still. How our lads cheered as some of our shots got home on the German packets, causing them to burst into flame. The last I saw of the ill-fated *Invincible* was the stern and bows pointing tragically out of the ocean; the explosion had broken her amidships, and in this way she sank to her last resting place. With her went hundreds of gallant men and boys answering to the last great Call as nobly and as bravely as they responded to the call of King and Country.

Soon after that I had the grim satisfaction of seeing one of the enemy ships meet a similar fate. Events then flowed so quickly that it's impossible to remember exactly what happened. The sky became thick and overcast by vast clouds of dense smoke, belched out by scores of funnels. Picture to yourself the shafts at Jarvis Brook Gas, Water and Brick Works, smoking at full pressure; combine the lot, and you have an idea of the tremendous amount of smoke which one ship alone can make. The sun, which was shining at first, got blotted out by smoke and haze. Only once more did the sun shine all day, and that was for a few seconds, when it shone down in a single beam and showed up a German three-funnel battleship; it made pure white on a black background.

About 11pm the foe got away in the darkness, but our destroyers hunted them all night, and the flash and roar of guns went on all around us until early morning. At times, while the fiercest of the fight proceeded, it was difficult to distinguish our ships from the enemy. The way our brave little destroyers worked cannot be spoken of too highly. To make a comparison, they are like water rats compared with whales that is, among the huge battleships. When the fighting eased down, after about six hours each and all being at their posts the whole time, 'twas then that we discovered how hungry we were, and we who were in the open and exposed positions suddenly found that the air was very cold. I stretched myself on a bench about midnight, but, though tired out, was too excited to sleep much, and we were called out again at 2 a.m. but there was no more doing; and so ended the most awful sea fight in the history of the world.

How we came through the ordeal unscathed in this way is beyond my comprehension. Our ship's black cat must indeed be a lucky mascot! At times I wonder if we have been through that inferno and come out alive. One thing I felt proud of that day, when I saw the Union Jack and the White Ensign drive the German Eagle back to port, was that I did not have to be fetched to do my bit. Nothing was ever near approaching the thrill of the great battle and all of us can rest secure in the knowledge that the Navy will never fail to do its duty, and keep dear "old blighty" free from invasion. We were ready for them again the next day, and are always ready.

Albion stayed in the ship until 1917 when he was asked by Captain Crooke, who had been appointed in command of HMS *Excellent*, the RN Gunnery School at Whale Island, Portsmouth, to join him there. On arrival he was greeted with a laconic "So you've arrived!" He served there until the end of the war, when he returned to service in the Merchant Navy. On 1ˢᵗ October 1921 he married Violet Kirk and they made their home in London. Their two daughters, Iris (José) and Olive, were born in 1922 and 1924.

During the Depression in the 1930s, life became increasingly difficult for merchant seamen and Albion was fortunate to secure a position as Cook/Steward on the private steam yacht *Mandolin*, owned by wealthy landowner Mr David Hanbury. The yacht took part in King George V's Jubilee Review of the Fleet at Spithead in 1935 and his daughters were invited on board. He later worked for Mr Hanbury on his estate in the New Forest and became steward of the village hall in Minster, where he was involved in looking after thousands of soldiers billeted in the area during World War II. It was here that José met her future husband.

HMS *Caroline* not only survived the Battle of Jutland but stayed in commission until 1924, when she became the Headquarters of the Ulster Division of the Royal Naval Reserve in Belfast. She remains there to this day, the only surviving warship from the First World War still afloat. On the fiftieth anniversary of the Battle of Jutland, in 1966, Albion visited the ship with the only two other survivors of the action still alive at the time. In 2013, his daughter, José, was invited to visit the ship on the 97ᵗʰ anniversary of the battle. "It was the proudest moment of my life to stand in exactly the same position on the platform next to the bridge where my father's action station had been at the Battle of Jutland nearly a century before," was her heartfelt comment.

Roger Paine

At the end of his letter home, Albion wrote "It's not our own possible fate that ever worries us, but the thought of those we leave. So here's 'To sweethearts and wives' and may we soon talk of the war as a thing of the past." A century later many might add "Amen".

Chapter 3

HASTINGS FISHERMEN'S MUSEUM

I saw a little church today,
The quaintest I have seen,
It stood amidst the fishing fleet,
And made a charming scene.

This delightful verse from a poem, "The Fishermen's Church", was written by Eliza Veness. In 1885 she married a Hastings fisherman, James Veness, and the family attended the Fishermen's Church in Rock-a-Nore, the road at the east end of the town which runs behind the beach, or The Stade, a word based on the Anglo-Saxon for "landing place", at the east end of the town. On the south coast of England, in the county of East Sussex, the same building is now the Hastings Fishermen's Museum.

Designed by William John Gant, surveyor to the town, it was erected as a Chapel of Ease for the nearby parish churches of All Saints and St Clements with the specific intention of serving the needs of the large fishing community who lived in the Old Town. It was completed in 1854.

Roger Paine

Although never formally consecrated, it was dedicated to St Nicholas, patron saint of seafarers.

This mission church became increasingly popular with the fishing community until the outbreak of the Second World War when it was closed and used for storage by the military. Fishing in the traditional manner, by boats from the beach, continued throughout the war, except at night, the church suffered considerable damage to the stained glass windows and wall decorations. After hostilities ceased the dilapidated church was taken over as a warehouse by a local firm. In 1956, the Old Hastings Preservation Society, with the help of Hastings Borough Council, reopened the church as the Fishermen's Museum.

In order to preserve the building in its original form, and as it had always been known as the Fishermen's Church, the Society felt it was the ideal place to display the last of the traditional Hastings fishing luggers, the *Enterprise*, RX 278, built in 1912, when offered to the Society by owner Harold Pepper. These boats had been the standard fishing boat in the Hastings fishing fleet until the First World War. In April 1956 part of the church's south wall was demolished so that the boat could be pulled in and installed. Her robust build and excellent condition made the *Enterprise* an impressive centrepiece. It continues in this role to the present day.

The Fishermen's Museum was formally opened on 17th May 1956. A large extension on the south side, known as the Vestry Gallery, funded with grants from the Heritage Lottery Fund, was opened in 2001. Today the museum is the most popular visitor attraction in Hastings. Although comparatively small, the museum is a cornucopia of relics, artefacts, photographs, prints, paintings, models and

Ships and Sealing Wax

associated memorabilia, both large and small, all linked to the sea and fishing. Oozing a sense of easily understandable history, making few concessions to specialist conservation, thematic labelling, or ambient temperature control—the focus of many of today's health and safety-burdened and security-obsessed museums and galleries—this is an up-front, family-friendly museum of the traditional type.

Walk straight in off the street and you are immediately confronted by the solid bulk of the *Enterprise*. Without a harbour, Hastings remains home to the largest beach-launched fishing fleet in Europe. This hundred-year old fishing boat is a perfectly preserved example of the wooden, clinker-built vessels. These were specifically designed with a large hold for the catch, and were bluff-bowed for buoyancy and almost flat-bottomed so they could be dragged over the beach to sit upright on their broad beams while ashore. Until the 1990s, beach launching of the boats was done by as many men as it took putting their backs into pushing—a combination of synchronized shoving and concentrated cursing. Today, bulldozers and tractors undertake the task.

Climb carefully up the stairway leading onto the deck of the boat and note the solid craftsmanship of the teak decking, the cast-iron chimney poking up from the cabin below, the weathered masts, spars, sails and rigging, and the hatches to the fish hold and crew's quarters, which can be viewed through glass panels. A life-sized fisherman, in yellow oilskin apron and sou'wester, stands, hand on tiller, at the stern. His head was carved by a local sculptor, Clare Sheridan. On the floor, beneath the boat's bowsprit, is an original wooden capstan, one of many, which was used for hauling the boats out of the sea and onto the beach. Until the

1930s cart horses, used by the borough council for refuse collection, were harnessed to the capstan's long bar and walked in a circle, winding the hawser round the large central post. When the horses were withdrawn from council duties, it was thought that the fishing fleet would be forced to move to nearby Rye. But the ever-resilient Hastings fishermen installed motor-driven winches, protected by sheds, which remain in use to this day.

Along the east wall is a motley collection of unusual stuffed seabirds and fish. This includes a great wandering albatross, a massive conger eel—7 feet 7 inches long, weighing 63 lbs 3oz—a puffin, a turtle, the vertebra of a basking shark, a huge lobster claw and the ugly blade of a swordfish, objects to fuel any seafarer's tales of the deep. Children are enthralled. There are also photographs of some of the characters etched into fishing folklore, including Jimmy "Toller" Adams, Fisherman Bumstead, George "Nuckum" Haste and Old "Quiddy" Mitchell. All members of illustrious local families, many of whose descendants still continue to earn their living from fishing.

In the east window, the impressive stained glass includes a new panel by Alan Wright, incorporated in 2000 to mark the Millennium, which vividly depicts the hazards of fishing. A fitting memorial to those who have lost their lives at sea. On the shelf which once overlooked the church altar is a quotation from St Luke's Gospel: "And He Sat Down And Taught The People Out Of The Ship". A number of polished black pews and a sandstone font installed at the west end in 1917, which is still used on special occasions for the baptism of local children, remind of the building's original role.

Ships and Sealing Wax

Particularly interesting is the area set aside for the Winkle Club. This unique benevolent institution was formed in 1900 by fishermen and their friends, to help under-privileged families in Old Town. Its membership includes such distinguished names as the Duke of Windsor, Field Marshal Montgomery, the Duke of Edinburgh and Admiral the Lord Boyce, currently Lord Warden of the Cinque Ports. Although traditionally a "men only" club, when Queen Elizabeth II and the late Queen Mother visited Hastings in 1997 they were invited to become honorary members. Everyone joining the club is given a special winkle. The queen was presented with her winkle in the form of a gold brooch. A large painting of Sir Winston Churchill being presented with his winkle when he visited Hastings in 1955 hangs on the east wall. There is also a life-size model of Walter "Slogger" Hoad wearing a suit and hat he had made himself and on which are sewn hundreds of silver-painted winkles, reminiscent of London's famous pearly kings and queens.

Most seafaring communities have strong connections with the Royal Navy. This is evident with a large, fully-rigged model of the coastal blockade ship, HMS *Enchantress*, used in the early nineteenth century to patrol the English Channel to prevent smugglers from landing their contraband along the coast. Another display, with sepia photographs and facsimile copies of service documents, records two members of the Breeds family, fishermen and sailors, who served in the Royal Navy from the time of Queen Victoria to King George VI. A collection of Richard William Breeds' medals includes his China Medal, awarded in 1900. A key figure in the foundation of the museum in the 1950s was Rear

Admiral Hubert Dannreuther. His portrait hangs on the wall to the right of the entrance. The ship's bell of the sloop HMS *Hastings*, built in 1930 and involved in the Atlantic convoys during World War II, hangs nearby.

The Vestry Gallery is used for temporary exhibitions. The open area outside the museum has several boats which form part of the historic collection. These include the *Edward and Mary*, RX 74, dating from 1919, the first Hastings fishing boat to be built with an engine.

The 30 foot high black-painted "net shops", a unique feature of the Hastings shoreline, were designed to keep fishing nets and ropes dry and prevent them from rotting. In use from 1875 to 1950, they had three floors as each type of fishing had its own set of nets, whether herring nets, mackerel nets or those used for trawls. A traditional fishing boat, *The Golden Sovereign*, RX 40, is on show in two halves, in which there are displays of nets, chains, lobster pots and other fishing tackle. The stern section of the boat is appropriately named *The Half Sovereign*. To again quote Eliza Veness:

> *Do not despise the fishermen,*
> *Though humble they may be,*
> *For they are God's own special care,*
> *These toilers of the sea.*

Chapter 4

"HAVE REJOINED THE FLEET....GOD SAVE THE KING"

The words of this message, sent by the frigate HMS *Amethyst* at the mouth of the Yangtse River, to the Commander in Chief Far East Station in Hong Kong at 5.30 am on Sunday 31st July 1949, reverberated around the world. It also signified the end of a remarkable action, often referred to as the "Yangtse Incident", which has now passed into history but seemed at the time to almost shatter world peace as Britain and other countries slowly began to recover from the Second World War.

In April 1949 the Chinese People's Liberation Army had swept across the great natural barrier of the Yangtse River in their drive against the Kuomintang armies of Generalissimo Chiang Kai-shek. They also took the opportunity to shell and drive ashore by heavy gunfire one of His Majesty's ships, HMS *Amethyst*, on a routine mission to Nanking, which resulted in considerable loss of life. The reality of the Royal Navy being attacked by the Chinese Communists seemed almost unthinkable, in no less a way than when Argentinian marines landed on the British territory of South Georgia in April 1982.

HMS *Amethyst* had sailed from Shanghai on 19th April 1949, having left Hong Kong a week earlier. Sometime before 8 am the following morning she started up the Yangtse and attracted small-arms fire which completely missed the ship. Such firings were quite common and usually meant no harm. The only action taken was to hoist several white ensigns and two large Union Jacks. Shortly afterwards, however, heavy and accurate fire opened on the ship. The first shell went over the bridge; the second hit the bridge, mortally wounding the captain, Lieutenant Commander Bill Skinner, and disabling everyone there; the third hit the wheelhouse, killing the quartermaster on the wheel and the seaman on the engine-room telegraphs. With the steering jammed, the ship turned towards Rose Island in the middle of the river. Fortunately, as one telegraph had been put to full astern the artificer in the engine room correctly assumed both engines should also be put astern, and the ship grounded comparatively gently before control of the ship was resumed.

Heavy fire from the Communist batteries continued for almost an hour. With the ship firmly aground it was not possible to bring the ship's main guns to bear. First Lieutenant and second-in-command, Lieutenant Geoffrey Weston, although wounded and with shells exploding around him, managed to send a final transmission, "Under heavy fire. Am aground in approx. position 31.10' North 119.50' East. Large number of casualties." The wounded were being collected on the quarterdeck, ready for getting them ashore, but when the ship's doctor and the sick-berth attendant came to attend them both were hit by a shell and killed instantly. This left no one in the ship with expert knowledge of the use of morphine and other measures necessary for care of the wounded.

By this time, with dead and wounded crew lying all over the ship, Weston decided to get the wounded, and as many men as could be spared, ashore to the Nationalist side of the river. With the ship's motor boat destroyed by gunfire, ferrying ashore was started using the whaler, rafts and men swimming, but fire was immediately diverted onto them so this had to be abandoned. Eventually those who survived and did get ashore were met by the Chinese Nationalists and the following day were taken to a missionary hospital in Kiang-Yin. About 60 unwounded men remained on board the ship. By the time the shelling stopped at about 11 am the ship had received over 50 hits, 22 men had been killed and 31 wounded. Holes below the waterline were plugged with hammocks and bedding, although no one dared move in case of attracting the attention of Communist snipers.

Vice Admiral Alexander Madden, Flag Officer Second in Command Far East Station, having been informed of the perilous situation by signal, ordered the destroyer HMS *Consort* from Nanking to go to the *Amethyst's* assistance, and the frigate HMS *Black Swan* from Shanghai to Kiang-Yin, downriver from the stricken ship. Those in *Amethyst* later reported that when *Consort* eventually arrived she was an inspiring sight, racing downriver at 28 knots with her guns blazing at the Communist batteries. She turned two miles below *Amethyst* in an attempt to take her in tow, but came under such heavy fire that the plan had to be abandoned. A second attempt also failed and *Consort* sustained further damage and casualties, during which her steering was affected. She suffered 10 men killed and 23 wounded.

It was next decided that an RAF Sunderland flying boat should be sent from Hong Kong to *Amethyst,* with a naval doctor and a medical attendant to replace those killed, and an RAF doctor to give what assistance he could. The aircraft landed on the Yangtse and the crew immediately started transferring medical stores by sampan. But the Communists then began firing at the plane, and the pilot, judging the situation to be too dangerous, had to take off, leaving the RAF doctor on board *Amethyst*, where he stayed and was to be invaluable in treating the wounded.

Just after midnight on 21st April, after lightning the ship, *Amethyst* was refloated and managed to move up river. The following day, the Assistant British Naval Attaché, Lieutenant Commander John Kerans, came down from Nanking and assumed command of the ship. After he had assessed the situation he ordered that all the wounded, including Lieutenant Weston, should be sent ashore.

On 30th April the PLA demanded that Britain, the United States, and France withdraw their armed forces from all parts of China. Negotiations, however, reached stalemate because Kerans would not accept the demand from Colonel Kang Yushao, the PLA representative, that Britain had invaded Chinese national waters and had fired upon the PLA first. For ten weeks throughout the swelteringly hot days of May, June and July, *Amethyst* remained under guard by the Communists. A major worry was the supply of food, essential spares and particularly oil fuel. Some food could be bought locally and on a few occasions stores did arrive from Shanghai. But after endless days of negotiation, the situation

Ships and Sealing Wax

became mired in frustration. An unlikely hero was the ship's cat, Simon, who, despite having had his fur singed and having been wounded by shrapnel, was kept busy killing the many rats intent on decimating the ship's stores.

With negotiations for safe conduct of the ship getting nowhere, Kerans, with the approval of Admiral Madden, finally decided that at the first available opportunity he would make a dash for it, and, if he failed, would blow up the ship. The necessary conditions were that there should be a typhoon about, preferably just gone past, so that the banks of the Yangstse would be flooded, and all batteries on low lying ground would be removed. It should be a dark night with no moon. New moon was on 25th July, so it had to be done sooner, or never.

News then came of another typhoon which would miss them by a comfortable margin, and on the afternoon of 30th July, with only 55 tons of oil fuel remaining, Kerans decided to break out that night. This was running it decidedly late to get out before dawn, but he dared not start earlier because the moon did not set until 11 pm.

Immediately it was dark they started altering the silhouette of the ship with canvas screens etc. to confuse any alert sentries into mistaking her for a merchant ship. Then at 10 pm, just as they were going to slip, a fully lighted merchant ship appeared and went on down the river ahead of them. They let her get well past and at 10.12 pm weighed anchor to follow in her wake. The open sea was nearly 150 miles away.

As they steamed downriver *Amethyst* frequently came under fire, but her speed and the use of smoke and helm, and Kerans's cool-headed navigation, enabled them to get away without further hits. The crucial point of the passage came at Kiang-Yin, about fifty miles from their starting point, which was heavily defended with well-placed batteries and a boom consisting of a line of sunken ships with a gap near the middle. No one, of course, could be certain where the gap was. With everyone's hearts in their mouths and trusting to good fortune, although under heavy fire, the ship managed to get through without damage.

At 2.30 am, having covered 100 miles, a signal "100 up" was made to the Commander-in-Chief.

Exceeding everyone's hopes, and fears, *Amethyst* passed the forts at Woosung just as first light was breaking on 31st July. Shortly afterwards they could see HMS *Concord* and it was then that they made the historic signal, "Have rejoined the Fleet. Am South of Woosung. No damage or casualties. God save the King." After one hundred and one days they were out.

A memorable black and white film, *Yangtse Incident: The story of HMS Amethyst* was produced in 1957 starring Richard Todd as Lieutenant Commander Kerans, Donald Houston as Lieutenant Weston and William Hartnell as the quartermaster, Leading Seaman Frank.

To participate in the film, HMS *Amethyst* was brought out of reserve, but as her engines were no longer operational HMS *Magpie* (another ship of the same class) stood in for the shots of the ship moving and firing her guns. The Rivers Orwell and Stour in Suffolk doubled as the Yangtse River.

Chapter 5

WAR AT SEA: USA VERSUS GREAT BRITAIN

The United States of America declared war on Great Britain on 18th June 1812. This declaration, signed by President James Madison, was the first time the USA declared war on another country, and the vote by Congress would prove to be the closest vote to formally declare war in American history.

Critics of the war labelled it "Mr Madison's War" but other, more hawkish elements, called it the Second Revolutionary War, quoting Benjamin Franklin in the American War of Independence: "The War of Revolution is won, but the War for Independence is yet to be fought." In those days there was no "special relationship" and it would be over a century before the USA and Great Britain became allies in war.

Despite losing thirteen American colonies to George Washington and the American revolutionaries over thirty years previously, Great Britain, like many European countries, did not take the United States very seriously. In 1812 it was fighting its own war against France under

Roger Paine

Napoleon Bonaparte, and supporting Spain and Portugal on the Iberian Peninsula.

The majority of Britain's supplies for the long-running Napoleonic war came from America and Canada, especially the raw materials essential to maintain the Royal Navy, which had expanded to nearly 1,000 ships. The US, however, was increasingly angry over Britain's arrogance on the high seas, and the Navy competed with privateers and merchantmen for a diminishing pool of experienced sailors required to maintain a large fleet at sea in wartime. This resulted in impressment, or "the press gang".

Anger grew when Britain refused to recognize British-born sailors on American ships as legitimate American citizens. Many had deserted for the more favourable conditions, and British frigates stationed themselves in territorial waters outside US harbours to search ships for contraband and impress crew members, including Americans. These violations, together with Britain seizing Yankee ships trading with France, inflamed controversy. "Free trade and sailors' rights" became a rallying cry in the United States throughout the conflict.

It was against this background that HMS *Java*, a 38-gun, fifth-rate frigate, sailed from Portsmouth on 12th November 1812. A former French ship, the *Renommée*, she had been re-named *Java* after capture at the Battle of Tamatave in the Indian Ocean eighteen months earlier. She had been commissioned in August under command of Captain Henry Lambert, an experienced officer who, although only 28 years old, had already been involved in a number of conflicts at sea. His task was to escort a small convoy of merchant ships to Bombay. Also on board were the newly appointed

Ships and Sealing Wax

Governor of Bombay, Lieutenant General Sir Thomas Hislop and his staff officers, as well as their baggage and stores for ships in India. *Java* also had a number of additional personnel taking passage to join other RN ships, including Master and Commander John Marshall on his way to command HMS *Procris*. The ship had a complement of nearly 400, plus the supernumeraries, but many of her crew were untrained in warfare at sea, "pressed men" or young boys.

On the passage across the Atlantic Ocean, *Java* encountered a disabled American merchantman off the coast of West Africa and took her as a prize joining up with the other ships in the convoy. She then headed towards the coast of South America in order to take full advantage of the favourable trade winds before continuing southwards around the Cape of Good Hope to India. Near San Salvador in Brazil *Java* encountered two American warships, the heavy 44-gun frigate, USS *Constitution* and the sloop, USS *Hornet*. They had sailed from Boston, Massachusetts on 27th October, tasked with engaging, and capturing, British merchantmen.

The *Constitution* was famously nicknamed "Old Ironsides", as a result of a successful engagement with HMS *Guerriére* earlier in the year, when British shot had bounced off her thick oak sides before the British ship was sunk. This had been an embarrassing episode for the Royal Navy but the *Constitution* was now under the command of Commodore William Bainbridge, 38 years old and with the dubious distinction of having surrendered his ship to the enemy without fighting on three previous occasions. He was known in the service as "Hard Luck Bill". The meeting of the American and British ships on 29th December 1812 was as much by chance as intent, for upon their respective sails being sighted, neither was initially aware that they had sighted the enemy.

The opening phase of the action comprised both ships attempting to get the better position from which to fire upon and rake the other. Bainbridge initially sailed to a matching course and opened fire with a broadside at half a mile, but this achieved little and he was forced to risk raking and getting closer to Java. Although severely out-matched, both in terms of the experience of her crew and the weight of her broadside, shots from *Java* carried away *Constitution*'s helm, disabled her rudder and left Bainbridge severely wounded, although he continued in command. Both ships continued to fire broadsides but by now *Java* had a mast and sails falling over her starboard side, which prevented most of her guns on that side from firing. It also prevented her from lying alongside *Constitution*. The guns that attempted to fire only managed to set the fallen sails and rigging ablaze.

Constitution's accuracy of fire put the *Java* at enormous disadvantage. Within an hour, after several close encounters involving the rigging of each ship becoming entangled with the other, *Java*'s masts collapsed. During this encounter a sharpshooter aloft in *Constitution* fatally wounded Captain Lambert, and command of the ship passed to Lieutenant Chads, his twenty-four-year-old first lieutenant, assisted by Commander Marshall. Bainbridge used this opportunity to make immediate repairs, but before *Java* could begin clearing the masts and fallen rigging, the American ship returned and immediately took a raking position from which the smaller ship was unable to defend herself. After three hours of desperate fighting, with his ship dismasted,

Ships and Sealing Wax

Lieutenant Chads had no choice but to strike the ship's colours and surrender. Bainbridge sent an officer and boarding party to take possession of the British ship.

As the *Java* had been rendered a "perfect wreck" and was considered not fit to be taken as a prize, Bainbridge removed her helm and installed it on the Constitution, to replace the one that had been shot away. On New Year's Day 1813, two days after the battle, the order was given to set the stricken vessel on fire, and when the flames reached the powder store she blew up.

Java suffered 24 men killed and 110 wounded. *Constitution* suffered 14 dead and 25 wounded, including Bainbridge. The wounded and the prisoners from *Java* were taken ashore where, on 5th January 1813, Captain Lambert and others who had died of their wounds, were buried in Fort St. Pedro. Upon learning of the death of *Java*'s captain, Commodore Bainbridge expressed deep sorrow for a commander he credited as brave and noble, although neither he nor any of his officers attended Lambert's funeral.

On 6th January, the *Constitution*, requiring more repairs than could be undertaken, sailed back to Boston, where she arrived on 18th February 1813. But such was her fame in the War of 1812 that she was repeatedly saved from being broken up and only retired from active service in 1881, becoming a museum ship in 1907. Today, "Old Ironsides", as she is still known, is the oldest commissioned warship afloat in the world, open to visitors all the year round in the former Charlestown Navy Yard, Boston, only a broadside's distance from where she was built.

Lieutenant Chads and other surviving officers and crew of the *Java* were put on board two transport ships and

Roger Paine

returned to Britain. On 23rd April 1813 they faced court martial in Portsmouth for the loss of their ship. They were honourably acquitted. Chads continued to serve in the Royal Navy, became an admiral and was knighted. He died in 1868. The War of 1812 was eventually settled when both sides felt they had achieved their objectives, although many of the grievances which had led to war were ignored. The Treaty of Ghent was signed on 24th December 1814.

Chapter 6

"THE FLYING ANGEL"

The Mission to Seafarers was founded officially in 1856, although it had first come into existence over twenty years earlier.

It was in 1835 that the Reverend John Ashley, a young Anglican priest, began visiting ships at anchor in the Bristol Channel. The realisation that no one from the Church took any notice of sailors in ships had been brought home to him by his daughter who, when walking on the cliffs and seeing the ships at anchor, had asked her father, with the innocent wisdom of a child, "Daddy, where do sailors go to church?" With his interest aroused by this simple question he soon discovered not only that the majority of sailors never did go to church, but also that no one from the ministry ever went to visit them.

He was so moved by their isolation and need that he gave up a secure living to devote his life to serving those who served at sea. John Ashley's work soon inspired other ministers in other ports, and it was decided in 1856 to coordinate and expand this mission. It was called The

Roger Paine

Missions to Seamen and in the same year adopted a flying angel as its sign, inspired by a verse from the Book of Revelation: "Then I saw an angel flying in mid-heaven with an eternal gospel to proclaim to those on earth, to every nation and tribe, language and people."

It became known as The Mission to Seafarers in 2000, to reflect more accurately what in reality it had always been, namely a missionary society of the Anglican Church which cares for the spiritual and practical welfare of all seafarers, regardless of gender, nationality or faith.

Lord Shaftesbury, the Mission's president, opened the first reading room for sailors in Deal in 1861, and a network of chaplains soon extended to ports around the country. One notable Mission figure in the late nineteenth century was the Reverend Stanley Treanor. He was chaplain in the Downs from 1878 to 1910 and spent 200 days a year afloat, visiting ships. He was also a frequent visitor to the Goodwin Lightship, anchored on the notorious stretch of sandbanks off the Kent coast. It was reported that his seamanship was of a high order, even by professional standards. He could board sailing vessels from his Mission boat before the ships had come to anchor and leave them after they had weighed.

At the outbreak of the Second World War, the Mission was involved from the first day. The SS *Athenia*, which had just left Liverpool for Montreal, carrying more than 1,400 people, was torpedoed off the Irish coast, with the loss of 112 lives. Survivors were visited in hospital by the Glasgow chaplain, and from then on the Mission was heavily committed to providing accommodation, food and support for thousands of sailors. In Dover a disused building was "fitted up" for the crews of minesweepers to have somewhere to rest. After the end of hostilities, in appreciation of the way the Mission had looked after seafarers, the Admiralty made a gift to the society of 1,000 guineas.

The 1950s saw the beginning of enormous changes in the shipping industry. One of these changes, containerization, brought larger ships and smaller crews. It also led to quicker turnaround times and the practice of flying crews to their ships. This cut the lengthy waiting periods in port and there was less need for accommodation. So the big hostels in port centres were phased out and the Mission opened smaller, more accessible clubs. By the 1980s changes in the world economy had led to differences in the nationalities of seafarers. Previously the world's merchant navies had predominantly come from the West; now two thirds came from developing countries such as India, the Philippines and China.

Today the Mission has a network of chaplains, staff and volunteers in 260 ports worldwide, reaching out to visit seafarers on board their ships and offering a welcome when they arrive in port. In over 100 ports the Mission runs centres where crews can relax away from their ships, obtain local information, discuss problems and share worship. In an average year the Mission makes 72,000 ship visits, distributes 175,000 bibles and other items of Christian literature, connects 230,000 telephone calls on behalf of seafarers, and visits almost 600 seafarers in hospital.

"Technology, multiculturalism and criminalization," the Mission says, "are now the key issues affecting sailors' welfare." But some things remain the same. Loneliness and homesickness are still a problem, and today's seafarers suffer the dehumanising effects of corner-cutting and cost-cutting, practised by an unscrupulous minority of ship owners, especially as regards safety. The characteristic problems that so many chaplains and volunteers in the Mission face are anxieties about security, which lead to isolation for seafarers in port for they cannot visit the shore, and chaplains cannot visit them.

To address these problems in Dubai the Mission built the world's first floating seafarers' centre. This purpose-built 27-metre boat was named MV *Flying Angel* by The Prince of Wales at a ceremony in Dubai on 28th February 2007. It is designed to serve seafarers whose ships use the east coast anchorage of the United Arab Emirates, the second largest bunkering anchorage in the world. At present as many as 2,000 seafarers who crew these ships are unable to go ashore to contact their families. Since the boat commissioned, seafarers have been able to enjoy the facilities on board which include an internet café, telephones, a medical clinic and a paramedic, and a book and DVD library. The Mission's two Dubai chaplains each spend a week on board, operating around the anchorage five days a week during daylight. This support boat is the 21st century equivalent of the cutter *Eirene* built by the Reverend Ashley for visiting ships in the Bristol Channel 150 years ago.

The Mission to Seafarers, like all major charities, relies heavily on a devoted band of volunteers. Throughout the British Isles dozens of men and women act as the parish link between their church and the Mission.

In paying tribute to the work of the Mission, HRH The Princess Royal, the Mission's President said, "We know that many seafarers' lives would be much harder if they were not able to turn to the Mission. If it did not exist, someone would have to invent a similar organisation." Fortunately, thanks to John Ashley's foresight and dedication over one 180 years ago, there is no need.

Chapter 7

FELINES AFLOAT

Although no one can be sure of the exact date when cats were first kept on board ships, there is plenty of evidence that from earliest times sailing ships kept livestock, such as goats, pigs and chickens, to provide a ready source of fresh meat during long ocean voyages. It is also known that the crew sometimes became so fond of an animal that it would be kept as a pet instead of ending up on the dinner table. Parrots, with their remarkable powers of mimicking the human voice, were popular pets with seafarers, and, thanks to Long John Silver's parrot "Captain Flint" in Robert Louis Stevenson's *Treasure Island*, have become inextricably linked with pirates.

At the same time, many cats, normally regarded as domestic pets, have spent their lives on board ship where they have also served a practical purpose. From the time of the ancient Egyptians, who took them on their Nile river boats to catch birds in the thickets along the riverbanks, cats, with their remarkable feline ability to adapt to new surroundings, have provided a ready means of keeping a

36

ship's stores free from rodents. As the ship's official rat-catcher, a cat often became a much cherished ship's pet or mascot.

Since 1975 all animals have been banned from Royal Navy ships and British-flagged merchant vessels on Health & Safety grounds. This, together with increased European legislation to prevent the spread of disease and concerns over security, has seen the virtual demise of ships' cats, although In other countries, where the enforcement of such regulations is less rigorous, ships' cats can still be found alive and well.

Stories of ships' cats in the past provide a glimpse of their usefulness, sociability and bravery. When it comes to these, few can match a cat named Oscar. Originally a survivor of the German battleship *Bismarck* when it was sunk in 1941, Oscar was picked up by the destroyer HMS *Cossack*, and when that ship was torpedoed a few months later, he again survived. This time he was taken on board HMS *Ark Royal*, but shortly afterwards that ship, too, was sunk. Again Oscar was saved. Re-named "Unsinkable Sam", although with the stigma that any ship to which he belonged was likely to be sunk he was put ashore to become official mouse-catcher to the Governor of Gibraltar. Despite demonstrating the legendary nine lives of a cat, Oscar finished his days in a Sailors' Home in Belfast where he died in 1955.

Equally brave was Simon, the black and white tabby cat on board HMS *Amethyst* when the frigate was shelled by Chinese Communists on the Yangtze River in 1949. With 25 of the crew killed, Simon, singed and wounded by shrapnel, continued with his rat-catching duties, which were vitally important in protecting the ship's dwindling food supplies from rat infestation. Sadly Simon died in quarantine after

Ships and Sealing Wax

the ship returned to the UK. He is buried in the PDSA cemetery in Ilford beneath a specially designed monument with the words, "His behaviour was of the highest order". He was also posthumously awarded the Dickin medal, often referred to as the "Animal's VC".

So highly regarded were ships' cats in the Royal Navy that some were given their own hammock, complete with mattress, blanket and pillow. On Sundays an "HMS" cap ribbon would often be tied around their necks. In World War I, the crew of the cruiser HMS *Chester*, present at the Battle of Jutland, thought so highly of their cat, Hoskyn, that his image was embroidered for perpetuity on a cushion cover which was presented to the ship's doctor.

In World War II, the cruiser HMS *Hermione*'s cat, Convoy, so called because of the number of times he had accompanied the ship on convoy duties, was listed as an "Able-Bodied Cat" on the ship's books. The ship's cat on board the steam gunboat HM SGB-7, like the ship, had no name. He was known simply as, "TBC"—"That Bloody Cat"!

A ship's cat that achieved lasting fame was Mrs Chippy, who sailed with Sir Ernest Shackleton's ship *Endurance* on his ill-fated expedition to Antarctica in 1914-15. The cat, a tiger-striped tabby with dramatic dark markings and which, despite its name, was a male, belonged to the Scottish-born master shipwright Harry "Chippy" McNeish. It was his carpentry skills which ensured that a ship's lifeboat, after *Endurance* had been crushed in the ice, withstood the battering of some of the roughest seas in the world during its legendary 800-mile journey to South Georgia. In 2004 a life-size bronze statue of Mrs Chippy was erected over McNeish's grave in New Zealand.

Roger Paine

The battleship HMS *Hood*, sunk by the *Bismarck* in 1941 with the tragic loss of over 1,400 lives, was well known for the variety of ship's pets acquired during a career spanning 21 years. These included a goat, an opossum, a squirrel, beavers and a wallaby. The ship's two cats, Fishcakes and Ginger, are believed to have perished with the ship.

While recognizing that ships' cats have served a wide variety of useful purposes, and some still do, there seems little doubt that they also provide companionship, amusement and the enjoyment of looking after a dumb animal, thus allowing the seafarer a rare opportunity of expressing feelings of love and affection at sea.

Over a century ago an American newspaper published an article entitled "Pets in the Fo'castle". This aptly summed up a sailor's feelings about ships' cats. "It affords him deep pleasure to hold in his loving but rough embrace an innocent soft-furred creature who with a responsive purr, assures him that his attentions are appreciated." Few who have experienced the pleasure of a feline afloat would disagree.

Chapter 8

DESPERATE TIMES

The Latin proverb *"Extremis malis extrema media"*, "Desperate times call for desperate measures," was never more true than in the early years of World War II. By the end of April 1941, the Battle of the Atlantic was exacting a terrible toll of ships and men. The "wolf packs" of Admiral Doenitz's U-boats were savaging the supply lines that stretched from the United States across the North Atlantic; essential food stuffs were strictly rationed and reserves of raw materials, including oil and iron ore, had fallen dramatically. The supply chain from North America was in serious danger of being severed. With the land war in Europe and North Africa also going badly, Britain had its back to the wall.

Winston Churchill, in an emotional letter to President Roosevelt, sought the assistance of the USA. This resulted in the famous "Lend-Lease Agreement" and Roosevelt's message to the American people: "We must be the great Arsenal of Democracy." The only proviso the President made was that all leased vessels, warships and merchant ships, together with 200 additional ships being built, must be British-crewed.

Such was the concern at the level of casualties amongst merchant seamen—5,622 lost out of a total of 23,922 forced to abandon their ships—and at the number of men threatening not to sign on or simply deserting, that a directive to find crews went out from the War Office. Whilst the days of recruiting sailors by impressment, or the "press gang" as it was colloquially termed, no such form of official recruitment had been used to crew British ships for nearly 150 years. But these were desperate times for the government and desperate measures were called for.

Glasgow had become the chief wartime port of the United Kingdom, handling some 80% of incoming merchant shipping. Although suffering badly from Nazi bombing, the work to build, repair, provision and munition a huge variety of ships proceeded relentlessly. Barlinnie Jail, built on an elevated position out of the local whinstone rock and looking every inch a fortress, had received its first prisoners in August 1882. In the following half century it had achieved a notorious reputation for being a tough institution in a tough city known at that time as "the gangster capital of the British Isles".

Gangs, usually formed on the basis of religion, Protestant or Catholic, waged bigoted street warfare in the slum areas of the city. Using knives, razors, coshes, hatchets and their fists, or anything that would maim or disfigure an adversary whilst stopping short of murder, they created a culture of violence. They were confronted by an equally tough police force who established a zero-tolerance regime aimed at putting ruthless gang members behind bars. These policemen, handpicked by

Ships and Sealing Wax

Glasgow's Chief Constable, Sir Percy Sillitoe, became the core of the 20th century press gangs.

In August 1941 the police force was tasked to recruit a crew of 500 for a one-time passenger ship, the 25,570 ton *SS George Washington*. Built in 1908 for the North German Lloyd Line and veteran of countless transatlantic crossings under the American flag in the halcyon days of liner travel, the US government had agreed to loan her for use as a troopship. From the Gorbals pubs to the gambling dens in Cowcaddens, the press gangs scoured Glasgow's notorious underworld for able-bodied men such as army deserters or criminals evading the law. Few questions were asked. As a final desperate measure, attention turned to local thugs and gangsters about to complete their sentences in Barlinnie Jail.

Prisons and ships have a long history. Converted wooden hulks in the River Medway were used for French prisoners in the Napoleonic Wars, and the former submarine depot ship HMS *Maidstone*, moored in Belfast harbour, was a jail for suspected Nationalist terrorists in Northern Ireland in 1972.

In August 1941, prisoners released from Barlinnie, normally five at a time, would suddenly find their way blocked by a posse of Sillitoe's officers after only a short walk from the prison gates. Told to "Just sign on and do your bit for your country, laddie. But if you don't, I'll see youse back inside in no time!", these men whose lives had been scarred by violence, anticipating a return to hard drinking, easy women, fighting and theft, had little alternative but to accept. Given contracts and money, which was promptly spent on liquor, or used to facilitate scams and bribes, these latter day pressed-men were eventually shipped off to Halifax in Canada in the modern French liner *Pasteur*, and then on to Montreal. Eventually traveling down to the United

Roger Paine

States, they arrived at the League Island Navy Yard of Philadelphia where the *George Washington*, the ship for which they had been recruited as crew, was being refitted after ten years rusting at her moorings, destined for the breaker's yard.

Work to get the ship seaworthy again continued throughout the autumn of 1941, and by the end of November it seemed that old "Rip Van Winkle" really had been given a new lease of life. But the calamitous Japanese bombing of Pearl Harbour on 7th December, which finally pushed the United States into the Second World War, accelerated plans for refitting the ageing liner and the embarkation of her crew who had been enjoying the licentious pleasures of cosmopolitan Philadelphia.

The man who would first captain the *George Washington* in wartime, with many of his crew acquired from unconventional sources, was 67-year-old Captain David Bone. Glasgow born and bred, he was senior captain in the Anchor Line and had been at sea for over 50 years, including serving his apprenticeship as a "brassbounder" under sail. He was well used to dealing with not only the worst of the natural elements at sea but also the toughest of seamen hardened by life and experience. By coincidence, Captain Bone had also encountered recruitment of crew members by force on his first sailing ship voyage to San Francisco in 1891. This was in the days of "Shanghai" Brown, a waterfront villain who for a price would "acquire" seamen for short-handed captains, usually by rendering them drunk and unconscious. Similarities with some of the crew Captain Bone now found himself saddled with seemed too close for comfort.

Ships and Sealing Wax

Although the *George Washington* did not sail as originally planned, she managed to reach New York, and then Halifax, where her ageing coal-fired boilers blew up on the day in February 1942 when she was due to leave on her first voyage as a troopship. Eventually fitted with new oil-fired boilers, the ship once again put to sea early in 1943 and served throughout the remainder of the war, making several successful journeys to and from the Far East and accommodating over 5,000 US Army soldiers on each voyage. Captain Bone, who had by now left the ship and was commanding the armed merchant cruiser HMS *Circassia*, met his former command in Bombay in 1943. Pleased to see her, as he termed, "back in the water", after enduring so many problems he added, "I had always known she would be a grand sea-boat." In 1951, after a series of fires on board, the *George Washington* was laid up in Baltimore when another fire broke out on the quay which spread rapidly and completed destroyed the once great transatlantic liner.

Captain Bone continued to serve with distinction in merchant ships until the end of the war. For his outstanding services to the Merchant Navy he received a knighthood in 1946. He retired to live in Surrey, a world away from the sea and ships, and died in 1959. What became of the ex-convict Glasgow hard-men, the majority of whom had been employed as stokers in the ship's engine rooms in those desperate times, is a matter of conjecture. Some were known to have deserted, but many, perhaps not surprisingly, were never heard of again.

Chapter 9

CORONATION FLEET REVIEW

Monarchs have reviewed the fleets of their countries since the fourteenth century. At the Diamond Jubilee of Queen Victoria in 1897, seven miles of ships were assembled at Spithead to honour her sixty years on the throne. There was no such review for the same landmark of Her Majesty Queen Elizabeth II in 2012. The last Fleet Review held at Spithead was to mark Her Majesty's Silver Jubilee in 1977. A huge reduction in the number of warships, together with devastating cuts in defence spending, has since prevented any similar tribute.

To celebrate Her Majesty's Coronation in 1952 it was very different. In Portsmouth, on Sunday 14th June 1953, Her Majesty was piped on board HMS *Surprise*, the ship selected to be the Royal Yacht for the Coronation Fleet Review. HM Yacht *Britannia* did not enter service until late 1953. The Queen was accompanied by HRH The Duke of Edinburgh, HM The Queen Mother, Princess Margaret and other members of the Royal Family. At 3 pm the following day Her Majesty made her way up to the specially built saluting

Ships and Sealing Wax

platform erected forward of the ship's bridge, and HMS *Surprise*, flying the Royal Standard and the Admiralty flag, preceded by the Trinity House vessel MV *Patricia*, in whom Sir Winston Churchill and Mr Clement Atlee had embarked, moved slowly away from South Railway Jetty into Portsmouth harbour to the accompaniment of 21-gun royal salutes fired from every major warship anchored in Spithead.

The noise, like distant rolling thunder, reverberated from the anchored warships across the crowded beaches of Southsea, over to the green fields of the Isle of Wight, around the sturdy Napoleonic forts which still guard the anchorage, and bounced off the rugged walls of Fort Blockhouse at the harbour entrance. As the smoke from the guns cleared, the strong breeze stiffened the flags and pennants of the ships, dressed overall from bow to stern. The Royal Yacht, with *Patricia* in the vanguard, followed closely by HM Ships *Redpole*, *Starling*, *Fleetwood* and *Helmsdale*, led the royal procession through the packed lines of anchored ships.

On each ship, the crew, officers and sailors, stood to attention along every available inch of upper deck. As the Royal Yacht passed, and on an order from the captain, "Three Cheers For Her Majesty The Queen!", followed by three "Hip, Hip, Hip!"s, and their bellowed "Hurrahs!"—each louder than the last—echoed across the intervening sea. With each "Hurrah!" every man, having removed his uniform cap and holding it at arm's length above his head, simultaneously flourished it in a clockwise gesture as a personal salute. Her Majesty, standing high on her platform, waved in acknowledgement. The first ship to welcome Her Majesty was the battleship, HMS *Vanguard*, flying the flag of the Commander in Chief, Home Fleet, Admiral Sir George Creasy, with a Royal Marines band on the quarterdeck playing the national anthem. It was this ship which had taken King George VI and Queen Elizabeth, and the two Princesses, on their visit to South Africa in 1948.

The Royal Yacht slowly moved down the lines of ships, to be greeted by the cheers of salute from the crews. Over 300 ships, including merchant ships and those from the fishing fleets, took part. There were 197 British warships, 13 from Commonwealth countries—Australia, Canada, New Zealand, India and Pakistan—16 from foreign navies, including the USS *Baltimore* from the United States, the French cruiser *Montcalm*, and the Russian cruiser, *Sverdlov*, about which little was known, on her first visit to a foreign port after commissioning two years previously. The ship was later to attract notoriety when her name was linked with the disappearance of Commander "Buster" Crabb in mysterious circumstances in 1956.

Also present were the aircraft carriers *Indomitable, Illustrious, Indefatigable, Implacable* and *Eagle*, successor to her namesake sunk ten years earlier escorting convoys to Malta. A reminder of the past was the three-masted, fully-rigged Italian sail training ship *Amerigo Vespucci*, with her crew of cadets standing on the yards. There were the depot ships *Maidstone, Montclare* and *Adamant*, floating bases for submarines, and many submarines manned by their crews standing along the casing or in the conning tower. The review also coincided with the news that the A-class submarine *Andrew* had just successfully completed the first submerged crossing of the Atlantic by a British warship, 2,840 miles. The days of nuclear powered submarines were some ten years in the future.

Lines of anti-submarine frigates, including *Brocklesby, Orwell, Termagant, Tenacious* and *Tyrian*, and the battle-

Ships and Sealing Wax

class destroyers *St Kitts, Barfleur* and *Finisterre*; the new weapon-class anti-submarine destroyers *Crossbow* and *Scorpion*; the fast minelayer *Manxman*; the Algerine-class minesweeper *Welcome*; fast patrol boats, descendants of HM Coastal Forces in World War II; the veteran three-funneled cadet training cruiser *Devonshire*; the light cruiser *Dido* (Flagship of the Reserve Fleet); cruisers *Sheffield, Swiftsure* (Flagship of Home Fleet Flotillas), *Superb, Gambia* (Flagship of Mediterranean Fleet Flotillas) and *Glasgow*, 9,000 tons, the largest cruiser and flagship of the Commander-in-Chief, Mediterranean.

Having sailed fourteen miles through the Fleet, the royal yacht anchored close to HMS *Vanguard*. It was now the turn of the Fleet Air Arm to fly past in salute, led by Rear Admiral Walter Couchman, Flag Officer Flying Training, in a Vampire jet. Over 300 aircraft, flown by RN pilots, and those from the Royal Naval Volunteer Reserve, Royal Canadian and Royal Australian Navies, took part. These included the aptly named Dragonfly helicopters, Meteor and Seahawk jets, Sea Furys, Sea Hornets, Skyraiders, Fireflys, Attackers and Avengers. The air was full of high-powered, piston-engined whines, and the Queen shielded her eyes as she looked upwards into the bright afternoon sky at formation after formation of aircraft flying overhead. Later she went on board the Commander in Chief's flagship for dinner. From there, at 10.30 pm, Her Majesty gave a signal and the fleet of hundreds of darkened ships lying at anchor was suddenly lit by millions of lights, as each ship became illuminated in brilliant, twinkling outline. It was a memorable sight. A dazzling firework display concluded the Review.

Nearly every ship which participated at Spithead over sixty years ago is now gone from the seas upon which they

Roger Paine

once so proudly sailed. Her Majesty Queen Elizabeth II, to whom their crews paid handsome and heartfelt tribute at the Coronation Fleet Review in 1953, continues to sail majestically on. Rule Britannia.

Chapter 10

CHRISTMAS WITH THE FLEET

The media has been awash with commemorations and events marking the centenary of the beginning and the end of the First World War. Many have concentrated, with good reason, on the conditions experienced by soldiers in the trenches of Flanders. But, one hundred years on, it is worth recalling what conditions were like in the Royal Navy at Christmas 1916.

The magazine *The War Illustrated* was published regularly from 1914 to 1919 and covered the war in all its aspects, and in every sphere of action. The 23rd December 1916 edition contained an article headlined "Christmas with the Fleet".

It was said when the Kaiser shattered the peace of the world over two years ago that it would need something more than a European war to upset the routine of the British Navy. It was an extravagant thing to say, however closely the peace training of the Navy since 1904 had been assimilated to the expected conditions of the "real thing". To give an instance— and it is only a small one, no matter how large it may seem at

Roger Paine

this particular time of the year—the Navy was always most punctilious, and even generous, in its celebration of Christmas. Depots and training establishments were closed down for the principal service holiday of the year, and every ship in home waters returned to her "home port"—or as near to it as she could conveniently get—to put herself virtually out of commission for three weeks. Every ship's crew was divided into two "watches", and each watch had ten days leave, the first getting home for Christmas and the second for New Year.

Things are different today, when a man's only chance for anything approaching "long leave" is when his ship is temporarily in the hands of the dockyard mateys. As for the seasons the war has levelled them out in everything but temperature. The first Christmas day of the war we sent over our flotillas and a bevy of seaplanes to drop a few souvenirs around Cuxhaven—and some of those who went over in a sea-plane carrier, and then spent an hour or two over the guns of the German defences, were picked up later and ate their Christmas dinner in the bowels of a submarine.

Whatever the day of the month or the year there can be no relaxation of the navy's vigilance. The patrols—from motor boats and trawlers up to those antennae of naval power, the light cruisers—can never be withdrawn nor reduced, although, as every ship cannot be at sea all the time, a certain proportion of officers and men will still be lucky enough to spend their Christmas ashore. Nor need anyone imagine that in any ship, great or small, the festival will be allowed to pass without due observance—subject always to the paramount call of the war. No unnecessary work is done —which is a useful concession in a big ship, but does not

Ships and Sealing Wax

count for much in a destroyer or a drifter on patrol—and as far as possible the day is treated as a Sunday.

At Christmas time the sailor loves to decorate the mess deck with festoons of coloured paper, while every man provides his photographs of "home" and anything else that may serve to take off the bare service look of his surroundings". A Christmas tree used to be hoisted to the top of the mainmast as the ship's own yuletide decoration. One hundred years ago RN ships in harbour would have represented a small forest of fir. Today, it is more likely ships will be illuminated with floodlights, or a necklace of lights from bow to stern. But the underlying theme in the Royal Navy today remains attempting to enjoy Christmas in the same way as at home.

In a warship on Christmas Day the crew's quarters will be visited by the ship's captain, traditionally accompanied by the youngest sailor on board. In the days of rum issue the captain would have been offered a "Christmas tot". This was always politely refused, for if accepted it is doubtful whether the "skipper's rounds" would ever have been completed! *The War Illustrated* magazine described this ritual:

> In the "happy ships" of the Navy—and that means in nearly every ship—you would find not only the decorations, but also a few pointed suggestions to the officers as to what they might do to make things happier for the ship's company. In such ships the captain and the whole of the officers make a round of the mess decks at dinner-time and for once in a way the barrier of discipline is broken down, and officers and men exchange the ordinary greetings of the season.

Roger Paine

Ships' Christmas puddings have traditionally contained a generous amount of rum. Another long held tradition requires the rum—which now has to be purchased ashore—to be poured into the pudding mix by the captain, whilst the ingredients are stirred into a large tub with a boat paddle. As well as rum-flavoured puddings and cakes, Christmas fare enjoyed by sailors has rarely been lacking. The meals enjoyed by Aubrey and Maturin in the Patrick O'Brian novels provide a glimpse of what might have been on the table in the eighteenth century. "The porpoises rather strangely jointed by the ship's butcher were served out for Christmas dinner and declared better, far better, than roast pork." Two hundred years later, a menu from an RN aircraft carrier at sea in the Persian Gulf on Christmas Day showed that nearly 50 separate dishes were available at the four meals served to the 1,800 crew.

Other traditional events take place on ships at Christmas. Before satellite links, videos, i-phones and emails, a concert, or music from the ship's band to accompany carol singing, was popular. Ship's pantomimes, colloquially known as "Sods Operas" ("Sods" being the "Ship's Operatic and Dramatic Society"), were often enjoyed, and gave the crew an opportunity to dress up as outlandish characters in bizarre costumes. Although full of bawdy humour, they kept to recognised stories. Forty years ago the pantomime "Dick Whittington" was performed on HMS *Endurance* when patrolling the frozen seas of Antarctica. The opening chorus contained the appropriate words, "But if you don't like it, or it's not nice, then come back next year, we're doing it—on ice!"

Ships and Sealing Wax

Accompanying the Christmas 1916 article was an evocative black and white illustration "Pudding in Peril: Tense Moments on a Warship" with the caption

> If the Christmas pudding is proverbial among soldiers and civilians as a symbol of the festive season, in the Fleet it is something of a rite, and no sailor-cook would dare to face the ship's company after having omitted it from the Christmas menu. Furthermore, on its way from the cook's galley to the mess-deck the pudding is often beset with peril of wind and wave, and it is certain not to be trusted to anyone who is not absolutely assured of his sea-legs, even though a gale be blowing.

For those spending Christmas at sea it will never be exactly the same as at home. Yet thanks to some long held traditions, the festive season in the Royal Navy is still a time to be enjoyed, and remembered. Even if making your way along the upper deck balancing a Christmas pudding on a tray is no longer necessary, the ingredients of the pudding will not have changed!

Chapter 11

CHRISTMAS DAY HAS NOT ALWAYS BEEN A DAY FOR CELEBRATION.

This was especially true for the inhabitants of Hong Kong in 1941. Prime Minister Winston Churchill's statement on 21st December 1941, "Every day that you are able to maintain your resistance you help the Allied cause all over the world," sounded strangely at odds with what he had written six months earlier: "There is not the slightest chance of holding Hong Kong or relieving it. It is most unwise to increase the loss we shall suffer there." He may, however, have later been persuaded by the then General Officer Commanding Hong Kong, Major General Grasett, who felt that by re-enforcing the Crown Colony the defending forces would be able to hold out for considerably longer—enough, possibly, for the war in Europe to have ended. Churchill agreed, and two Canadian battalions were deployed to Hong Kong in November 1941. But it proved to be far too little and much too late.

The period between the two World Wars was the heyday of the Royal Navy on the China Station. The fleet based in Hong Kong consisted of: the 5th Cruiser Squadron, one ship

Ships and Sealing Wax

of which flew the flag of the Commander in Chief, China Station; the 4ᵗʰ Submarine Flotilla of 12 boats; the Yangtse Flotilla of 10 gunboats; the West River Flotilla of five boats; and the 8ᵗʰ Destroyer Flotilla, consisting of nine ships and usually an aircraft carrier—frequently HMS *Hermes*. In 1937, as the Japanese invaded Manchuria and then China itself, the Royal Navy became involved in the large-scale evacuation of British citizens from Shanghai to Hong Kong. The Japanese bombed and shelled its ships.

Since September 1939 and the outbreak of war with Germany, Britain had been fighting an increasingly bloody and costly war in Europe and the Mediterranean. It had also become clear that Hong Kong was ever more isolated from Europe and its defence would be limited. There were good strategic reasons for choosing Singapore rather than Hong Kong as the British Far Eastern base. A cruiser squadron operating from Singapore could, within two days, be either in the Indian Ocean or off the southern coast of China. Singapore lay at the end of a peninsula that was British territory and protected by a solid bloc of British, Dutch and French possessions. Only independent Thailand (Siam) was identified as a likely jumping off point for Japanese aggression. Hong Kong, on the other hand, although well situated for action in the China Sea, was uncomfortably close to Japan. The Japanese occupation of China and Taiwan (Formosa) meant that Hong Kong was increasingly vulnerable to attack at any time.

In 1941 Hong Kong's own forces consisted of both regulars and volunteers from all three services. Conscription had been introduced in 1939 for men ages 18 to 41. In addition, many European and Commonwealth nationals had signed up for the volunteer defence forces. So had many

Chinese, although they served mainly as drivers, orderlies and medics.

Naval forces comprised approximately 1,600 Royal Navy, Royal Marines and Hong Kong Royal Naval Volunteer Reserve personnel. Since it was considered there could be no serious naval defence of Hong Kong, two of three available destroyers were ordered to Singapore on 8th December. This was the day after the Japanese had attacked the United States at Pearl Harbour and two days before the battleship HMS *Prince of Wales* and the battlecruiser HMS *Repulse* were sunk by the Japanese with enormous loss of life off the east coast of Malaya.

The Japanese, under General Takashi Sakai, commenced their attack on Hong Kong at 8 am on 8th December. About fifty aircraft bombed and strafed Kai Tak airfield, destroying the five small out-of-date Royal Air Force planes stationed there. The strength of the naval forces was equally unimpressive. Comprising a third destroyer, HMS *Thracian*, built in 1916, with a maximum speed of 21 knots and a total armament of three four-inch guns; an Insect-class Yangtse River gunboat, HMS *Cicala*; two smaller gunboats; and a flotilla of six ageing motor torpedo boats of the 2nd MTB Flotilla. If something of the Nelson spirit was called for in those dark December days it might be said to have been provided by the only one-armed captain in the entire Royal Navy, veteran of Coastal Forces in World War One, Lieutenant Commander John Boldero of HMS *Cicala*. It was, nevertheless, remarkable what the Royal Navy—only a shadow of the impressive fleet on the China Station ten years earlier—was able to achieve with such limited resources.

In the fight for Hong Kong the Royal Navy had several roles: to support by bombardment army action on land, to

Ships and Sealing Wax

evacuate troops, to intercept Japanese landing craft attempting to cross the harbour from the mainland, and, finally, when all else had failed, to destroy shipping too valuable to be allowed to fall into enemy hands. The Navy was even involved in a miniature Dunkirk evacuation. Between 12th and 13th December, *Thracian* was instrumental in evacuating one of the resident Indian Army battalions from the Devil's Peak area, coming as close in shore as her captain dared. Even so, shells and mortar bombs exploded around the troops as they waded out to the ship, which then took them to Aberdeen, rapidly becoming the centre of resistance on the island because it was on the coast furthest away from the Japanese guns.

Having established themselves on the mainland, the Japanese attempted to cross the main Hong Kong harbour on the night of 15th December but *Thracian* sailed from Aberdeen, with darkness providing sufficient cover; however, by keeping close inshore the ship went aground. Desperate attempts to refloat her succeeded just before dawn and revealed two large junks packed to the gunwales with invasion troops. The ship promptly blew these out of the water before limping back to dry dock. Three days later five motor torpedo boats, three commanded by officers of the Hong Kong Royal Naval Volunteer Reserve, managed to sink three heavily laden landing craft—enough to make the enemy stop its ferrying service, even if only temporarily. The Japanese then called in their airpower and the ships were sunk.

The last ship to be put out of action was HMS *Cicala*, which had been engaged in the unwelcome task of sinking merchant ships to stop them being taken over by the enemy. Under heavy air attack, and before the ship was sunk, the crew managed to get away in life rafts and were soon ashore fighting as soldiers. As the battle on shore raged from 22nd to 24th December, brave pockets of resistance held up the Japanese advance. But the end was in sight. Repulse Bay, where a large number of Europeans lived, fell on the 22nd and many of the defenders were killed, or captured and later executed at Eucliffe Castle. Despite Churchill's fine words, and the promise of "lasting honour" to those who "maintained resistance", the outcome was inevitable.

On Christmas Day 1941, at Queens Pier, after bitter fighting ashore and afloat, Sir Mark Young, Governor of Hong Kong, and General Christopher Maltby, General Officer Commanding, offered an unconditional surrender. The Japanese had successfully captured Hong Kong in eighteen days at a cost of around 3,000 casualties and had taken 12,000 prisoners. Naval forces had suffered 148 casualties, 119 of which were killed.

A contemporary account by a naval officer describes his Christmas seventy-five years ago. *In the morning of the 26th the Japanese Army marched into the dockyard and took all our arms. The Japs informed us we were their prisoners and would have to obey their orders. We were then ordered to the China Fleet Club (formerly the Royal Naval Canteen) a few hundred yards down the street. When we got there, other Japs, apparently very angry, ordered us back to the Yard. Eventually I arrived at Shamshuipo camp at about 1700 with all my gear including my bed which I had started off with, completely deadbeat. The camp was in a filthy mess, about a foot of rubble everywhere, no beds or furniture, no windows and very few doors to the huts. I was one of the few who had a bed, the others had to lay down in*

Ships and Sealing Wax

the dirt for the night. Now we started our life as prisoners of war.

Another three Christmases passed before the Royal Navy, led into harbour by the cruiser HMS *Swiftsure*, returned to Hong Kong on 30th August 1945.

Chapter 12

CHARTING THE SEAS

The science of hydrography, the methodical recording of navigational information for the seafarer in charts and other forms, is as old as navigation itself. It was through the development of the sea chart, with its visual representation of exploration and trade, conquest and colonization, that the world took shape.

While the early maps and charts are fascinating in their often strange and distorted views of newly discovered lands, the hydrographic surveying work of the eighteenth and early nineteenth centuries, frequently carried out in small open boats, was extraordinary in its level of accuracy. Seafarers had relied on local knowledge for centuries, generally keeping close to the coast, and although the cultures of the Far East and Persian Gulf had developed the ability to use wind against sail to propel ships across the oceans, the Mediterranean is the commonly accepted birthplace of navigation.

It was the magnetic compass, in the hands of the twelfth-century navigators, that was the key to accurately recorded

Ships and Sealing Wax

information, and it is from this period that the earliest charts survive. These were known as portolans (from *"portolano"* meaning an Italian pilot book with sailing directions), and were used by the Venetians and Genoese. By the sixteenth century, manuscript charts for use at sea were produced, including the early Portuguese charts of the coast of Africa and those by Jean Rotz, a Frenchman much respected for the accuracy of his charts which included a world map in 1542..

Out of sight of land, across the vast oceans, the means of pinpointing position were haphazard and many ships were lost with their crews and valuable cargoes. Latitude, the lines that run parallel to the equator, and longitude, the lines running north and south to converge at the poles, had been the grid lines used to mark out the globe for thousands of years and were used by Ptolemy in his first maps of the known world in AD 150. In order to determine longitude, and fix a ship's position, the difficulty had always been in designing a timepiece that could keep the time at Greenwich accurately at sea. It was the Yorkshire-born clockmaker John Harrison, born in 1693, who was the first to do so by designing a clock with moving parts that were perfectly balanced in relation to one another, regardless of ship movement and atmospheric changes, and ran to time. It was called the H4 chronometer and can still be seen at the Greenwich Royal Observatory. Captain James Cook, who made three long voyages across the Pacific Ocean in the eighteenth century, was so impressed that he had an exact replica made and called it "our never failing guide".

It was not until 1795 that King George III appointed the Scottish geographer Alexander Dalrymple to be the first Hydrographer to the Admiralty. In the same year the Hydrographic Office (now known as the United Kingdom

Roger Paine

Hydrographic Office, or UKHO) was founded. Dalrymple set to work reviewing the "difficulties and dangers to His Majesty's fleet in the navigation of ships" and in 1800 the first Admiralty chart appeared. Rear Admiral Sir Francis Beaufort was appointed Hydrographer in 1829 and he began organising surveys all around the world to improve chart coverage, encouraging international co-operation. Among his many accomplishments was the Beaufort Scale of wind strength, still familiar to mariners today. By 1855, the Chart Catalogue listed 1,981 charts, with 64,000 copies issued to the Fleet. Thanks to the vision and efforts of Beaufort, the Admiralty now led the world in the techniques of hydrography and cartography.

More than 150 years later, the UKHO is still at the forefront of charting the world's oceans. Today, its primary activity, as a part of the Ministry of Defence, is the provision of navigational products and services to the Royal Navy and Merchant Navy, which must all comply with the Safety of Life at Sea (SOLAS) regulations. As such, the UKHO is the power behind the world-renowned Admiralty brand of products and services. This portfolio now includes a remarkable 3,300 standard navigational charts and 220 navigational publications, as well as an ever-expanding range of leading digital and web-based products.

While the seas are being mapped, a base on land is also needed. The UKHO's headquarters is at Taunton in Somerset. Here it employs approximately 1,000 staff, including a small number of naval officers who also serve on board the RN's five surveying ships which operate throughout the world. The information they gain from practical work done on the waves is used for producing Admiralty charts and nautical publications. The global

Ships and Sealing Wax

interests of the UKHO are reflected in the diversity of data received, including approximately 400 hydrographic surveys every year. From 1795, when masters of HM ships were instructed to deposit all original survey drawings with the Admiralty, these documents were stored in the cellars of Admiralty buildings in London. Now at Taunton, this collection of original survey data has grown to include over 2.5 million graphical items.

The archive contains a unique record of the exploration of the maritime world, including original manuscripts, books and atlases relating to the history of maritime cartography and exploration, as well as print and manuscript sailing directions, coastal views and ships' remark books from around 1750. Early charts were often embellished with beautiful artwork depicting the strange flora, fauna and native peoples encountered by explorers for the first time. Specially selected hand-coloured prints of the most attractive documents, known as "The Admiralty Collection", can be purchased from UKHO.

Until the availability of the meticulous charts which are produced today—without which no self-respecting mariner, including weekend yachties, would ever go to sea—seafaring was always an extremely hazardous profession. It is sobering to reflect that today's Global Positioning Systems (GPS) can fix a ship's position to within a few feet, day or night. Most recently introduced are Port Approach Guides providing information on a single chart to help simplify port entry and exit.

All the more admiration must go to those early explorers and voyagers, such as Vasco da Gama, Magellan, Columbus, Cook and Bligh, who achieved so much with relatively unsophisticated equipment. Original hand-drawn charts

Roger Paine

from centuries past, and the 21st century electronic navigational charts and digital tide-prediction programmes now sit under the same roof in the English countryside. UKHO is the world's largest hydrographic agency and has recently declared net profits of over £10 million. Not only is charting the seas a global science, it is also big business.

Chapter 13

A WARSHIP NAMED SUSSEX

The Royal Navy has a long tradition of naming ships after British counties. Over a period of three hundred and sixty years, five ships have been named "Sussex", although there is no warship of this name at present.

The first *Sussex* was a 40-gun frigate launched in 1652 when Oliver Cromwell was establishing a strong navy. As the Netherlands was sympathetic to the Royalists exiled there during the Civil War, in the race for maritime supremacy in the waters that divided the two countries the scene was set for armed conflict. It was to be a war fought entirely at sea. The two fleets met three times in 1652 and 1653.

At the Battle of Portland in February 1653, although the outcome was inconclusive, the Dutch Admiral Maarten Tromp claimed victory. But this was premature, for five months later, at the Battle of the Gabbard, more commonly known as the North Foreland, an English fleet of over one hundred ships again clashed with Tromp's ships. This time the English, under Admiral George Monck, were successful. Tromp was killed and the Dutch coast blockaded. *Sussex* took part in both these actions and every warship with this name since has the battle honours, "Portland 1653" and "Gabbard 1653".

Forty years later, when the monarchy had been restored and Britain, under King William III, formerly Prince of Orange, was in formal alliance with Holland, the combined navies of both countries suffered a heavy defeat in a sea battle against France. Mastery of the Channel was again being disputed and at the Battle of Beachy Head in July 1690 the French were victorious. The Anglo-Dutch fleet, under Admiral Herbert Torrington, was humiliated. King William immediately ordered a major warship building programme. Twenty ships of 1,200 tons, 160 feet long, 80 guns and 500 crew, were ordered. One of these new vessels was named HMS *Sussex*.

In December 1693, a huge fleet of forty warships and four times as many merchantmen gathered at Portsmouth. The flagship of the fleet, commanded by Admiral Sir Francis Wheeler, was HMS *Sussex*, launched ten months earlier. Ordered to sail to the Mediterranean, the admiral had also been given sealed orders to carry ten tons of gold and silver coins packed in iron chests in order to buy the loyalty of the Duke of Savoy. It represented about £1 million in cash. In today's terms the money is estimated to be worth around £2.6 billion. One night out of Gibraltar, in February 1694, a severe storm struck the fleet. Weighed down by the vast cargo of gold, the ship was unable to stop the sea pouring through the open gun ports, and sank. Except for two men, everyone on board drowned.

For the next three centuries the tragedy remained largely forgotten. But following discovery of contemporary documents in 1995, the giant US undersea exploration

Ships and Sealing Wax

company, Odyssey Marine Exploration, has been attempting to salvage the ship. But international controversy over ownership has prevented the ship's cargo being brought to the surface, except for a few gold coins and other artefacts. The ship remains lying at the bottom of the Mediterranean. If the ongoing disputes can be resolved, the second HMS *Sussex*, one of the richest treasure ships in the world, could become a household name.

The third ship to bear the county name was a 90-gun second rate, one of England's "wooden walls", launched in 1756 as HMS *Union*, before being re-named HMS *Sussex* in 1802. She later served as a floating barracks and hospital ship before being broken up in 1816.

The fourth HMS *Sussex* was a 9,750-ton "London" class heavy cruiser built as part of the 1926 Ship Build Programme. Laid down in February 1927, she was built by Hawthorn Leslie at Hebburn-on-Tyne and launched twelve months later. A magnificent looking ship, she was 633 feet long with three raked funnels, 8 x 8 inch and 4 x 4 inch guns, a maximum speed of 32 knots and a peacetime complement of 650. Initially part of the Mediterranean Fleet in the halcyon days of the Royal Navy in that region, she later took part in a two-year exchange with the cruiser HMAS *Australia* of the Australian Navy. Returning to the Mediterranean in 1936 she was on hand to protect neutral shipping along the coast of Spain during the final days of the Spanish Civil War.

At the outbreak of World War II in September 1939 she operated in the South Atlantic, taking part in the search for the German battle cruiser *Admiral Graf Spee*, later to be scuttled after the Battle of the River Plate. Over the next six years HMS *Sussex* was involved in many important naval operations. Her only period not on active service at sea followed a direct hit by a 250-pound bomb, dropped on 17 September 1940 during an air raid, whilst undergoing machinery repairs in Prince's Dock, Glasgow. This caused extensive fires in the engine room which threatened the ship's magazines and required the local community to be evacuated. In an attempt to control the fires, the dry dock was flooded, but water entered several internal compartments, making the ship unstable so that she capsized. Extensive structural repairs were needed to make the ship fully operational again. This work was carried out in Govan where, for almost two years, she was under repair before rejoining the First Cruiser Squadron at Scapa Flow in August 1942. Details of this major damage were not made public at the time.

In early 1943 the ship was deployed to the Eastern Fleet on convoy escort duties based in Durban, Mombasa and Colombo, before coming home for refit at Chatham in June 1944. She then returned again to the Indian Ocean and off the coast of Malaysia took part in operations against the Japanese, which included being attacked in July 1945 by two Kamikaze suicide bombers. As the flagship of Rear Admiral Cedric Holland, HMS *Sussex* was in Singapore on 5 September 1945 when General Itagaki, commander of the Japanese garrison, and Vice Admiral Fukudone, were brought on board to formally sign the surrender of Singapore to the Allies.

The ship remained with the Eastern Fleet until after VJ Day before returning to Chatham in March 1946. After a period employed in trooping duties bringing back personnel from the Far East she paid off in Devonport. In April 1947, on completion of refit, she re-commissioned for service with the British Pacific Fleet. At the end of 1948 she was relieved

Ships and Sealing Wax

in Singapore by HMS *Belfast*, the ship now permanently moored by Tower Bridge in London, returning to finally pay off at Portsmouth in February 1949. During the Second World War she gained two further battle honours, "Norway 1940" and "Burma 1943". In 1950 she was sold for scrap and broken up at Arnott Young's yard in Dalmuir, a sad end for a proud ship, whose motto, "Bravely in action", could hardly have been more appropriate.

The name HMS *Sussex*, however, was to live on for another forty-four years. The Sussex Division of the Royal Naval Volunteer Reserve (RNVR), later the Royal Naval Reserve (RNR), had established its headquarters at Hove in November 1903. For the first forty-eight years of its existence the unit had no name. It was simply titled HQ Sussex RNVR Division. But at noon on Saturday 28 April 1951 the Division was formally commissioned with the ship's name "HMS Sussex". The commissioning warrant was read by the Mayor of Brighton at a ceremony held at the Hove Battery. Commodore Earl Howe, who as the Right Honourable Viscount Curzon had been Commanding Officer of the Sussex RNVR Division from 1907 to 1939, was also present. On this occasion, too, the ship's bell from the cruiser HMS *Sussex*, which had been obtained by the Sussex Motor Yacht Club after the ship was scrapped, was handed over by the club's Commodore, saying, "It is no ordinary bell. It is a bell with a wonderful record. Whenever this bell rings it should bring to your minds memories of a great ship."

Training at sea for the Reserve Divisions has always been carried out in ships on loan from the Royal Navy. For a period of over twenty years from 1960 these ships were usually Ton-class minesweepers which were given a new "local" name appropriate to that Division when used by the

Roger Paine

RNR. HMS *Fittleton* was the ship belonging to the Sussex Division, where she was known as HMS *Curzon*. In 1976 she reverted to her HMS *Fittleton* name but remained operating from HMS *Sussex*, manned by reservists of that Division, and others from the London Division. Tragically, she was sunk in collision with an RN ship on 20 September 1976 whilst on exercises in the North Sea. Twelve volunteer reservists lost their lives in the worst peacetime accident involving the RNR.

The Division's HQ at Hove transferred to a new purpose-built building at Maxwell Wharf, Shoreham, opened on 12 July 1968 by Princess Alexandra. HMS *Sussex* remained there until March 1994 when the unit was disbanded following defence spending cuts. With this demise went the name "HMS *Sussex*." The original ship's bell, engraved "Sussex 1928", from the fourth warship of that name, was presented to Chichester Cathedral, where it hangs to this day.

Chapter 14

THE HISTORY OF SMUGGLING

The dictionary definition of smuggling, "defrauding the government of revenue by the evasion of custom duties or excise taxes", goes a long way to explain why stories of smuggling, and smugglers, have been a source of fascination for centuries.

Few people want to pay the full price for something if they are able to purchase it more cheaply, or possibly pay nothing at all! Especially if this means that the government, or the monarchy, is being deprived of money which they want to use to wage wars or indulge in personal excesses. This aspect of "us versus them" has traditionally helped to provide a veneer of legitimacy to an otherwise illegal activity.

The history of smuggling can be directly linked to the earliest recorded imposition of customs duty. This was approved at the Winchester Assize of 1204 in the reign of King John. From that time customs—customary payment of dues of any kind—were payable to the King on the import or export of goods. Collectors of customs were appointed by King Edward I in 1298 to collect customs for the Crown in certain ports. One of the first duties to be levied was on the export of wool, which was in great demand in Europe. The initial duties imposed were small, but as the Hundred Years War progressed, so the tax increased in order to fund troops and further fighting. Smuggling, to avoid paying these taxes, began in earnest.

Smuggling of wool, which was known as "owling" after the owl-like noises made by smugglers to communicate with each other, was made punishable by death in 1661. Ten years later, King Charles II created the Board of Customs and during the same period the Board of Excise was established to levy inland duties on articles at the time of their manufacture. The next two hundred years saw taxes imposed on beer and tobacco, cheese and hard soap, salt and pepper and, at one point, playing cards and windows.

In the eighteenth century customs duties were imposed on imported luxuries such as silk, lace, tea, tobacco, rum and brandy. At each port, staff from the Customs House searched cargoes and collected dues. At sea, Customs Revenue cruisers watched for vessels illegally offloading cargo. Ashore, Riding Officers patrolled the coast to catch smugglers as they beached cargoes and carried them inland to secret hiding places in inns, barns, caves and cellars. The coastlines of Kent and Sussex, with their proximity to the Continent, were in the front line of this activity.

As attempts to apprehend smugglers became more organized, so smugglers became more ruthless. In the 1740s the Hawkhurst Gang, so named as they hailed from the village of that name in Kent, terrorized the south coast from Deal to Portsmouth. It was said that they could raise 500 men in an hour and were prepared to murder to protect their trade. They even broke into the Poole Customs House to retrieve goods confiscated by the Customs service. The gang's reign came to an end when its leaders were executed in 1749.

Nevertheless, the government was hugely worried about the extraordinary quantities of smuggled goods. In 1779, in response to estimates of £7 million lost in revenue each year, Parliament passed another act against smuggling. Yet in some areas, despite all the official efforts, whole communities were dependent on smuggling for their existence. In the Scilly Isles the population faced starvation when stricter preventative measures were introduced.

Smuggling continued throughout the early nineteenth century but began to decline after the conclusion of the Napoleonic Wars. The anti-smuggling effort had been stepped up with the formation in 1809 of a disciplined coastal force, the Preventative Water Guard, and of the Coastguard in 1822. But it was simple economics that ended smuggling's golden era. Britain's adoption of a free trade policy in the 1840s reduced import duties significantly and made smuggling no longer a viable occupation.

Although smuggling, in one form or another, has continued unabated for the past 800 years smugglers now have little in common with their predecessors. HM Revenue & Customs (HMRC), as it became known in 2005, now tackles some of today's most serious and organised criminals who attempt to smuggle illegal goods such as drugs, weapons, endangered species, and obscene material into the country. Around £110 billion in VAT, duties and taxes is collected every year but it is estimated that £2.7 billion per annum in revenue is lost as a result of tobacco smuggling, and a further £215 million through alcohol smuggling. The

UK alone spends more than £1 billion each year tackling the problem of drug smuggling.

Whilst some of the goods now smuggled into the country are dramatically different from those of years ago, the practice of apprehending smugglers and their vessels at sea has changed little. The UK Border Force now has four customs cutters stationed at strategic ports around the UK. The latest is HMC *Valiant*, a 42-metre fast patrol craft which came into service at a cost of £4.3 million in 2004. With a skilled crew of 12 using the latest surveillance technology, it is aimed at meeting the challenge posed by today's well-financed smugglers. HMC Valiant seized an estimated 300 kg of cocaine off the south coast of the Isle of Wight during 2010 and HMC Searcher seized cannabis said to be worth £12 million off the Sussex Coast in 2011.

That is a far cry from the days described by poet and author, Rudyard Kipling, who lived at Burwash in East Sussex, a village on a smugglers' route inland from the coast. His poem, "A Smuggler's Song", reflects the respect local communities once had for smugglers where, euphemistically, they were known as "the gentlemen":

If you wake at midnight, and hear a horse's feet,
Don't go drawing back the blind, or looking in the street,
Them that asks no questions isn't told a lie.
Watch the wall, my darling, while the Gentlemen go by!

Chapter 15

THE ROYAL NAVY AT GALLIPOLI

By the spring of 1915 the war in Europe had reached stalemate. Troops stared at each other from a line of opposing trenches that stretched from the English Channel to the Swiss border. Neither opponent was able to outflank its enemy, resulting in costly and unproductive direct attacks on well-fortified defences. The war of movement that both sides had anticipated at the beginning of the conflict had literally, in many instances, become bogged down in mud.

Allied leaders, including Lord Kitchener, appointed as Secretary of State for War by Prime Minister Asquith, and Winston Churchill, First Lord of the Admiralty, sought a way out of the impasse. The Dardenelles Strait, the only outlet from Russia to the Mediterranean, came under scrutiny. Over 100 years earlier, in 1807, a successful naval operation under Vice Admiral Sir John Duckworth had forced the passage of the Dardanelles, and his squadron of "wooden walls", including veterans of the Battle of Trafalgar, destroyed eleven sail of the Turkish Navy and anchored eight miles off Constantinople. It was believed that a successful attack in this same area could therefore open up a sea lane through the Black Sea, and provide a base for attacking Germany and its allies though what Churchill described as the "soft underbelly of Europe", thus diverting attention from the Western Front.

Although the idea of gaining control of the Dardenelles and seizing Constantinople, in order to reduce the Turkish threat to Russia, was plausible, in execution it failed totally because of poor planning and a complete absence of coordination between Allied land and naval forces. The original plan was that the Royal Navy and the French Navy together should force the passage; even if this had been successful, it is difficult to see how any advantage could have been consolidated without control of the nearby surrounding shores. At sea, the stumbling block was the extensive Turkish minefield, which was covered by shore batteries equipped with searchlights. Minesweepers were unable to operate because of the covering artillery, and until the minefield was cleared the big ships could not get close enough for the accuracy required to silence well-sited field guns.

On 18th March 1915 the battleships HMS *Irresistible*, HMS *Ocean*, and the French battleship *Bouvet* were sunk by mines and Turkish gunfire from ashore. HMS *Inflexible* was severely damaged. The Navy then withdrew until the troops arrived. A month later, on 25th April, a landing on the Gallipoli peninsula attempted to secure the shoreline and silence the Turkish guns. Trouble brewed from the beginning. Amphibious operations were a new and largely untried form of warfare. Poor communications, troop deployments and re-supply problems were recurring difficulties.

Ships and Sealing Wax

The Turks entrenched themselves on high ground, pouring artillery and machine gun fire upon the hapless British, French, Irish, Australian and New Zealand troops as they came ashore and tried to establish a beachhead. The focal point for landing the troops on the beach was HMS *River Clyde*, a former 4,000-ton collier put aground on "V" beach. Six awards of the Victoria Cross were made to officers and men of the Royal Navy, including two to midshipmen, for their outstanding bravery on the first day of the landings. A further two awards of the same honour for gallantry were made in May 1915 to Lieutenant Commander Edward Boyle and Lieutenant Commander Martin Nasmith for their conspicuous bravery whilst commanding HM submarines *E. 14* and *E.11* during operations in the Sea of Marmora beyond the Dardenelles.

Within weeks the battleground ashore began to resemble that of the Western Front, with both sides confronting each other from fortified trenches and being forced to sacrifice lives in futile frontal attacks on well-defended positions. The campaign continued for nine months, until the Allied forces withdrew. It was the first major military action of Australia and New Zealand as independent dominions and is often considered to mark the birth of national consciousness in those nations. The date of the landing, 25 April, is known as "Anzac Day", and continues to be commemorated in those countries every year.

In addition to the part played at sea by ships and men of the Royal Navy, the campaign marked a significant contribution by the Royal Naval Division. Established at the outbreak of war by Winston Churchill, it was composed largely of Royal Navy reservists who were not required in seagoing ships. The Division was composed originally of eight battalions, each named after a famous British naval commander—e.g. Anson, Benbow, Collingwood—plus four battalions from the Royal Marine depots at Deal, Chatham, Portsmouth and Plymouth. The 63rd Division, as the RND was officially known, was one of two British Divisions who took part in the Gallipoli landings. Initially shipped to Egypt, it fought in both the Anzac Cove and Cape Helles battles. But by the end of the campaign, the Division's casualties were so high that it no longer contained a significant number of naval servicemen, so in July 1916 it was redesignated and totally integrated into the British Army for the reminder of the war. A memorial to the 45,000 men who lost their lives serving in the RND in World War One is in the north-west corner of Horse Guards Parade in London, where it was moved from the Royal Naval College, Greenwich in 2003.

Signalman Eric Peacock was a Royal Navy sailor at Gallipoli. After qualifying at the Signal School in Portsmouth I was allocated to HMS *Irresistible*. Early in January 1915 we sailed from Chatham in the company of the battleship *Majestic*. We arrived via Malta at Tenedos, an island near the entrance to the Dardanelles. We were told we were going to bombard the area and force a passage through and shorten the war! The day of 18 March 1915 remains clear in my mind, as it was our biggest attack on the Turkish gun positions. Many battleships and destroyers, British and French, moved into position from west of the entrance to the Dardenelles. My action station was in the foretop, high on the foremast, manning the voicepipe to the captain. So I knew what was going on, and also had a magnificent view of the whole area.

The first real shock was hearing a heavy explosion and seeing the French battleship *Bouvet* listing and gradually disappearing, all in seconds. Suddenly there was an awful crunch, and the ship shuddered and began to list to starboard. I remember looking towards the bridge and seeing the captain leaning against the rails at the same time as I heard the order "Abandon Ship". I slipped into the water was soon picked up and taken to the battleship *Queen Elizabeth*. I then transferred to *Phaeton* and we travelled to Mudros. Here I was chosen as part of a landing party to land at "W" beach, Cape Helles. We disembarked from the *Euryalus* with the Lancashire Fusiliers. Rifle fire came from every point along the clifftop. There was barbed wire in the shallow water and on the shore. Somehow we got in bows-on, between the bodies and wire. I jumped out of the boat as I had to try and keep hold of my signaling equipment because that was vital—I wasn't any good without it, for, as soon as we hit the shore, and despite enemy fire, we had to keep up our signals to our ships covering the troops landing.

The Turks made several determined efforts to drive us into the sea. We slept where we could, when we could. Living in dugouts and lying on sandy soil meant that everyone became infected with lice. The heat, the unburied dead carcasses, and the rubbish brought in a plague of flies. Mealtimes were a nightmare, as everything was black with flies. As the months went on, we saw Turkish prisoners. We all admired them as fighters but they were mostly filthy, with torn and tattered uniforms. They'd had no pay for months and very little to eat. Yet they still shelled and shot at us. Rumours of a possible evacuation came through to us before anyone else. Units began to disappear. We heard that Suvla and Anzac beaches had been successfully evacuated with no casualties. By now, December, the weather was raw cold. Yet we couldn't believe the Turks would let us simply slip away. But they did, and on 8 January 1916 we left. Of that 20-man naval party I was one of the first onto the beach on 25 April 1915 and one of the last to leave. I was ten days off my eighteenth birthday.

In short, the Gallipoli campaign, despite countless individual acts of bravery and self-sacrifice, was a fiasco. On the Allied side, the reputation of one the key promoters of the expedition, Winston Churchill, was badly tarnished and took years to recover. Casualties were high, approximately 252,000, or 52% of the Allied Forces, while the Turks suffered about 300,000 casualties or a rate of 60%.

For the Allies the campaign was a dismal failure, yet for the Turks it was considered one of their greatest victories and a defining moment in the nation's history, a final surge in defence of the motherland as the Ottoman Empire crumbled, leading directly to the founding of the Republic of Turkey eight years later.

Chapter 16

"IF YOU HEAR THE GUN, YOU SHOULD RUN!"

On 15th November 1928, just a mile or so out at sea from Camber Sands and the village of Rye Harbour in East Sussex, there occurred a lifeboat tragedy that was front-page news at the time, and which reverberated around the world. It still reverberates today. Especially as many of the descendants of all seventeen crew members who drowned still live in Rye Harbour and the surrounding towns and villages.

Every year in November a special service of remembrance is held in the Church of the Holy Spirit, Rye Harbour's parish church. Many of those who attend are relatives and close family friends of those who perished in the tragic circumstances of that fateful night. In the churchyard, after the service, wreaths of roses and laurel leaves are laid on the impressive memorial with individual plaques which record the names and ages of all who lost their lives. The statue above the communal grave, depicting a lifeboat man in sou'wester, oilskins and lifebelt, is of Manx stone, a gift from the people of the Isle of Man.

Roger Paine

A lifeboat station for Rye was first established in 1805, but thirty years later the boat was transferred to Camber on the east side of the River Rother, although the name of the station remained unchanged. In the same year another lifeboat station was established at Winchelsea. The Rye station was closed in 1901 and in 1910 Winchelsea was re-named Rye Harbour. In May 1914 a new lifeboat was offered to Rye Harbour to replace the self-righting ten-oar pulling and sailing boat that had been in service since the turn of the century. The boat chosen was a fourteen-oar 38ft Liverpool class non self-righting pulling and sailing boat, weighing three tons. The cost of the new lifeboat was met by a legacy in memory of Mary Stanford, after whom the boat was named. It was built by J. E. Saunders of Cowes in the Isle of Wight and sailed from there, arriving in Rye Harbour on 19 October 1916. For the sake of practicality, the crew had rejected a self-righting boat as it would have been difficult to drag across the shingle to launch in the surf conditions of Rye Bay.

The night of 14th November 1928 was extremely dark and fiercely stormy. A Force 10, gusting Force 11, southwesterly gale was sweeping up the Channel, with winds in excess of 80 mph, forcing the sea into viciously large waves. Many ships along the coast were wrecked. Just after 4am on the 15th, a small Latvian steamer, *Alice of Riga,* laden with a cargo of bricks, was in collision with a larger German ship, *Smyrna*. In the collision, *Alice of Riga* lost her rudder and had a hole torn in her side. The weather was too bad for the *Smyrna* to attempt a rescue, and at 4.27 am the Ramsgate coastguard station received a message, passed on by North Foreland radio, "Steamer. Alice of Riga. Leaking. Danger. Drifting SW to W 8 miles from Dungeness". The message was then passed to Rye Harbour coastguard station, where it was received at 4.55 am. Immediately the coastguard, Bert Caister, fired the maroons, or rockets, to alert the lifeboat crew and the launchers.

The noise awoke most of the village, where the ferocious storm was rattling windows and doors and dislodging tiles from the rooftops. As a young man Fred Southerden recalled hearing his brother Charlie, a lifeboat man, tumble out of bed saying "Best go. Someone may need help." In addition to the coxswain and crew of the lifeboat, some thirty volunteers, both men and women, were required to launch the *Mary Stanford*. Schoolchildren, too, felt it was their duty to help, and from an early age were told "If you hear the gun, you should run!" On that pitch-dark morning in November 1928 everyone did run. For a mile and half against wind and rain so strong it was difficult to stand up, down the path across the shingle and mudflats which now form the Rye Nature Reserve, to the boathouse on the shore.

The maroons were fired just after 5 am, but because it was low tide and the weather so appalling, it took three attempts and almost two hours before the boat managed to get away. Then, just as daylight was beginning to break, a message was received by the coastguard in Rye Harbour that the crew of the *Alice of Riga* had been rescued by the *Smyrna*. This message had originally been received by Ramsgate coastguard station at 6.12 am. But as it was not, strictly speaking, a distress or "life saving message" it was regarded as "entitled" and not therefore requiring priority action. There had also been a further delay in sending the recall signal to the coastguard after an attempt to call Dungeness via Lydd had failed.

Roger Paine

Coastguard Bert Caister made frantic efforts, using a large signal lamp, to recall the lifeboat. But to no avail. The *Mary Stanford* had been launched some five minutes before the recall message reached the lifeboat station. With the crew soaking wet from their exertions in launching, and all the activity in the lifeboat whilst they did their best to keep her head to sea with the oars, it is hardly surprising that in the early morning murk, blinding spray and driving rain the recall signal was not seen.

At around 9 am the mate of a passing ship, the S.S. *Halton,* reported seeing the *Mary Stanford* three miles WSW from Dungeness, and a little later a sailor on the *Smyrna,* the ship involved in the collision, reported the same. All appeared well. But at about 10.30 am a boy, Cecil Marchant, collecting driftwood at Camber believed he saw, in a sudden shaft of sunlight, the lifeboat capsize. He ran home to tell his parents and promptly got a clip round the ear for making up stories, although just in case this was true his father reported it to the coastguard. Almost immediately rumours that "the Mary Stanford has gone over" went round the village. By 12 noon it had been confirmed and the boat could be seen floating upside down towards the shore.

Within ten minutes the maroons were fired and over one hundred people rushed to the beach where the upturned lifeboat lay. Over the next two hours the bodies of the crew were washed ashore. A total of fifteen that day. No effort was spared in trying to revive them, but all had drowned. Henry Cutting's body was washed ashore at Eastbourne three months later. The body of John Head has never been found. An Army tank from Lydd was brought to help right the lifeboat.

Ships and Sealing Wax

Speculation was rife as to the cause of the capsize. The most likely explanation, which exists to this day, was that Henry Cutting, the bowman, or John Head, the youngest member of the crew, had been washed out of the boat and the others were searching for them. This could be the answer as to why the lifeboat was in the position where it was last seen. On 20th November the funeral was held for those crew members whose bodies had been recovered. Hundreds of mourners from all over the country attended. Among the dignitaries present were members of the Latvian Government, recognizing that the men had lost their lives going to the assistance of the *Alice of Riga*. The Royal National Lifeboat Institution awarded pensions to the dependents of those who were lost. A local fund raised over £35,000, a colossal sum in those days, equivalent to nearly £2 million today.

An Inquest was opened with the Rye Borough Coroner, Dr. T. Harrett, presiding. Witness accounts were heard and the sea worthiness of the lifeboat and the competence of the crew called into question, although it was stated emphatically that the boat and her crew were totally efficient. A Board of Trade Court of Inquiry sat later at Rye Town Hall. After much deliberation, the Court finally announced: "As there were no survivors, the cause of the Lifeboat capsizing is a matter of conjecture, but we are of the opinion that she was suddenly capsized and the crew were thrown into the water. The broken water and heavy surf caused the loss of the crew."

The crew of the *Mary Stanford*, several of whom were members of the same family or closely related, were Coxswain Herbert Head, aged 47, and his two sons James (19) and John (17); 2nd Coxswain Joseph Stonham (43);

Roger Paine

Bowman Henry Cutting (39), and his two brothers, Robert (28) and Albert (26); brothers Charles (28), Robert (23) and Lewis (21) Pope; brothers William (27) and Leslie (24) Clark; cousins Arthur (25) and Morriss (23) Downey; Albert Smith (44), Walter Igglesden (38) and Charles Southerden (22). They had all grown up together, worked and laughed together, and died together.

After the loss of the lifeboat the Winchelsea lifeboat house was closed and never used again. It still stands to this day, defiant but not derelict, high above the shoreline overlooking Rye Bay. The *Mary Stanford* remained at Rye Harbour until the Inquiry was completed. In January 1929 she was taken to the RNLI depot in London where she was dismantled and broken up. The present lifeboat house at Rye Harbour was opened in 1996.

In the Parish Church of St Thomas, Winchelsea, a magnificent stained glass memorial window, the gift of Lord Blanesburgh, depicts St Nicholas and St Augustine and a lifeboat putting to sea to help a ship in distress. Figures on the shore are watching as it goes. The inscription in glass includes the words:

> *These men of Rye Harbour, crew of the lifeboat Mary Stanford, are here recorded in acknowledgement that we have received in trust for England the memory of their faithfulness and loving kindness.*

Chapter 17

ROYAL YACHTS

Her Majesty Queen Elizabeth II would always refer to the Royal Yacht *Britannia* as "the one place where I can truly relax". And it was the Duke of Edinburgh, at the time of the Queen's Silver Jubilee in 1977, who wrote: *Britannia* is rather special for a number of reasons. Almost every previous sovereign has been responsible for building a church, a castle, a palace or just a house. William the Conqueror built the Tower of London, Edward I built the Welsh castles, Edward IV built St George's Chapel at Windsor and Edward VII built Sandringham. The only comparable structure built in the present reign is *Britannia*. She is a splendid example of contemporary British design and technology and much admired wherever she is seen, particularly on official visits overseas. As such, the Royal Yacht became the defining, seagoing symbol, across the world, of Queen Elizabeth's reign during the second half of the twentieth century.

It was in May 1954 that Her Majesty embarked in *Britannia* for the first time, prior to a tour of the

Roger Paine

Commonwealth. But the history of royal yachts goes back much further than that. *Britannia* was the eighty-third vessel to be used for this specific purpose, although official and private yachts had been used by British sovereigns since the time of the restoration of the monarchy in 1660. King Charles II had three yachts. Two, the *Mary* and the *Bezan* were Dutch, and the third was the *Royal Escape*, formerly the fishing smack *Surprise*, in which the King had escaped to France after the Royalist defeat at Worcester in 1651.

Over the next two centuries numerous royal yachts were built as the accession of the House of Orange, and later the House of Hanover, entailed frequent royal journeys across the Channel. The last sailing royal yacht, the *Royal George*, was built for George III in 1817. Although used in 1842 by Queen Victoria, she found sea voyages under sail tedious, and the first steam yacht, named the *Victoria and Albert*, was commissioned one year later. This yacht was succeeded by another of the same name in 1855 and it was *Victoria and Albert II*, with large paddle-wheels powered by steam, which was able, for the first time, to take the Queen to visit, and be seen by, a greater proportion of the people of her kingdom than any of her predecessors. The ship's ornate figurehead, with gilded Royal Coat of Arms and Crown, can be seen in the National Museum of the Royal Navy in Portsmouth.

Although the ship was Queen Victoria's favourite for nearly fifty years, the monarch continued to lobby Parliament for a more modern yacht. She finally won agreement after pointing out that both the Russian Tsar and German Kaiser had larger and more state-of-the-art yachts. Sadly the Queen died seven months before the *Victoria and Albert III*, built at Pembroke Dock and launched in 1899, was completed. At 4,700 tons, 380 feet in length and 40 feet in the beam, she was designed by Sir William White, the Royal Navy's Chief Constructor. A magnificent ship which served four sovereigns, she took part in two Fleet Reviews, commemorating King George V's Silver Jubilee in 1935, and the Coronation Review of King George VI in 1937. At the outbreak of World War II she was decommissioned and served as an accommodation ship at Whale Island, Portsmouth, until finally broken up at Faslane in 1954.

Plans to build a new royal yacht had to be suspended at the outbreak of war, although King George VI was known to support a modern replacement. The King died in 1952, four months before the keel of the new royal yacht was laid. The new Queen, Elizabeth, together with Prince Philip, took a guiding hand in the design of this yacht, approving plans prepared by consultant architect Sir Hugh Casson, and selecting furniture, fabrics and paintings.

HMY *Britannia* was built at the shipyard of John Brown & Co on Clydebank, from which had come the great liners, the *Queen Mary* and the *Queen Elizabeth*. At 5,769 tons, 412 feet in length, 55 feet in the beam, and powered by steam turbines with a maximum speed of almost 22 knots, she was launched by Her Majesty the Queen on 16th April 1953 and commissioned on 11th January 1954. The ship was also designed with three masts, the main mast and foremast being hinged to allow the ship to pass under bridges.

An additional requirement was that the ship could be converted into a hospital ship in time of war. At the time of the Falklands War in 1982 this was given serious consideration. In the end it did not happen as this role was performed by the former educational cruise ship, SS *Uganda*. Nevertheless, *Britannia* was at Aden in 1986 to evacuate over 1,000 refugees fleeing from the civil war in the Republic of Yemen.

In 1997 the Conservative Government under John Major committed itself, if re-elected, to replacing the Royal Yacht *Britannia*. But following the landslide victory of the Labour Party, it was announced that the vessel would be retired and no replacement built. Despite differing views expressed in Parliament—many believed its role in foreign policy and promoting British interests abroad was hugely important—Prime Minister Tony Blair vehemently argued that such expenditure could not be justified in view of other pressures on the defence budget, from which the ship was funded. Rumours still circulate that Her Majesty The Queen has never forgiven Mr Blair for that decision. Although if a replacement had been built as planned, it is unlikely it would have survived the savage cuts to the Royal Navy announced by the Coalition Government as part of the Strategic Defence and Security Review in October 2010.

Britannia's final foreign mission was to convey the Prince of Wales and the last Governor of Hong Kong, Chris Patten, away from the Colony after the handover to the People's Republic of China on 1st July 1997. Five months later, on 11th December, Her Majesty The Queen, together with senior members of the Royal Family, attended the ship's decommissioning ceremony in Portsmouth. Her Majesty's Royal Yacht *Britannia,* which had been her royal home-from-home for nearly half a century, was to be no more. The emotion of the occasion caused the normally undemonstrative monarch to publicly shed a tear after disembarking for the last time.

During her forty-four year career as the Royal Yacht, *Britannia* conveyed the Queen, other members of the Royal

Ships and Sealing Wax

family and various dignitaries on visits to 696 foreign ports around the world—from Aberdeen to Antarctica, from Portsmouth to Polynesia—and made 272 visits to ports in Britain, clocking up a total of 1,087,623 nautical miles (2,014,278 kms), the equivalent of sailing once round the world for each year of her service. Whilst *Britannia* followed in a long line of royal yachts, she was also a much-loved royal residence. Furnished to the Queen's personal taste, each room had photographs of her children, treasured family heirlooms, and gifts from across the globe. Even with a full complement of over two hundred officers and crew, known as Royal Yachtsmen, and Royal Household staff, no matter how exotic or remote the location in the world, stepping onto the deck of *Britannia* was always a "home-coming" for the Queen. Her guests were entertained as they would have been at a royal palace on British soil.

The ship also provided a honeymoon sanctuary for four royal couples. In 1960 Princess Margaret and Anthony Armstrong-Jones were the first royal honeymooners to enjoy the Yacht's inimitable status when *Britannia* took them on a 6,000 mile voyage to the Caribbean. Princess Anne and Captain Mark Phillips were next to honeymoon on board, cruising the West Indies in 1973. Eight years later it was the turn of the Prince and Princess of Wales, who flew to Gibraltar to meet *Britannia* at the start of their sixteen-day honeymoon in the Mediterranean. The Royal Yacht's final honeymoon cruise was around the Azores for the Duke and Duchess of York in 1986. Had the ship been in commission today, it would surely have been the odds-on favourite to have provided a similar honeymoon haven for Prince William when he married Kate Middleton, now the Duke and Duchess of Cambridge.

Roger Paine

Today the ship is cared for by the Royal Yacht Britannia Trust, a non-profit making charity which receives no public funding. Permanently based in Leith, Edinburgh, alongside Ocean Terminal, the ship is a five-star visitor attraction and corporate hospitality venue. Around a quarter of a million people now visit the former Royal Yacht every year.

This popularity seems to indicate that, even though nearly two decades have passed since *Britannia* was decommissioned, the vessel not only has a special place in the heart of Her Majesty The Queen but also in the affections of a large proportion of her subjects and of visitors to Britain.

Chapter 18

ROGUE WAVES

Seafarers have a reputation for spinning yarns. Especially when it comes to describing the seas they have encountered. An old salt once remarked, "Rough? It was so rough we had to put a canvas cover over the funnel to stop the stokers falling out!"—an amusing exaggeration, but stories of terrible storms, huge seas and freak waves are part of seafaring folklore.

Nevertheless, in recent times scientists have discovered strong evidence to indicate that massive freak or rogue waves do exist and should be taken seriously. No longer can they be regarded as a figment of a mariner's imagination or, as often insisted upon in the past, a nautical myth. Neither are they tsunamis or tidal waves which are caused by seismic conditions, such as undersea earthquakes or landslides. Rogue waves are colossal breaking walls of water that come out of the blue.

The realization these were fact, not fiction, happened in December 1978 when the 37,000-ton German freighter *Munchen* sent out a garbled Mayday message while on a routine voyage across the Atlantic. When rescuers arrived they found only "a few bits of wreckage", including an un-launched lifeboat which, although stowed 20 metres (70 feet) above the water line, had one of its attachment pins "twisted as though hit by an extreme force". It is now believed that a rogue wave hit the ship and caused it to capsize and sink. No survivors from the crew of 27 were ever found. A maritime court concluded that "bad weather had caused an unusual event". Many seafarers believed it was a rogue wave.

In the past, oceanographers have insisted that such freak waves only happen "once in 10,000 years". Now they are being reported with startling frequency. Over the last three decades more than two hundred supercarriers, cargo ships over 200 metres long, have been lost at sea. Although several losses can be put down to poor seamanship or bad weather, it now seems likely that a percentage of these sea disappearances are the result of rogue waves. Eyewitness reports suggest many were sunk by high and violent walls of water that rose up out of calm seas. Off the South African coast since 1990 twenty vessels have been struck by waves that defy the normal pattern of wave height predictions. In the North Sea, on New Year's Day 1995, a giant wave hit the Draupner oil platform. The oil rig swayed a little, suffering minor damage, but its on-board measuring equipment successfully recorded a wave height of 26 metres. When visiting Trafalgar Square in London, look up at Nelson's Column, 51 metres high, and imagine a wave half the height of this famous landmark.

In the open sea waves can regularly reach seven metres, even up to fifteen in extreme conditions. In contrast, some reported rogue waves have exceeded thirty metres in height. Curiously, rogue waves are often seen traveling against the prevailing current and wave directions, and, unlike a tsunami, are localized and very short-lived. Most modern vessels are designed to withstand about fifteen tons of pressure per square metre, but the unusual waves exert a pressure of about one hundred tons per square metre. A rogue wave can mean disaster for any ship it meets.

In 2001 two reputable ships, designed to cope with the world's worst ocean conditions, were crippled within a week of each other. The *Bremen* and the *Caledonian Star* were both on cruises in the South Atlantic. The *Caledonian Star's* First Officer, Goran Persson, saw a 30-metre wave bearing down on them, "Just like a mountain, a wall of water coming against us. The ship went down like freefall." The wave smashed over the ship and flooded the bridge, destroying much of the communication and navigation equipment. In the *Bremen* all power was lost, leaving them helpless in tumultuous seas. Only after two hours of frantic work were the engines restarted. Both ships were fortunate to survive.

Investigating these and other South Atlantic incidents, oceanographer Dr Marten Grundlingh plotted the strikes on thermal sea surface maps. All the ships affected had been at the edge of the Agulhas Current, the meeting point of two opposing flows mixing warm Indian Ocean water with a colder Atlantic flow. Satellite radar surveillance confirmed that wave height at the edge of this current could grow well beyond normal predictions, especially when the wind opposed the current flow.

But ocean currents could not explain another nearly disastrous wave strike. In February 1995 the cruise liner *Queen Elizabeth II* met a 29-metre monster wave—the height of a ten-storey building—in the North Atlantic. Her Master, Captain Ronald Warwick, reported "Out of the darkness came this great wall of water.... It looked enormous, like the white cliffs of Dover." Displaying expert seamanship to avoid being overwhelmed, he positioned his ship so that it managed to "surf" the wave.

Scientists now think that freak waves observed in the deep ocean are due to unstable waves self-focusing in bad weather conditions. It seems there is a separate population of unstable waves that can grow into rogues. American Professor Al Osborne is one of the world's leading wave mathematicians. Waves can suck the energy from their neighbours. Adjacent waves shrink whilst the one at the focus can grow to an enormous size. An almost vertical wall of water preceded by a trough so deep like a "hole in the sea". Profiling the rogue wave which hit the Draupner oil platform confirms this theory.

To study the phenomenon, a consortium of 11 organizations founded MaxWave in 2000. The European Space Agency tasked two earth-scanning satellites to monitor the oceans. The survey detected 10 massive waves, some nearly 30 metres (100 feet) high. Another project, called WaveAtlas, used the data to create a worldwide atlas of rogue waves and carry out statistical analyses. "These waves exist in higher numbers than anyone expected," says Dr Wolfgang Rosenthal of the GKSS Research Centre in Germany. "Our goal is to find out exactly how these strange cataclysmic phenomena may be generated, and which regions of the seas are most at risk. We know some of the reasons for rogue waves, but we do not know them all."

While it is easy to be skeptical about things rarely seen or even less likely to be encountered, rogue waves are now a measurable phenomenon. They have been upgraded from legend to reality. Krakens and sirens may have been consigned to myth, but the threat of a rogue wave remains real. Recent scientific findings illustrate, once again, how little is really known about the world's oceans and how many secrets the sea still holds.

Chapter 19

UP SPIRITS!

"Yo! Ho! Ho! And a Bottle of Rum!" sang the pirate Long John Silver in Robert Louis Stevenson's *Treasure Island*. As this memorable jingle never fails to remind, and as every advertising copywriter worth his salt knows, rum is inextricably linked with the sea, ships and the navy. The Royal Navy in particular. Yet not a glass of it has been regularly issued to Her Majesty's sailors since 31st July 1970.

This was known as Black Tot Day and marked the last issue of rum in the Royal Navy. The Portsmouth Evening News recorded, "Sailors in ships and establishments in the area ... said farewell to the last issue of 'Nelson's Blood' by conducting mock funerals and wearing black armbands..."

But in the same way that rum has always been synonymous with everything nautical, the same might also have been said of rum's two most licentious companions, which together formed a notorious triumvirate and were descriptive of the Royal Navy for nearly two centuries, namely "Rum, Bum and Baccy". They are, however, no longer a true reflection of life on the lower deck. In the same way that the rum issue was abolished, so the others have been mortally wounded: "baccy" by the government's ban on smoking in public places, and "bum" by the legalisation of such behaviour between consenting male adults in private. The salty and rumbustious days which spawned this derogatory description of the senior service are gone for good!

Rum as the special naval tipple, however, has a fascinating history. Originally it was the quality of beer on board ship, once referred to by a seventeenth-century sea captain as "stinking", and the difficulties of obtaining and keeping fresh water, that led directly to the issue of rum. In spite of Samuel Pepys' improvements in administration and victualling, there were no overseas bases, and with British expansion in the Americas and West Indies it became commonplace for individual ships, when visiting the islands, to stock up on the cheap local brew.

On 14th February 1727 the captain of HMS *Greyhound* in Port Royal, Jamaica, complaining about the lethargy of his crew in helping to build a new jetty wrote to the Admiralty, "If anything can make life agreeable to them, it may be a double allowance of rum being joined to what extra pay may be thought proper." As his ship's company were already receiving half a pint of rum per man per day as an alternative to their allowance of beer, which was eight pints per man per day, the captain's recommendation implied that his men should have a pint of rum every day to make them work harder!

Against this background, and with more ships visiting the West Indies, the first official approval to issue rum on a daily basis was given in 1731. By the end of that decade, although still largely confined to ships deployed to the Caribbean, the practice of daily rum issue had become widespread. The rum was drunk undiluted and this inevitably led to many accidents at sea, as well as drunkenness on board in harbour. The press-ganged crews were not allowed shore leave, but this did not stop them smuggling quantities of rum on board in coconuts which had been cleverly drained of their milk. This was known as "sucking the monkey", and, together with the custom of permitting local women to share a sailor's hammock, resulted in further indiscipline and calls for stringent action.

Vice Admiral Edward Vernon, as Commander in Chief of the West Indies Station, was appalled at the drunkenness of his fleet. In 1740 he ordered: "Whereas the pernicious custom of the seamen drinking their allowance of rum in drams, and often at once, is attended by many fatal effects to their morals as well as their health, the daily issue of half a pint is to be diluted with a quart of water to be mixed in one scuttle-butt... in the presence of the Lieutenant of the Watch."

This mixture immediately become known as "grog" due to the Admiral's nickname "Old Grogram", so called because he wore a boatcloak made of grogram ("grosgrain"), a coarse waterproof mixture of mohair and silk. The issue was permitted twice per day, at noon and sunset. As a result, drunkenness become less prevalent and the rate of sickness, which hitherto had such a debilitating effect upon the crews of ships serving in tropical waters, was reduced.

In the years that followed, grog drinking spread as more ships from the West Indies arrived back in England with full casks of rum in their holds. It also became necessary to have a separate stowage where the neat rum could be safely stored. This compartment, which became known as the

Ships and Sealing Wax

"Spirit Room", was built into every warship constructed for the next two hundred years.

Nevertheless, it took another 40 years for the Admiralty to reluctantly accept that rum was in the Navy to stay. It was not until 1784 that James Man, a merchant dealing in imported goods from the West Indies, was appointed as official rum broker. The rum was shipped direct to bonded warehouses, where it was bought by the Navy's victualling department and stored at the new yards being built at Gosport and Devonport. The raw rum was specified as 40% over proof and the firm, which became known as E D and F Man, continued to supply rum to the Royal Navy until the final issue.

Throughout Nelson's time in command in the Caribbean and his later triumphs in the Napoleonic War, grog as originally constituted continued to be issued twice daily. However, in 1824, on the recommendation of Admiral Lord Keith, still concerned at the habitual drunkenness in the fleet, the issue was reduced further to one of gill of rum, to which was added two equal parts of water. This was issued once per day "to every victualled member of the Ship's Company who were over the age of 20 years and who were not temperant".

Although the Board of Admiralty might have felt that this reform would reduce drunkenness, a gill was equal then to a quarter of a pint. So the navy rum issue, equivalent in strength to four double whiskies today, and in spite of being diluted with water to form grog, was still a lethal drink, irrespective of the time of day when it was consumed. It was this ration, although later reduced in 1850 to half a gill (equal to one gill, or an eighth of a pint in modern terms) that continued to be issued until 1970. Then senior service officers and a campaigning parliamentary lobby, recognising the increased technological complexity of ships and naval warfare, recommended that the issue of grog to sailors, and neat spirit to chief petty officers and petty officers in the traditional strength and quantity, should be discontinued.

It was recognised, however, that abolition would be universally unpopular. So the Navy Minister, Dr David Owen, Labour MP for Devonport, reluctant to be involved in what he perceived as a vote-losing act with serving sailors and thousands of ex-matelots, many of them in his constituency, proposed instead that a reasonable daily beer ration should be provided to junior ratings, and that chief and petty officers should be permitted similar drinking privileges, both beer and a range of duty-free spirits, to those that officers had always enjoyed. He also argued that the equivalent of three pence per day, which was the sum paid to those sailors who did not "draw a tot" and who were known as "T" for "temperance", should be paid by the government for every rating serving at the time. This, together with £2.7 million provided by the Treasury, to compensate for the purchase of rum from traditional sources, was used to set up a fund known as The Royal Naval Sailor's Fund. Immediately this became known as "The Tot Fund" and it exists to the present day, helping to finance a range of sporting and welfare amenities for sailors not provided by the Ministry of Defence.

The unenviable task of informing the Royal Navy that, after nearly two hundred and thirty years, the issue of rum was finished fell to the First Sea Lord, Admiral of the Fleet Sir Michael Le Fanu. Nicknaming himself, not least because of his sandy hair and this historic act of temperance, "Dry Ginger", he signalled to the fleet:

Ships and Sealing Wax

"Most farewell messages try to tear-jerk the tear from the eye, But I say to you lot, very sad about tot, And thank you, good luck and goodbye."

The Board of Admiralty introduced the compensatory measures already approved and then, in 1979, in a remarkable act of foresight and entrepreneurial flair, sanctioned the sale of the special blending formula which for so long had been a closely guarded secret to an American millionaire businessman, Charles Tobias, together with the distillery in Tortola in the British Virgin Islands which had been supplying rum since the earliest days. The rum is distilled in a process not unlike that used for the best single malt whiskies. By using the original pot stills the rum has a unique flavour which is absorbed from the wood from which they were first constructed. It is alleged that Nelson, before capturing Tortola and proclaiming it a Crown Colony, had trained his guns on the capital, Road Town, and threatened to blow the inhabitants into the Caribbean, only to grant a reprieve when the island offered, in exchange for clemency, an unlimited supply of rum to the Royal Navy in perpetuity.

Mr Tobias, in partnership first of all with the long-established E D and F Man, began marketing the rum worldwide as "Pusser's Rum", using the white ensign as his company's logo. "Pusser", a corruption of the word purser, the officer aboard ship responsible for providing food and stores, was also naval jargon for anything that was official. Hence rum that was "pusser" was Admiralty approved and issued from the purser's department. Mr Tobias has also been a generous benefactor, using the profits of his sales to make a royalty donation to the "Tot Fund" for every case of "Pusser's Rum" sold.

Roger Paine

Despite the elaborate funeral rites enacted a generation ago, there will be only a handful of sailors today who will have experienced rum's sacrosanct traditions. For the issue of rum, and grog, like so many naval customs had a time-honoured routine as well as its own special language. Sailors were expected to remove their headgear in respect to the monarch when receiving their rum ration, issued from the tub on which was emblazoned in large brass letters "The Queen God Bless Her". The daily issue of grog was supervised, as tradition demanded, by the officer of the day and a petty officer, assisted by the "tanky", usually a long-serving sailor whose designation derived from the days when the sailing master's assistant looked after the fresh water tanks, and the "Jack Dusty", another sailor, so called after his original storekeeping duties in the dusty breadroom, whose job it was to account for the rum and take care of the assortment of copper measures and lipped jugs.

The rum was collected by sailors in receptacles known as "fannies". Reputedly called after Fanny Adams, a lady of dubious repute, whose remains, after her murder in Deptford victualling yard in the late nineteenth century, were said to have been mixed with the preserved mutton which was then issued to the fleet in large round tins. It was also the sailors' ribald explanation of why members of the Women's Royal Naval Service (known as Wrens) did not receive an issue of rum, because if they did, "They would have to hold out their fanny and say 'Sir'!" Neither did officers ever receive rum. Except on the occasion of the order "splice the mainbrace" when an extra tot was issued to every person serving on board, or possibly the entire fleet. This could be in recognition of a special event, e.g. a visit by the Sovereign, the Coronation, a Fleet Review, or before or after

Ships and Sealing Wax

a battle. The expression derived from the days of sail when if the mainbrace parted in a storm—the braces were the lines used to trim the sails, and in the heaviest rigging could be up to 20" in diameter—it had to be spliced together again, still in bad weather. This was a tough and skilled job, so those who carried it out were rewarded with an extra tot of rum for their efforts.

Drinking a tot of rum also had its own vocabulary. "Neaters" was the neat rum issued to senior ratings; "Queen's" was anything left over after the issue—and so called as belonging to the Queen—or, alternatively, "Plushers"—and traditionally passed around those present at the time. A "Wet" was just enough to wet your lips, "Sippers" a small, polite sip from a friend's issue, "Gulpers" a good swallow, probably in return for a favour granted or a duty carried out on a friend's behalf, and "Sandy Bottoms", the invitation to drink whatever was left in a shipmate's mug or glass. Rum was also a form of shipboard currency which had its own equivalent values. Three "wets" equalled one "sip"; three "sips" equalled one "gulp"; and three "gulps" equalled one tot. Woe betide anyone who tried to abuse the system! A sailor who had a good nose for where he might find, or be given, an extra tot, or even a sip of rum, was known as a "Rum Rat".

Today, selected shops will stock Pusser's Rum and duty-free outlets around the world do a brisk trade in it. But reaching for a bottle of the dark, mahogany-hued liquid from a shelf is a far cry from being on board one of Her Majesty's ships and hearing, at precisely 11.50 am each day, "Up Spirits" trilled on the boatswain's call, to announce that the daily rum issue was taking place, then hurrying to a friend's

Roger Paine

messdeck to drink the "gulpers" he offers from his tot to celebrate your birthday!

In the same way that old salts would mutter, "Stand Fast the Holy Ghost!" on hearing the hallowed words "Up Spirits", so all such phantoms and fantasies are now permanently laid to rest. Epitomised in a poem written by a sailor in Portsmouth on the day rum issue in the Royal Navy finally came to an end:

> *At ten to twelve each forenoon*
> *Since the Navy first began*
> *Jack drank the health of Nelson*
> *From Jutland to Japan*
>
> *He's always done his duty*
> *To country and the throne*
> *And all he asks in fairness*
> *Is leave his tot alone*
>
> *You soothed my nerves*
> *And warmed by limbs*
> *And cheered my dismal heart*
> *Procured my wants, obliged my whims*
> *But now it's time to part*
>
> *And so the time has come, old friend*
> *To take the final sup*
> *Our tears are shed, this is the end*
> *Goodbye and Bottoms Up!*

Chapter 20

BATTLE OF BEACHY HEAD

It has not always been the "English" Channel, neither has Britannia always ruled the waves. Some twenty-five miles from where the French defeated the English at the Battle of Hastings in 1066, another defeat was inflicted by the same adversary, this time at sea, six hundred years later at the Battle of Beachy Head in 1690.

After the death of King Charles II in 1685, his younger brother, James, a Catholic, became King James II of Protestant Britain. This led disgruntled noblemen to invite King James' Protestant son-in-law, William, Prince of Orange, in Holland, to invade and take the throne. In November 1688, William, with a force of five hundred ships, landed at Torbay in Devon, and at the head of his army marched to London. This so called "Glorious Revolution", led to the fall of James and brought about the end of the wars which Britain had been fighting with the Dutch for thirty years. William was crowned King William III. This also signalled a complete rearrangement of Europe's political map, with the French King, Louis XIV, soon declaring the first of a series of wars that would last for over a century.

James fled to Ireland where he hoped to enlist the support of the Irish Catholics to regain his crown. He also had the help of Louis XIV, who provided a force of 6,000 French troops which landed in Ireland in March 1690. Three months later, William decided there was no alternative but for him to go to Ireland, leaving Queen Mary in control at home. In June he landed at Carrickfergus with 15,000 men. At the end of the month the French fleet, under the young Admiral Comte de Tourville, aboard *Soleil Royale*, was sighted off Cornwall.

The British fleet, under Admiral Torrington, flying his flag in *Royal Sovereign,* sailed from the Nore. They were joined by a Dutch squadron under the command of Admiral Cornelis Evertsen. The combined Anglo-Dutch fleet comprised 56 ships (4,153 guns), compared with Tourville's nearly 100 ships (4,600 guns). Torrington, on reaching the Isle of Wight, and realizing he was heavily outnumbered and outgunned, announced his intention to return to the Straits of Dover. But on 9th July he received orders, signed by Queen Mary's advisers, ordering him to fight.

On 10th July, off Beachy Head, just a mile or two from the Sussex coastline, Torrington sailed towards the French in line of battle. At about 8 am, the Allies, being to windward, ran down together in line abreast, elongated to cover the greater number of enemy ships, but leaving a leading division of French ships "unmarked", who promptly cut across Evertsen's path and inflicted heavy losses. The Dutch, with little assistance from the rest of the Allied fleet, maintained the unequal contest but lost two ships sunk, and

Ships and Sealing Wax

another shattered, dismasted, and captured. Many others were badly damaged.

The action was fought almost in a calm, but by late afternoon it was evident to Torrington that the French had the upper hand, so taking advantage of the tide and a change in wind direction, he dropped anchor. The French were carried away by the tide, out of cannon range, and the battle ended. Torrington's flagship had not fired a single shot. At around 9 pm, when the tide turned, the admiral took his chance and, having burned seven badly damaged ships to avoid capture by the French, headed for refuge in the Thames estuary. Here he ordered all navigation buoys to be removed, thus making any attempt by Tourville to follow him too dangerous. Nevertheless, the eight-hour battle was a complete success for the French, who did not lose a single ship and had, in one day, gained command of the English Channel. In Paris the news was greeted with huge rejoicing and the minting of a special silver medal depicting King Louis XIV dressed as a Roman warrior.

Despite news the following day that King William had decisively overcome the forces of James at the Battle of the Boyne in Ireland, the defeat at Beachy Head caused panic in England. The diarist John Evelyn wrote, "The whole nation now exceedingly alarmed by the French fleet braving our coast even to the very Thames mouth". Recriminations over the battle at sea began and Torrington was accused of treachery. On 13th July King William was informed, "In plain terms, Torrington deserted the Dutch so shamefully that the whole squadron had been lost if some of our ships had not rescued them." The King was furious and Torrington was sent to the Tower of London to await Court Martial at Chatham.

110

Roger Paine

The charge was that he had withdrawn and not done his utmost to damage the enemy or to assist his own and the Dutch ships. Torrington blamed his defeat on poor intelligence and inadequate preparation and gave an ingenious, but much debated, defence for not fighting when ordered to do so. "Most men were in fear that the French would invade; but I was always of another opinion, for I always said that, whilst we had a Fleet in Being, they would not dare to make an attempt." To the outrage of King William, but to the delight of the English seamen, who regarded him as a political sacrifice to the Dutch, the court acquitted Torrington. As Earl of Torrington he took his seat in the House of Lords. The King refused to meet him and in December he was dismissed from the Navy and never again actively employed.

Although for a year after the Battle of Beachy Head the French reigned supreme in the Channel, they failed to capitalize on their opportunity, and two years later there was a complete reversal when Tourville's fleet was defeated by the English off Cape Barfleur on the Cherbourg peninsula. Since that time, the Channel has remained "English", despite mastery of this narrow stretch of sea again being threatened a century later by the French under Napoleon, and by Germany when Hitler's plans to invade were thwarted in 1940.

Chapter 21

THE BATTLE OF THE ATLANTIC
AND CAPTAIN "HOOKY" WALKER, RN

It was in February 1941 that Winston Churchill coined the name "Battle of the Atlantic", and it has been called the "longest, largest and most complex" naval battle in history. The campaign lasted for six years, with the most significant period from mid-1940 to the end of 1943.

It involved thousands of ships in more than 100 convoy battles and perhaps 1,000 single-ship encounters, in a theatre covering thousands of square miles of ocean. For an island nation it demonstrated, yet again, that control of the sea to provide a highway for the transport of food, fuel, raw materials, munitions and troops, to maintain the nation's security, was both essential and of enduring importance. Britain required more than a million tons of imported materials every week in order to be able to survive and fight.

The defeat of the German U-boat threat was a prerequisite for winning the war. Churchill later stated: "The Battle of the Atlantic was the dominating factor throughout. Never for one moment could we forget that everything that happens elsewhere, on land, at sea or in the air, depended ultimately on its outcome."

Victory, however, was achieved at enormous cost. Between 1939 and 1945, 3,500 Allied merchant ships (totalling 14.5 million gross tons) and 175 Allied warships were sunk, and some 72,000 Allied sailors and merchant seamen lost their lives. The Germans lost 783 U-boats and approximately 30,000 sailors, three quarters of Germany's U-boat fleet.

Against these grim statistics it might seem invidious to single out the exploits of one man. But in the same way that Admiral Lord Nelson is remembered for his defeat of France under Napoleon Bonaparte, who was poised to invade Great Britain, so in the Battle of the Atlantic another naval officer came to his country's rescue in its hour of greatest need.

The Battle of the Atlantic was finally won as a direct result of the daringly innovative tactics employed by the Royal Navy's "little ships", under the inspirational leadership of Captain F J Walker RN. Frequently known as "Johnnie" Walker (after the whisky), but more affectionately by the crews of the ships he commanded as "Hooky", the nickname always given to every Walker in the RN.

Frederick John Walker was born in Plymouth on 3rd June 1896, the second son, in a family of three brothers and four sisters, of Captain Frederick Murray Walker RN and his wife Lucy Selina. He joined his first ship, the battleship HMS *Ajax*, as a midshipman after passing out from the Royal Naval College, Dartmouth in June 1914. He served throughout the First World War, including time in the destroyers HMS *Mermaid* and HMS *Sarpedon*, and after the war in the battleship HMS *Valiant*.

However, keen to get back to destroyers, he volunteered for a new course at the recently founded school of anti-submarine warfare, HMS *Osprey*, at Portland. He also married Jessica Eillean Stobard, with whom he was to have three sons and a daughter. He enjoyed his time ashore in Dorset but left there to spend the next five years at sea as Fleet Anti-Submarine Officer in the Atlantic and the Mediterranean fleets.

In 1933 he was promoted to Commander and took command of HMS *Shikari*, a World War One destroyer, and later the same year commanded the sloop HMS *Falmouth* on the China station. This was followed by appointment as second-in-command of the battleship HMS *Valiant*. Although an important job, it did not turn out to be to Walker's liking and his straight-talking did not always find favour with superiors. After two years he returned to be Commander of the Anti-Submarine Warfare School at Portland. But with his specialisation regarded as "unfashionable", and despite war clouds gathering, it seemed that by 1939 Walker's career was at an end. He had been passed over for promotion and was scheduled for early retirement. But the old adage, "Cometh the hour, cometh the man", rarely has been proved more apposite.

Due to the commencement of hostilities Walker was retained and in 1940 was appointed Staff Officer Operations to Vice-Admiral Sir Bertram Ramsay at Dover. During his time there the safe evacuation of over 330,000 British and French troops from the beaches of Dunkirk took place, and he was Mentioned in Despatches for his contribution to the success of this legendary operation.

After much lobbying of the Admiralty, Walker finally received a command in October 1941. He was appointed to the sloop HMS *Stork* and in command of the 36th Escort Group. Based in Liverpool, home of Western Approaches Command, the Group comprised two sloops and six *Flower*-class corvettes. His first chance to test his methods came in December, when five U-boats were sunk whilst he was escorting a convoy to and from Gibraltar. In January 1942 he was awarded the Distinguished Service Order (DSO) "For daring, skill and determination while escorting to this country a valuable Convoy in the face of relentless attacks from the Enemy".

Summoned to the Admiralty to discuss anti-submarine tactics, he made several key recommendations, including that "All escorts should be used as striking forces for offensive lunges away from the convoy, attacking U-boats detected as far away as thirty miles." Although this was dismissed as impracticable, Walker was determined to rely on success to prove his point. His 36th Escort Group succeeded in sinking at least three more U-boats during his time as commander. He was awarded a Bar to his DSO in July 1942.

During that year, Walker was given time to recuperate after continuous operational service, but in January 1943, keen to return to sea, he was appointed in command of the 2nd Support Group. This consisted of six sloops, with Walker commanding the newly built *Black Swan*-class sloop, HMS *Starling*. The Group was intended not simply to protect convoys but to actively hunt and destroy U-boats. Walker had outlined his ideas to the new Commander-in-Chief Western Approaches Command, Admiral Sir Max Horton, based in Derby House, Liverpool, who gave unequivocal support. Like Nelson, he was determined "to engage the enemy more closely". In June 1943 Walker's own ship was

Ships and Sealing Wax

responsible for the sinking of two U-boats by depth charges, gunfire and ramming. A charismatic leader much-loved by his sailors, he introduced the playing of "A Hunting We Will Go" over the ship's loudspeaker system each time *Starling* entered and left harbour.

At sea again in November 1943, Walker's Group sank two more U-boats, and in early 1944 it again displayed ever-increasing proficiency by sinking six in one patrol. The ships returned to Liverpool to a hero's welcome. The First Lord of the Admiralty was present to greet Walker, who was promoted to Captain and awarded a second bar to his DSO.

In March the following year, Walker's Group provided the escort for a convoy to Russia. They sank two U-boats on the outward journey and a third on the return. He then undertook protecting the invasion fleet during the D-Day landings in June 1944. No U-boats managed to get past Walker and his ships, with many sunk or damaged in the process. Walker's dedication to his task was recognised by a third bar to his DSO, and he was again Mentioned in Despatches.

On July 2nd, the 2nd Support Group returned to Liverpool. After a few days leave, he and Mrs Walker met some of his officers for lunch. On the way home, having complained of a severe headache and giddiness, he was admitted to the Royal Naval Hospital at Seaforth, Merseyside. By the next day it was apparent that something was seriously wrong and Eillean returned to his bedside, where she stayed until midnight. Two hours later, on July 9th, Captain Walker was dead.

According to doctors he had died of cerebral thrombosis. In fact, at the age of 48, he had died of overstrain, overwork and war weariness. He was renowned for staying on the open bridge of his ship for hours on end, often having only two hours' continuous sleep in twenty-four. He would constantly and vociferously encourage the crew of his own ship, and the Commanding Officers of others in his Group, to relentlessly pursue the U-boats they had contacted. When such supreme dedication was added to the appalling weather conditions the ships frequently encountered in the Atlantic month after month, especially in the winter, the strain on his mind and body in the service of his country had become too great. The formal message informing the Admiralty said, "Captain Walker's death is considered to be aggravated by and attributable to the conditions of the Naval Service."

That night, the 2nd Support Group, steaming into the Channel, received a signal to say that Captain Walker had died. A contemporary report recalled "numbing shock seemed to hang over the Group like a pall." On the afternoon of July 13th more than a thousand people filled Liverpool Cathedral for his funeral service. The Address, read by Admiral Sir Max Horton, included the words, "May there never be wanting in this realm men of like spirit in discipline, imagination and valour, humble and unafraid. Not dust, nor the light weight of a stone, but all the sea of the Western Approaches shall be his tomb."

His flag-draped coffin, accompanied by the singing of "Abide With Me", was carried out of the cathedral by six petty officers and placed on a gun carriage. With hundreds following, the cortege moved slowly through the streets of Liverpool to the quayside where the coffin was taken on board the destroyer HMS *Hesperus*. When the destroyer reached the edge of the rolling Atlantic ocean, the coffin was tilted over the stern into the sea.

Ships and Sealing Wax

A statue of Captain Walker in typical pose—a tall, lean figure in grey pullover and patchwork waistcoat on *Starling's* bridge, directing operations against U-boats—made by Liverpool sculptor Tom Murphy, was unveiled by HRH the Duke of Edinburgh in 1998. It stands on the Pier Head in Liverpool, a fitting memorial to the man who, in the words of the Admiralty, "did more to free the Atlantic of the U-boat menace than any other single officer".

Chapter 22

WHEN BRITANNIA REALLY DID RULE
THE WAVES

The Spithead Fleet review of 1897 marked the zenith of the
Royal Navy in the nineteenth century. The occasion was
Queen Victoria's Diamond Jubilee and seven miles of ships
were assembled to celebrate it. No other display in any single
place could so directly have symbolized the might and
integrity of the British Empire. The Royal Navy was the bond
that held together the scattered lands, and its unquestioned
mastery of the sea was their protection. Ordinary people may
have known little about the Empire, but the Royal Navy was
a visible, magnificent and seemingly inextinguishable source
of national pride and affection. This was particularly true in
Devon where the Senior Service has been held in the highest
esteem and ships have been built, and crews provided to man
them, for hundreds of years.

At the turn of the last century the Fleet had grown to its
enormous size because it had the whole world to police, and
because of Britain's policy to maintain a navy larger than
those of any other two nations put together. But the policy

Ships and Sealing Wax

had a weakness. It put too much emphasis on sheer numbers, and too little on fighting power. In addition, the huge fleet had been built at a time when technical skill, in ship design, machinery, propulsion and armament, was advancing rapidly. The introduction of new inventions had proceeded at such a pace that it had been possible for a ship to be outdated before it was launched. Within a year of the Review another, greater problem arose. Germany, who had no tradition of power at sea, decided to disregard the past and build a modern and more effective fleet. This could only be intended for one purpose. To challenge British seapower.

It was essential that the Royal Navy found someone who understood these weaknesses and potential problems. Fortunately, history has been good at producing the right man at the right moment. It did so now. He was Admiral Sir John Arbuthnot Fisher. Already in his sixties, he was a pugnacious, stocky little man, known throughout the Fleet as "Jacky". The Navy had been his whole life since the time he had joined at age 13 and, as a midshipman, served in the Crimean War. To him, inefficiency in naval affairs was akin to sacrilege and he had a reputation for weeding it out.

Appointed Second Sea Lord in 1902, Fisher was responsible for the Navy's personnel, including its training. He held this appointment for only just over a year, but in that time he swept away the practices of training both officers and ratings which had been relied upon for generations, and revolutionized the establishments where this was carried out. Most of the officers responsible for the Navy's training were understandably upset. He called them "Fossils" or "Naval Rip van Winkles". He had no time for anyone who refused to accept his way of thinking, and "Get on or get out" was one of his favourite sayings.

Roger Paine

After a short period as Commander-in-Chief, Portsmouth, Jacky Fisher returned to the Board of Admiralty in 1904 as First Sea Lord, the most senior post in the Royal Navy. This position gave him the chance to be as ruthless about the Navy's strategy and ships as he had been about training. "Scrap the lot" was his best-remembered phrase. He wrote it across a list of 154 ships, including 17 battleships, which he said were out-of-date devices for wasting men. It was as shocking as it sounded.

But the decision turned out to be absolutely right and heralded a period of warship building never seen before and unlikely ever to be seen again. Existing battleships had speeds of only 11 or 12 knots when their engines were running well—which was frequently not the case. But now it had become possible to build ships of the same tonnage or more with almost twice the speed. The Navy's ships were, as Fisher put it, "too weak to fight, too slow to run away". By the time he took up his new post, Fisher had carefully laid his plans and was determined to push through his requirements. The resulting design was the famous Dreadnought.

The first of the class was laid down in Portsmouth on October 2nd 1905, launched by King Edward VII on February 6th 1906 and, through a mixture of Fisher's bullying and persuasion, went to sea for trials a year and a day from the time work had started. HMS *Dreadnought* was the most revolutionary British battleship since Charles the First's "Sovereign of the Seas" and immediately became the model for all future battleship development. Devonport Royal Dockyard, too, was ordered to build the new ships. A much improved Dreadnought-class battleship, HMS *Téméraire*, was ordered in 1906 and launched at Devonport in 1907. The speed of shipbuilding at that time was astonishing. With a

Ships and Sealing Wax

crew of over 700, the majority of whom would have been West Countrymen, she was one of the largest, fastest, most powerful battleships in the world.

Britain soon had seven more Dreadnoughts in commission or being built, and a corresponding number of new cruisers, destroyers and submarines. One was the battlecruiser HMS *Indefatigable*, laid down in Devonport in February 1909 and launched only nine months later. This fine "Guzz" ship was sunk at the Battle of Jutland in 1916. Of her crew of 1,017, only two survived.

Another famous ship of this era built in Devonport Dockyard was the Iron Duke-class, "super-dreadnought" battleship HMS *Marlborough*. Launched in 1912, the ship served in World War I, and later, whilst in the Black Sea in 1919, rescued members of the Russian Imperial Royal family fleeing from the civil war.

Fisher astutely encouraged the Press to support his programme, and never has there been a time when the British public was more "Navy-minded" than during the decade at the beginning of the last century. The slogan "We want eight, and we won't wait!", referring to the number of Dreadnoughts being built, became the man-in-the-street's rallying cry. By the time of King George V's Coronation Review of the Fleet in 1911, there were 32 battleships and Dreadnought-class battle cruisers amongst the 165 warships anchored in Spithead. When Britain finally went to war with Germany just over three years later, in 1914, it was the Royal Navy, thanks to Fisher's vigilance and energy, which had the most capital ships ready at the outset.

Given the latest emasculation of the Royal Navy, as a result of successive strategic defence and security reviews, the British government has managed to achieve what enemies of Britain have failed to do over centuries. A heavy price may yet be paid for this short-sighted political and economic expedient. It is a wonder that Jacky Fisher has not risen from his grave in protest over how much has been forgotten.

Chapter 23

"FAITHFUL UNTO DEATH"
A story of the Titanic

For over a century, countless books, articles, feature films and documentaries have described the dramatic story of one of the greatest maritime disasters ever, the sinking of the *Titanic*. On its maiden voyage from Southampton to New York in April 1912, the huge ship struck an iceberg, with the loss of over two-thirds of the 2,200 people on board. "It was an event that made the world awake and rub its eyes," said a surviving passenger.

Those who lost their lives included aristocratic passengers, impecunious immigrants, the ship's captain, many officers and crew, and the eight members of the ship's orchestra. One of these was cellist John Wesley Woodward. His untimely death is recorded on a little-known memorial under the promenade facing the bandstand on Eastbourne's seafront in East Sussex.

The idea for a memorial had been put forward by the Eastbourne Gazette of 1st May 1912, less than a month after the ship's sinking. While the horror of the *Titanic* disaster is

Roger Paine

still fresh in the public mind...would it not be as well to give a little thought to those who did not survive? This question finds some response in the feeling which has been expressed in several quarters that a memorial should be erected in Eastbourne to Mr J Wesley Woodward, a member of that heroic orchestra, who went down with the ship. A memorial to Mr Woodward, who was so well known and so deservedly popular for so long a time in the town, would, we feel sure, be welcomed by all residents, musical and non-musical alike.

The marble memorial plaque, with a bronze embossed medallion of Mr Woodward surmounting a depiction of his cherished cello, alongside an engraving of the ship about to sink beneath the waves, includes the inscription: "This tablet is erected as a tribute to the self-sacrifice and devotion of John Wesley Woodward (formerly a member of Eastbourne Municipal Orchestra, the Duke of Devonshire's Orchestra and the Grand Hotel Orchestra) who with other of the hero-musicians of the ship's band perished in the Atlantic through the sinking of the White Star liner *Titanic* on 15th April 1912. Faithful Unto Death. The unveiling ceremony was performed six months after the tragedy by the celebrated opera singer, Dame Clara Butt. Over one hundred years later the memorial remains in good condition.

John Wesley Woodward, the youngest of six brothers and two sisters, was born to Joseph and Martha Woodward in West Bromwich, Staffordshire, on 11th September 1879. His father was manager of the local Holloware Iron Foundry. The family later moved to Headington, Oxford. John was trained on the cello, having displayed musical talent from an early age. His high standard of musicianship soon became well known and he played both solo engagements and in a number of string quartets, eventually leaving home to join

Ships and Sealing Wax

the Duke of Devonshire's band in Eastbourne. But finding military service not to his liking, and although playing in prestigious local orchestras, he decided to become a musician on ships of the White Star Line.

His first voyage was in 1909 and he made a number of journeys across the Atlantic, and three to the Mediterranean. He was on board the *Olympic*, sister ship of the *Titanic*, narrowly escaping injury when it was in collision with the battle cruiser HMS *Hawke* in 1911. Hand-picked by Wallace Hartley, bandmaster of the *Titanic*, Woodward and the seven other musicians joined the ship at Southampton on Wednesday 10th April 1912. In view of the importance of this maiden voyage, it was the first occasion he had taken his prized best cello with him to sea.

By the time they joined the *Titanic*, Woodward and his fellow musicians were not employees of the shipping company, but of Black Brothers, artistic agents in Liverpool. Although Blacks had sought out the best musicians available, and they enjoyed free room and board, they were poorly rewarded for their efforts. In 1912 their pay was £4 per month with no uniform allowance. Two weeks after the ship's sinking, the father of one of the musicians, (John Hume, aged 28), was to receive a short and unwelcome letter from Blacks: "Dear Sir, We shall be obliged if you will remit to us the sum of 5s 4d, which is owing to us as per enclosed statement. We shall also be obliged if you will settle the enclosed uniform account. Yours faithfully, C W & F N Black". The uniform account included items such as: lyre lapel insignia (2 shillings), sewing White Star buttons on tunic (1 shilling). The total bill was 14s 7d. Equivalent today to 75 pence.

Roger Paine

Being a musician on a transatlantic liner a century ago was hard work and the repertoire extensive. On board *Titanic* they were divided into two ensembles, a five-piece string orchestra and a string trio section. The five-piece orchestra was led by Hartley, who played violin, with Woodward on cello. They played in the first-class dining saloon and first-class reception room. They also played regularly at the Verandah and Palm Court next to the first-class smoking room. The trio played mostly in the a la carte reception room and the second-class dining room.

Within minutes of the collision taking place at 11.40 pm on the fateful night of 14th/15th April 1912, water started to pour into the ship. Wallace Hartley, quickly realizing the seriousness of the situation, decided that he and his musicians should try to calm the passengers by playing up-tempo music. It was probably the only time the two groups had played together during the short voyage. Many of the passengers had made their way to the lounge near the first-class staircase which entered onto the boat deck, and where an upright piano was located. Here the band struck up a variety of waltzes, polkas and ragtime tunes to provide entertainment as passengers made their way from their cabins out to the lifeboats. As one surviving passenger later remarked, "There was a feeling of gaiety."

As the *Titanic* took in more water, the ship began to list, causing widespread panic. Hartley, however, continued to encourage his musicians, even when it became apparent that there were insufficient lifeboats and there was the likelihood that many would perish, they kept on playing. It is impossible not to marvel at their character and resolve. They also played, among many other tunes, what has been described as a hymn of sacrifice, "Nearer, my God, to Thee".

Ships and Sealing Wax

This became a lasting musical memory for those fortunate enough to be in the lifeboats, as well as a requiem for the many who never again would see the light of day.

Without a rescue ship, all the lifeboats gone and the end getting ever closer, Hartley called to his fellow musicians that they should try and save themselves. None chose to do so. They remained playing together on the boat deck until the slope of the ship made it impossible to stand upright and forced them to stop. A surviving passenger, Colonel Archibald Gracie, later remembered that the band only stopped playing and laid down their instruments about half an hour before the ship sank. The final moment came at 2.18 am. A large crowd of passengers and crew, including members of the orchestra, had gathered on the stern of the doomed ship before it plunged almost vertically downwards into the icy Atlantic waters.

As soon as word of the disaster filtered through, the bravery of the band in their efforts to convey hope and comfort to others, without any consideration for their own safety, caused an outpouring of sympathy around the world. A newspaper at the time reported, "The part played by the orchestra on board the *Titanic* in her last dreadful moments will rank among the noblest in the annals of heroism at sea."

The bodies of only three of the musicians, dressed in their uniforms with green facings and wearing overcoats, were recovered from the sea. John Wesley Woodward, aged 32, whose bravery is still recognized in a corner of East Sussex, was not among them.

Chapter 24

"ENGLAND EXPECTS"

Horatio Nelson was born at Burnham Thorpe in Norfolk on September 29th 1758, one of eight children of the Reverend Edmund Nelson, whose father had also been a country clergyman. There was nothing, therefore, particularly remarkable about his parentage on his father's side. But his mother, Catherine, who died when he was nine years old, could trace descendancy from Sir Robert Walpole, Britain's first Prime Minister, and one of her brothers, Captain Maurice Suckling, was a successful naval officer.

At the age of twelve and still at school in North Walsham, young Horatio heard that his Uncle Maurice had been appointed to command the *Raisonnable*, fitting out for overseas service. Excited by this news, he begged his father to write and ask if he could go with him. Captain Suckling agreed, writing back, "What has poor Horace done, who is so weak that he, above all the rest, should be sent to rough it out at sea? But let him come and the first time we go into action a cannon-ball may knock off his head and provide for him at once."

Ships and Sealing Wax

Undeterred by this reply, he went with his father in early 1771 by stagecoach to London. From there he took the Brompton stage to Chatham, which stopped outside the Main Gate to the Dockyard. This building with the coat of arms of George III above the entrance remains unchanged to this day. The naval career of Mr Midshipman Nelson, and what was to be a lifelong association with the county of Kent, had begun.

His introduction to the navy, however, was inauspicious, for no one knew where the *Raisonnable* was berthed. It was not until a kindly former naval officer took pity on the young man that he found his way to the ship. At that time ships which had just left the dockyard were moored in the River Medway opposite Upnor Castle. This required Nelson to walk through the dockyard to what was known as Prince's Bridge and from there get a boat out to his ship. He would certainly have walked past the dock where, by coincidence, the *Victory* was being fitted out. This famous ship had been ordered in the year of his birth and the keel laid down in Chatham a year later. It is not hard to imagine how thrilled the young midshipman must have been on seeing his very first warship, the same ship which thirty-four years later was destined to be the scene of his greatest triumph and heroic death.

However, as the *Raisonnable* was not after all required for service overseas Captain Suckling was given command of the *Triumph*, a guardship in the River Medway. It was from this ship that young Nelson piloted the ship's sailing cutter and learned to navigate the shoals and tides of the rivers Thames, Medway and Swale. The confidence he gained in such restricted waters was to stand him in good stead for the remainder of his career.

Roger Paine

Chatham in the latter half of the eighteenth century was Britain's premier naval dockyard and most of the buildings of that period have survived to this day. Between 1700 and the end of the Napoleonic wars Chatham dockyard built over 100 ships for the Royal Navy. Repairs and maintenance of other ships provided work for nearly 1,500 men throughout this period. The *Victory* took six years to build, at a cost of £63,176, equivalent to around the cost of an aircraft carrier today. Construction required the wood of 6,000 trees—mainly oak, plus elm, pine and fir—27 miles of rope for the rigging and 4 acres of canvas for the sails.

Because of Chatham's distance from the open sea it could sometimes take twelve weeks for large vessels to sail down the River Medway. This led to the establishment of a naval dockyard in Sheerness. It was also close to the important anchorage of the Nore, the name given to the waters off the north Kent coast across the mouth of the Thames to Essex. On April 9th 1777, when Nelson had completed six years' sea service, he received his commission as Second Lieutenant of the frigate *Lowestoffe* which he joined at Sheerness. The ship did not sail immediately, so he took the opportunity to visit London and have his portrait painted by Francis Rigaud, but because this was not finished until 1780 it was altered to show him as a proud twenty-one-year-old captain in the West Indies, although his features remain those of the fresh-faced young man he was when the painting was started. It is now in the National Maritime Museum, Greenwich.

Nelson returned to Sheerness in 1787 as captain of the *Boreas* after his second cruise to the Caribbean. His ship was used as the receiving ship for men recruited by the press gangs which were then operating in many Kentish towns. Shortly afterwards hostilities with France came to an end

Ships and Sealing Wax

and as there was no employment for Nelson he returned home to Norfolk for five years.

It was not until war clouds were again gathering that Nelson returned to Kent, this time to take command of his first ship-of-the-line, the *Agamemnon*, fitting out at Chatham. The circumstances were very different from his first visit. He was now an experienced captain, married and with a midshipman stepson, Josiah, who joined the ship with him. On February 7th 1793 he called on the Resident Commissioner of the Dockyard in the magnificent house which still exists. It is the oldest British naval building to survive intact. Captain Nelson, in full dress uniform, cocked hat and sword, then walked the few hundred yards to what is now known as the Assistant Queen's Harbour Master's Office on Thunderbolt pier to be rowed out to his new command.

His ship did not go downriver until mid-March, and although he visited his wife on a number of occasions he did not ask her to join him at Sheerness where The Three Tuns was acclaimed by naval officers, with a sort of perverted pride, as "The Worst Inn in the World". In a month at the port he never slept ashore, and his cabin in the *Agamemnon*, in which he was to see continuous service in the Mediterranean for the next three years, was his home. It was during these years that he first met Emma, wife of Sir William Hamilton, the British ambassador in Naples.

It was also during this time that the infamous mutinies took place on board ships anchored at the Nore. This was especially frightening for those in the dockyards at Chatham and Sheerness, who feared the Revolution which was sweeping France might spread to the entire British fleet. Richard Parker, the ringleader of the mutineers, was hanged on board the *Sandwich*, anchored at the mouth of the

Roger Paine

Medway, on June 30th 1797. Twenty-nine of his fellows suffered the same fate in the following weeks.

Nelson did not return to England until September 1797. By then he had lost the sight of his right eye at Calvi in Corsica and his right arm at Santa Cruz in Tenerife. Although hailed as a hero after his exploits at the Battle of Cape St Vincent and promoted to Rear Admiral, his victories at the Battle of the Nile and the Battle of Copenhagen were yet to come. But, returning home from these in 1801, it was natural he would be first choice to repel the threat of invasion by Napoleon which once again was very real. Nelson was therefore appointed in charge of the naval forces and went on board his flagship, the *Unite*, at Sheerness. The country was on war alert, particularly in Kent, where the citizens of Margate, Ramsgate, Dover and Folkestone were making plans for evacuation.

On July 28th 1801 Nelson issued orders to the ships under his new command, some of which had appropriate names—*Defender, Conflict, Attack, Boxer, Bruiser, Gallant, Ardent*—and by the next day was ready to leave, by post chaise, for Deal and Faversham. His arrival in Faversham attracted large, cheering crowds and he inspected the reservists, who looked "with wild but affectionate amazement at him who was once more going to step forward in defence of his country".

Deal was important to the navy as it was the port for the Downs, the protected anchorage in the lee of the Goodwin Sands, where as many as 300 ships could lie safely offshore. There was also a walled dockyard which built small sailing vessels, carried out ship repairs and supplied stores, provisions and fresh water to the anchored ships. It covered a large area of the town with the main entrance adjacent to

Ships and Sealing Wax

The Port Arms public house and the Time Ball Tower, which both still exist. In August 1801, with invasion from France—just twenty-two miles away—likely, Deal was a scene of great activity.

Nelson took the opportunity to not only command his ships from there but also to have a brief family holiday by the sea. Lady Nelson as well as Sir William and Lady Hamilton arrived in Deal to stay at the Three Kings (now The Royal Hotel) where Nelson booked rooms with a gallery overlooking the beach. A bathing machine was hired for the ladies. During this time they made excursions to Ramsgate, Dover Castle and Walmer. This was an unusual *"ménage à quatre"* as Nelson had also become the father of a daughter, Horatia, born to Emma Hamilton earlier the same year.

Using knowledge gleaned from local smugglers who brought back information as well as brandy and tobacco, Nelson planned to attack the enemy flotilla in Boulogne harbour with ships and flat-bottomed barges loaded with explosives. The expedition, however, was a failure, with 44 men killed and 128 wounded. Captain Edward Parker, one of Nelson's most promising young officers, was severely wounded and the admiral took lodgings for him at 73 Middle Street so he could recover. This narrow street of Georgian houses still exists, largely unchanged. However, the young man died and is buried in the churchyard of St Georges's Church. Nelson attended the funeral as chief mourner and was observed leaning on an oak tree, weeping bitterly.

During the so-called "experimental peace" with France that followed it seems likely Nelson visited Sheerness again and, with Lady Hamilton, stayed at Church House in nearby Queenborough, where it is believed they worshipped in Holy Trinity Church. He was then sent to command the

Roger Paine

Mediterranean fleet in the *Victory*, which between 1800 and 1803 had been completely refitted in Chatham dockyard, at a cost greater than building the ship there forty years earlier.

Nelson's final return to Kent was after the Battle of Trafalgar in his battle-scarred flagship *Victory*. Under makeshift masts and sails the ship anchored off Deal on December 19th 1805. This time the flags in the dockyard and the town were at half mast. Delayed by two days of gales, the ship eventually sailed round to the Nore, where the surgeon Sir William Beatty performed an autopsy on the admiral's body, preserved in a cask of brandy after the battle, and extracted the fatal musket bullet. Nelson was in his forty-eighth year. His body was transferred to a coffin which he had had made especially for himself from the wood of the main mast of the *L'Orient*, a captured French ship.

Although Horatio Nelson was neither a "Man of Kent" nor a "Kentish Man", he had a long and distinguished association with the county. He had come home for the last time. The nation was in mourning.

Chapter 25

SECOND AGE OF SAIL

Wind has propelled boats and ships across seas and oceans from earliest times. Throughout the world many original sailing craft, dhows in the Indian Ocean, junks in the South China Sea, feluccas in the Eastern Mediterranean, still rely on wind power as they have done for centuries.

As far as the Western world is concerned, the greatest age of sail commenced in the early seventeenth century. For the next two hundred and thirty years, until the advent of steam power around 1830, there was a huge growth in merchant shipping. But there was little specialisation, and vessels such as East Indiamen and colliers, irrespective of their nationality, were determined by size and cargo space rather than any special features of design. Yet they all had one thing in common. They relied on wind for their source of power.

Although the famous clipper ships with cargoes of wool and tea were still racing across the oceans as late as the 1880s, they were fighting a losing battle against steam and the internal combustion engine. A lasting reminder of those halcyon days of sail is the *Cutty Sark,* permanently preserved

Roger Paine

in dry dock at Greenwich by the River Thames in London. Her fastest voyage was 67 days from Australia to Britain, with her best run 360 nautical miles in 24 hours, a phenomenal achievement for a ship of her size powered by wind alone. But by the time the four-masted barque *Moshulu* rounded Cape Horn in the last grain race in 1938 the days of sail had finally come to an end.

Or had they? Like many things apparently consigned to history, so the use of wind is now being considered not only as an alternative to conventional energy ashore but also as another form of marine propulsion. Yet the idea of exploiting wind energy for maritime transport is not wholly new. Experiments to design a modern wind ship have been ongoing for forty years and the majority of maritime countries have carried out studies, partly with the intention to save oil, partly to save on emissions for the benefit of the environment, and partly to save money.

In periods when oil prices were high, especially during the oil crises in the mid-1970s and early 80s, ship owners expressed interest in these ideas, but interest waned when oil prices dropped back. The pressure is now on again. Like it or like it not, the shipping industry is totally dependent on oil. The International Energy Authority estimates that the average price of oil, US $100 per barrel for the period 2009 to 2015, will have doubled by 2030. The underlying cause for this increase is the steady decline in the quantity of the world's oil in the face of rising demand.

Various projects have shown that, technically speaking, wind ships work. Now with huge improvements in modern satellite weather forecasting and the sophisticated technology which provides for routes to be planned to take account of prevailing winds, serious consideration is again

Ships and Sealing Wax

being given to wind power. The evidence gathered from computerised simulation of wind power has shown that on certain routes in the North Atlantic, e.g. Rotterdam to New York, savings on fuel of 21% to 27% were possible, depending on the ship's average speed. A Danish firm fitted one of their bulk carriers with a high-tensile steel mast with fibreglass panels fore and aft, which produced three times more power per square metre than a traditional sail.

More revolutionary are the plans of the Hamburg-based firm Skysails. They originate from the founders, engineers Stephan Wrage and Thomas Neyer, who came up with the notion of a kite-powered ship. Stephan explains that the idea, like many inventions, is very simple. Although he also readily admits that originally he was regarded as something of a crank! Now it is proving to be practical.

Kites of between 750 and 5,000 square metres can be launched from a ship and fly at anything from 100 metres to 300 metres above sea level, where the wind power can be twice as strong as that which would normally power conventional sails, and the practical problems of fitting a ship with masts and sails, as previously envisaged, can be avoided. Skysails generate five times more propulsion power per square metre of sail area than conventional types of sail. Fuel burned by ships accounts for 4% of global CO_2 emissions, twice as much as the aviation industry produces, as well as accounting for half the operating costs of a ship. The Skysails system boasts that the annual average fuel costs of a vessel, depending on wind conditions, can be reduced by anything from 10% to 35%. The same applies to CO_2 emissions.

Kites can be fitted on any type of conventional ship up to and including the very largest. Skysails, who have attracted millions in investment in this new technology, started by equipping a gigantic yacht before moving to bigger vessels.

The MS *Beluga Skysails* was the first commercial ship to use the system. The 132m, 10,000 ton vessel was fitted with a 160 square metre (700 square feet) kite and launched on 17th December 2007. The ship departed the German port of Brenehaven and returned in March 2008, having called at Veneguila, USA and Norway. While the kite was in use the ship saved an estimated 10-15% fuel. Annual savings in consumption on windy routes is around 5.5%.

The expense of between £300,000 and £2m for fitting a ship to operate under kite-power is relatively modest, and the firm believe they could be recouped in two to five years, depending on usage. The system consists of three simple components: a kite with towing rope, a launch and landing system, and a computer-controlled autopilot system for operation. The kites can easily be retracted by winch during poor weather, and there are therefore few manpower costs to consider. The company eventually expects to kit out 1,000 ships with Skysails. As the founder points out, it is not a case of a ship not using its engines, but rather of "throttling back a little" if there are good winds.

The viability of the shipping industry is now of great concern to governments, ship owners and economists. A green environment is high on the agenda of all industrialized nations. One thing is certain—wind is free. The expression "wind of change", once used by politicians, could now have a lasting resonance with those responsible for the world's maritime trade.

Chapter 26

THE SHIP'S WAKE

Stand at the stern rail and watch the light of the
    ship's wake,
It bubbles and tumbles like water in a washing
    machine,
But wakes bubbled and tumbled long before
    convenience appliances,
Vasco da Gama, Magellan, Columbus, Cook
    watched the light of the ship's wake.

Stand at the stern rail and watch the light of the
    ship's wake,
Stenciling the passage of a ship through the sea,
Marking the time and the speed and the distance,
Immeasurable in itself, yet an immemorial measure
    of time.

Stand at the stern rail and watch the light of the
    ship's wake,

Roger Paine

Look into the churning foam or the slowly
    stretching ripples,
The sea opens, is disturbed and closes again,
The wake is a signature in the sea that a ship has
    passed this way.

Stand at the stern rail and watch the light of the
    ship's wake,
Traditionally white but always reflecting the water
    it leaves behind;
Cobalt blue Atlantic troughs, iridescent
    Mediterranean chops,
Ochre Ganges silt and scum swilling out into the
    Indian Ocean.

Stand at the stern rail and watch the light of the
    ship's wake,
Stirring the water below, bringing to the surface
    food from the ocean's floor
Or the galley's gash, slung into the chute by a cook
    going off watch,
For gulls, terns, skuas and Mother Carey's chickens
    who swoop, soar and swallow.

Stand at the stern rail and watch the light of the
    ship's wake,
By night phosphorous without a moon, shimmering
    ethereal in the moonlight,
By day flashing brief rainbows, as the sea's spray
    filters the sunlight,
What matter created by turbines, generators, diesel
    motors, shafts and propellers.

Ships and Sealing Wax

A wake can stretch to the horizon, straight as a
    narrow road across the polders,
But bent as a dog's hind leg when a novice
    helmsman is 'getting the feel';
It mesmerises, tranquilises, energises, and satisfies
    that we're moving on.
Stand at the stern rail and watch the light of the
    ship's wake.

Chapter 27

EVERYONE HAD TOLD ME

Everyone told me it was unlikely I would hear from
    him for four months,
That was how long it usually took a ship to sail from
    Bombay to Plymouth.
So I had not expected that he would be home until
    August,
Because I knew his ship had left Bombay in April.

Everyone told me that the trip should take about 130
    days,
For it was in days that the length of a voyage was
    measured
And that was how I'd worked it out that it would be
    August before I'd see him.
By the time the end of that month came I was getting
    very excited.

Everyone told me that if anything had happened to
    the ship,

Ships and Sealing Wax

The owners would normally find out from another
    ship
And then some people in London called Lloyds would
    have to be told;
They were the people who said that a ship wouldn't be
    coming home.

Everyone told me the last letter from him came by the
    overland mail.
He said they were sailing on April 10th, he'd bought
    some Indian cotton I could make a dress with,
And a little carved ivory elephant for Bertie's first
    birthday.
That was in September so I was sure he'd be home by
    then.

Everyone told me the first I would know he was home,
Would be recognising his steps as he came striding up
    the path,
That was a sound I knew alright and I was sure he'd
    want to get ashore as soon as he could,
Although they said he might be required for
    something called anchor watch, on the first night.

Everyone told me as soon as his ship had arrived in
    the Sound. It was August 24th.
I was beside myself with joy, so was little Bertie
    although he didn't know why.
We waited all day and into the long sunset evening to
    hear his footsteps
But everything was silent although his ship was
    definitely back.

Roger Paine

Everyone told me the next day the watch would
    change and he'd get ashore.
It was a sunny morning, a westerly breeze blew off the
    Tamar,
I had put on my Sunday best dress, Bertie wore proper
    boots for the first time,
And I'd cooked a Devon ham for him, just the way he
    liked it.

Everyone told me he wouldn't recognise Bertie as he'd
    grown so much,
But difficult for me because when you're with a child
    all day you don't notice, do you?
I didn't hear anyone coming up the path but I heard a
    loud knock on the door,
Being so warm it was half open although I didn't
    expect a knock unless it was him, teasing like.

Everyone told me his Captain was a very experienced
    sailor, one of the best.
I pulled open the door while the echo of the knocking
    was still in our ears;
Bertie pulled at the apron I'd put over my dress and
    wrapped his arms around my knees,
A leathery faced man with a neat white beard and
    serge cap stood there. It had to be bad news.
Everyone told me that the ship's captain would come
    and tell you if something had happened.
They were rounding the Cape, he said, 71 days out
    from Bombay, everything taken in,

Ships and Sealing Wax

Only running with bare poles. None of it meant
    anything to me except that on a stormy, moonless
    night
In gales and high seas my John had been lost
    overboard. These things happened at sea, he said.

Everyone told me never to cry, so I didn't, but I
    thanked him for telling me, kindly like;
He wouldn't come inside but he patted Bertie on the
    head and said he was very sorry,
He gave me John's canvas bag which contained all his
    belongings and some money collected by the crew.
He said it was the worst thing about being married to
    a sailor, except you hoped it would never happen.

Everyone told me to be thankful I still had my Bertie,
    even if he never knew his father,
I had John's sailor's bag with his shirts, his jerseys, his
    thick trousers, all slightly damp and smelling of tar
    and hemp;
There was the roll of Indian cotton, too, which I never
    got around to making into a dress,
And the ivory elephant which Bertie played with on
    his birthday and in the years that followed until a
    tusk broke off.

I'm looking at it on the mantel shelf now, waiting for
    Bertie to come home from his first trip to sea.
Just like his father really.
Everyone had told me. Everyone had told me.

Chapter 28

HAMMOCKS REMEMBERED

The wardroom steward no longer serves pink gins,
Officers' stripes no longer have colours in between,
Sailors would wait for 'Up Spirits!' then sink a midday
    tot,
The ships's cat, or dog, or monkey was allowed to go
    below.
Only Navy sailors know what happened to the
    hammock.

Kitbag on your shoulder and hammock safe in hand,
When joining your new ship a slinging billet was
    always first in mind,
A stanchion to pull-up on, a mess deck table to put
    feet down on,
Over eighty snugly swinging hammocks, to and fro.
Only old salts know what happened to the hammock.

Lashings, clews and nettles, wooden stretchers carved
    in vees,

147

Ships and Sealing Wax

Rigid and upright in the netting, pliable and form-
    shaped when correctly slung,
A well-lashed hammock could stay afloat and save
    your life,
"In Which We Serve", filmed in black and white, was
    not made just for show.
Only timeless seas know what happened to the
    hammock.

Scrubbed with pusser's hard to make the canvas soft
    and white,
You 'slung your mick' before you went ashore,
But bunks, and more bunks were fitted for everyone
    in rows,
The boatswain's mate no longer pipes, "Wakey!
    Wakey! Lash Up And Stow!"
"Cooks To The Galley", like the hammocks, "Have
    Gone Long Ago!"

Chapter 29

RAIN IN MAY

Like the steel deck of a ship washed clean by waves,
The tarmacadamed road glistens underfoot.
In the May rain hedgerows are groaning with green,
Wild flowers, white, blue, yellow, deep pink are freshened
    by the shower.

High grey clouds scud on the wind, keeping a downpour
    at bay,
Or part sufficiently to allow Spring sunshine to anoint the
    fields.
A thrush, using the road as a scaffold, greedily
    demolishes a gorged snail
Lured out by the afternoon's unexpected wetness.

A cuckoo, rooks, doves, a blackbird and a robin
Add their song to the dancing raindrops warning of my
    footsteps.
My hair is damp, flattened; I turn up my collar, oblivious;
My face glows wetly as the May rain sweeps in like a
    squall at sea.

Ships and Sealing Wax

Issuing rum, HMS *Diomede*, c.1923. See Chapter 19

HMY *Britannia* entering Malta. See Chapter 17

Ships and Sealing Wax

1953 Fleet Review at Spithead. See Chapter 9

HMS Starling 1942. See Chapter 21

Chapter 30

INSIDE PARISH CHURCHES

In today's busy times, entering their parish church is a rare experience for many people, unless for a wedding, a christening or a funeral. These, together with the annual landmark festivals of Christmas and Easter, are sometimes the only occasions when parish churches appear to serve the purpose for which they were built and intended. While this may not be universally true, and whether or not the occasion is one of joy, sadness or traditional celebration, it is worth recalling how parish churches evolved and what are some of the interesting features that can be found inside. Parish churches encapsulate much of the complex history of the British Isles.

Nearly every town and village has its parish church and very often it is the oldest building, set apart from the houses of the people who live nearby. Many churches are extremely ancient, the first buildings in stone by early Christians, dating back to a time when religion was the cornerstone of society. It is not uncommon to find a Norman church built in the eleventh century, especially in Kent and Surrey, or East

Roger Paine

Sussex where William the Conqueror first set foot on English soil in 1066. Nevertheless, it is unusual for any church to date from only one century. Many have something to offer from every period of history, the architecture, decoration, furnishings and artefacts being governed by the services and worship held in them. Although there has been constant change over the passage of time, three distinct periods are often apparent.

The first is the six hundred years from medieval times to the Reformation in the mid-sixteenth century. It is easy to forget that the early churches were Roman Catholic, with Mass the dominant form of worship. There were few furnishings, apart from a font for baptisms which, because it was normally freestanding, has often survived intact, even if the church around it has been re-built. The patronage of wealthy benefactors, their names recorded on memorial plaques or elaborate tombs, later encouraged a proliferation of new aisles, steeples, porches, towers and windows, all of which fundamentally affected the appearance of the church. The thirteenth century was also a time of decorative innovation. Perhaps the most significant was the introduction of stained glass. Wall paintings, too, began to appear, covering the nave walls with biblical scenes such as the Day of Judgement depicted over the chancel arch. The Black Death, or bubonic plague, that swept the country in the mid-fourteenth century was a social and economic disaster which sometimes decimated whole villages and saw them moved away from the parish church to which they belonged.

The immediate effect of the second period, the Reformation, was equally far-reaching. This ended the religious unity of Western Europe and resulted in the establishment of Protestant churches. It was King Henry VIII who repudiated the Pope's authority in 1534 and dissolved the monasteries. The new religious order was based on preaching and the community, and its churches were plain and unadorned. The colourful scenes of the medieval saints were no longer acceptable and this required the destruction of almost all visible decoration. Wall paintings were whitewashed, fonts and monuments defaced, stone altars and the rood removed, plate and vestments confiscated, and much stained glass destroyed. In the seventeenth century a number of new furnishings appeared and the Anglican service, with emphasis on Matins and Evensong, was introduced. For the next two centuries preaching became the most important element and the pulpit was a key feature. These were set high above the congregation so that they could carry the preacher's words to the ends of the church. The display of the Lord's Prayer, Creed and Ten Commandments was made obligatory in churches in 1603, and the Royal Arms, signifying the monarch as Head of the Church of England, became a universal ornament after 1662.

Almost no new churches were built between the Reformation and the Great Fire of London in 1666, after which a radically different style of church design appeared. Architects such as Wren and Hawksmoor saw churches as preaching boxes, rectangular halls with galleries, plain glass in round-headed windows, box pews and a dominating pulpit. Parish churches that underwent alterations at this time frequently incorporated these styles.

In the third period, throughout the eighteenth and nineteenth centuries, numerous Church of England churches suffered serious neglect, becoming damp, dilapidated and in urgent need of repair. It was not until the 1840s and over the next fifty years, that the Oxford, or Tractarian, Movement

Roger Paine

built new churches and saved others from terminal decay, although some had their antiquity distorted in the process. Choir stalls and an organ in the chancel replaced the musician's gallery; new brass lecterns, altar cloths, vestments, new tiles on the floor and new stained glass in the windows were the order of the day. Since that time there have been many further changes, and today's parish church invariably contains a remarkable mix of many periods and architectural styles.

If you are able to turn away for a moment from the sermon you are listening to, or the ceremony you are attending, look up and around you. The sheer variety you can encounter gives a glimpse of living history combined with perennial fascination.

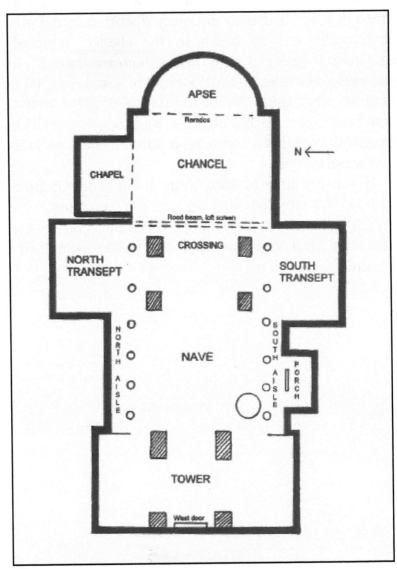

Plan of a typical church.

Chapter 31

ARLINGTON CHURCH

At the end of a country lane close to the popular Yew Tree Inn, some four miles from Hailsham, is the parish church of St Pancras, Arlington. Unless following the Wealdway footpath through the churchyard towards Arlington reservoir, from where the church's broached spire is visible in the distance, the church is almost hidden from view.

The dedication to St Pancras indicates the church's early history. Pancras, the son of a Roman nobleman, was executed at the age of fourteen in AD 304 for refusing to renounce his Christian beliefs; he was recognized by St Augustine as a martyr when establishing Christianity in Britain in the sixth century. The medieval priory at Lewes, later destroyed by Henry VIII, was also dedicated to St Pancras. It is believed that a wooden church stood on the existing site at Arlington until replaced by the present flint-built church, parts of which date back to pre-Conquest times.

Evidence of these Saxon origins can be seen outside the church, where large "long and short work" stones provide the corners of the flint walls. Another example is the exquisite round-headed window to the right of the porch. Distinctive Roman tiles, the legacy of a Roman road which passed through the village, form the arch of this window, which is set into walls two and a half feet thick.

Inside, an outstanding feature is the timbered roof with kingposts, trusses and beams dating from around 1450. Traces of its early covering in lath and plaster are evident from the rusty nail holes in the wood. On some walls can be seen remains of frescoes, probably dating from the fourteenth century, large red roses over the chancel arch, and St Christopher, patron of pilgrims, over the arcades of the north aisle. This period also witnessed the rebuilding of the Saxon chancel in Decorated Gothic style, including the impressive east window. Also dating from this time are the carved stone heads on the arch into the lady chapel of King Edward III, king from 1327-1377, and his lady, Queen Philippa.

A list of vicars on the north wall records an unbroken line, with the first shown as "1276-7, Henry is the Vicar". There are also complete church registers, the earliest dating from 1607. These record countless marriages, baptisms and funerals, including an unusual entry for 1613, "Baptized the 14th daye of March, Stephen the Sonne of John Williams executed fortnight before for stealing. God give his Sonne more grace". Later, another poignant entry reads, "Buried Stephen the Sonne of John Williams. The Lord will be more merciful". They also include names such as Charity French, Patience Tester and Zealous Foote, reminiscent of John Bunyan's Puritan characters Christian and Faithful in *The Pilgrim's Progress*.

The church's three bells, still in regular use, date from 1606, 1616 and the largest, a tenor, inscribed "William Hull made mee, 1677, weight 1 ton". The imposing square stone font, made by fourteenth century craftsmen, has miniature columns and capitals at the corners. The ironwork cover was made at Arlington forge.

By the mid-nineteenth century the church was being described by the Bishop of Chichester as "in a state of decay, dirt and ruin, worse than any other parish church in Sussex and bare of almost every decent requisite of worship". Fortunately, in 1889 Reverend Thomas Bunston was appointed vicar and soon embarked on a programme of restoration, raising funds by functions and appeals. The roof was re-tiled, the spire re-shingled and the stucco which covered the exterior walls was removed to reveal the original flints, allowing these to be restored and repointed. The west gallery and the old belfry floor at the rear of the church were removed. These had been supported by the trunks of four towering oaks, and the timber was sent to the Mayfield School of Carving where it was used to create the beautiful carved screen of the chancel.

It was also during this extensive restoration that the lady chapel, formerly used as a school and separated from the rest of the church interior, reverted to its original use. Stone coffin lids which had served as the floor of the school can be seen against the walls in various parts of the church. Particularly interesting is a stone coffin with an early English cross, which has now been raised above floor level between the chancel and the chapel to prevent further damage. When the lid was first lifted it revealed a solid chalk sarcophagus containing the remains of someone most likely buried six hundred years earlier, probably at about the same time the existing tower was built.

Ships and Sealing Wax

It was also while the foundations of the tower were being strengthened that a medieval pottery food storage jar, buried in gravelly sand, was discovered. Now displayed in a cabinet, there is nothing comparable in the British Museum, and it is the only specimen of its kind in Sussex. Also of interest is a twelfth century oak chest with two half lids, with all the boards rough cut from a tree. On the wall of the chancel a memorial to Reverend Bunston records, "Remember before God. His devoted labour and the help of many ensured this church was restored". After twenty-nine years as Vicar of Arlington he died in 1918.

Another incumbent, well remembered in the village, is the late Reverend Bill Hardy, along with his wife Jean, to whom the magnificent oak lychgate at the entrance to the churchyard is dedicated. Built to commemorate the start of the new Millennium in 2000, it was designed by distinguished Sussex church architect Ralph Wood. Following in the tradition of their many generous predecessors, the cost was met by parishioners and friends, for whom the ancient church of Arlington has provided an inspiration, and a place of worship, for over a thousand years.

Chapter 32

ASHBURNHAM CHURCH

If you look on a map for the village of Ashburnham you are likely to be disappointed. No definitive village, as such, exists. It is more a collection of scattered farms, houses and cottages in the vicinity of Ashburnham Place, now the Ashburnham Christian Centre, to the north of the A271, some five miles from Battle in East Sussex.

Situated in two hundred and twenty acres of heavily wooded parkland, with three spring-fed lakes, the church of St Peter lies adjacent to Ashburnham Place, formerly the home of the Earls of Ashburnham. But in spite of inextricable links with the history of the family, the church is by no means diminished in size or importance and attracts an enthusiastic congregation from a wide area, including volunteers and visitors to the Centre.

St Peter's was completely rebuilt, with the exception of the fifteenth century tower and north porch, by John Ashburnham in 1667, although there appears to have been a church at Ashburnham from as early as 1086. Originally the church belonged to the Prior and Convent of Holy Trinity,

Ships and Sealing Wax

Hastings, and the first vicar is recorded as "William the Churche" in 1399. After the Reformation, patronage of the church passed to the Ashburnham family.

The exterior reflects what might be termed "Gothic Revival", as it represents a style of architecture which, by the seventeenth-century, had been replaced by more Classical forms. The outside of the church is solid, almost severe, with many buttresses and battlements reminiscent of an earlier era. The interior, however, is bright and light, with high barrel-vaulted and painted ceilings in the nave and chancel. The ceiling in the latter, with its twin north and south chapels, was raised to accommodate the Ashburnham family vault, now bricked up, which lies beneath. It contains the coffins of forty-five members of the Ashburnham family, covering a period of more than 300 years, and includes Lady Catherine Ashburnham, the last of that name, who died in 1953.

Among many interesting features are the clear, unadorned windows and time-worn, oak box pews, which were cut down to their present size in 1893. The imposing wrought-iron railings and screens were almost certainly made locally at the Ashburnham forge, where the best Sussex iron was reputed to be smelted and whose furnaces were only finally extinguished in the early years of the nineteenth century.

The wooden gallery at the west end was given to the church by Baroness Cramond, wife of Sir John Ashburham, in 1649. It now houses the organ and is reached by a fine seventeenth century staircase with moulded balusters. On the wall leading up to the gallery, located beneath the bell tower, is an inscription sometimes known as "the bell-ringer's motto": "If a bell you overthrow, say your grace before you goe". The oldest of the six bells was cast by Thomas Giles of Lewes in 1621.

On the south wall of the nave hangs a magnificent oil painting in a gilt frame encrusted with china birds and cherubs. Dated 1676, this *Table of Commandments*, flanked by the figures of Moses and Aaron, is believed to be the work of an Anglo-Flemish painter and originally formed the reredos behind the communion table. The commandments are written not, as might be expected, in the words of the Authorised Version of the Bible of 1611, but in those from an earlier translation. The name of God is written in Hebrew, Greek, Latin and English. The painting was extensively renovated in 1977.

The historic links with the Ashburnham family are most evident in the north chapel, known as the Chapel of St James, which is dominated by two large monuments. The first, in black and white marble, commemorates John "Cavalier" Ashburnham (1603-1671), who lies on a tomb chest with his two wives, their hands clasped in prayer. On the frieze below are eight carved figures representing their children, four boys and four girls. John Ashburnham was only 17 when his father, Sir John, died penniless in Fleet Prison. Fortunately for subsequent generations, his son eventually reclaimed the Ashburnham estate in 1639. He also served King Charles I as Groom to the Bedchamber, traveling with the King when he was fleeing from Cromwell. Ashburnham was later imprisoned in Windsor Castle, and after the King's execution the estate was again seized and John was banished for eight years.

Personal belongings of Charles I, including a white linen shirt and silk drawers, said to have been worn by him on the scaffold, together with of a lock of his hair, although now removed for safekeeping, were at one time kept in the chapel. After the Restoration, John served Charles II in a similar capacity, and it was during this period that he and his younger brother, William, funded the rebuilding of the church.

The second tomb, on the west wall, is a monument to William, who died in 1679. This shows a be-wigged husband kneeling before his dying wife, Jane, Countess of Marlborough, as two cherubs pull back a marble curtain. Sculpted by John Bushnell, whose work is also in Westminster Abbey, it is considered the finest of its kind in Sussex. The estate later passed to "Cavalier" John's grandson, also John, as William died childless;he became 1st Baron Ashburnham. On the north wall are two funeral hatchments of the 3rd and 4th Earls of Ashburnham.

After the death of the last of the Ashburnhams, the estate passed to the grandson of the 6th Earl's sister, Reverend John Bickersteth, Vicar of Ashburnham. On 1st April 1960 he formed the Ashburnham Christian Trust, gifting to it the house and estate. He died in 1991, aged 65, but remains affectionately remembered by several of today's parishioners. The Ashburnham Christian Centre is his legacy, the church of St Peter a monument to his illustrious ancestors.

Chapter 33

BREDE CHURCH

The parish church of St George, Brede, is said to have "the happiest churchyard in Sussex". This comment, by the writer Sheila Kaye-Smith in *The Weald of Kent and Sussex*, refers to the view from the churchyard looking southwards across the Brede valley to the coast. It encapsulates the timeless beauty of rural England.

First mentioned in a charter of King Canute nearly one thousand years ago, the village of Brede, thought to be a derivation of the Anglo-Saxon word "bred", meaning "broad", in recognition of its proximity to the wide valley to the south, now straddles the busy A28 road some five miles north-west of Hastings. The River Brede, which took its name from the village, would then have been navigable from the sea at Winchelsea.

The Manor of Brede was granted to the Abbey of Fecamp in Normandy in 1031. Work on the present church, constructed mainly of sandstone and ironstone, and probably funded by the Abbot of Fecamp, began around 1180. Laurence, the first parson of Brede, arrived from

France in 1190. Benedictine monks from Normandy occupied the church until 1413. Substantially larger than might be expected for a rural village, St George's reflects not only Brede's key geographical location but also its important role in the early Sussex iron industry.

The dedication of the church to St George, the patron saint of England—best remembered for the legend of "St George and the Dragon"—is believed to date from around the time of the Crusades. Fine nineteenth century stained glass depicting this saint can be found at the west end of the north aisle in a small stone window, the oldest in the church and dating from the late Norman period.

The oldest parts of the church are still visible in the south arcade of the nave, where the distinctive round Norman pillars date from the twelfth century. This is about the same time the existing south aisle was added. In the late fifteenth century the Perpendicular style chancel, further east than its predecessor, was built. The octagonal font, too, dates from around the same period and is made from local fine-ground sandstone. The tower, also built at this time, contains a peal of six bells, the oldest dating from 1628.

The eastern half of the south aisle forms the Lady, or Oxenbridge, Chapel. The Oxenbridge family owned Brede Place, about a mile to the east of the church, and used the chapel for over 250 years. It contains many memorials, including a wall tomb of Purbeck marble commemorating Robert Oxenbridge and his wife, Ann, who died in 1494.

There is also is a magnificent tomb chest dated 1537, with a recumbent effigy of Sir Goddard Oxenbridge. Reputed to have been a man of unusually large stature, seven feet tall, he was known as "The Brede Giant". Although a deeply religious man, and a generous benefactor of the church, he gained an unfair posthumous reputation, enshrined in local folklore, as the "Giant Ogre" who ate small children! Sculpted in Caen stone, the knight is resplendent in full armour with his head resting on a helmet and his feet on a lion. On the sides are the coats of arms of the Oxenbridge, Etchingham, Dacre and Fiennes families.

Another impressive sculpture is "Madonna and Child", by the sculptor and writer Clare Sheridan, who was brought up and later lived at Brede Place. Carved from the trunk of a single oak tree, it stands in memory of her son, Richard, who died tragically in 1941.

Around the walls of the church are a series of unique paintings depicting the the Stations of the Cross. Commissioned by the rector, the Reverend Percy Hill, and painted by Tom Monnington (later Sir Thomas, President of the Royal Academy, 1966-1976), the artist originally wanted to execute the works as frescoes, but since the surface of the ancient walls did not allow this, painted them instead in tempera on panel. Using a style not unlike the fifteenth century Italian artist Piero della Francesca, although more abstract in execution, Monnington became deeply moved by his subject matter. The paintings were installed in 1960, with the cost met by donations from parishioners and friends.

One of several items of historical interest is the "Vinegar Bible" printed in Oxford in 1717 by the King's printer, John Baskett. It was given this name due to a printing error in the heading for Chapter 20 of St Luke's Gospel, which is rendered as "The Parable of the Vinegar", instead of "The Parable of the Vineyard". There is also a seventeenth century alms box made of wrought iron fixed to the floor by an oak pedestal. Etched into the cover with the date 1687 are the words "Sarve The Lord And Remember the Poor".

Ships and Sealing Wax

Outside the church, carved into lead where the chancel and chapel roofs join, is an unusual inscription: "This gutter was new cast by me, Anthony Griffin of Battel AD 1665". Against the boundary fence, on the west side of the churchyard, is a small wooden cross with a single name, "Damaris". The story is told that a young man, Lewis Smith, from the wealthy family who lived at Church House on the other side of the fence, fell in love with Damaris, a poor orphan girl, and they became unofficially engaged. Threatened by his parents with disinheritance if he married her, he succumbed to their wishes. Damaris, it is said, died of a broken heart and in 1856 was buried at the exact spot by the wall where she kept secret tryst with her lover on the other side. Lewis never married.

High on a buttress near the south entrance, above a brass sundial dated 1826, are the words "As time and hour pass awaye, so doth the life of man decay". Looking southwards from the historic church St George, across the "happiest" of Sussex churchyards, it is a phrase worth pondering today.

Chapter 34

BURWASH CHURCH

At the eastern end of the picturesque village of Burwash, on the road between Heathfield and Etchingham in East Sussex, is the parish church of St Bartholomew. The first stone church was built here in 1090, but only the walls of the tower, three feet thick and made of roughly embedded stones with wide mortar joints, provide evidence of these Norman origins.

As Burwash grew, so, too, did it become necessary to extend the church. Towards the end of the twelfth century the church was enlarged by removing the south wall of the nave and adding an aisle. The north wall underwent similar treatment fifty years later. The chancel was also replaced at this time and later still both aisles were widened, buttresses added to the south-west corner of the tower, and new widows put into both aisles. A porch over the west door was added and a vestry built in the north-east corner. At some point an impressive shingled spire was built on top of the tower.

Ships and Sealing Wax

Except for these alterations, the church remained largely untouched for almost 500 years, until 1856, when it was partially rebuilt and extensively restored. During rebuilding the opportunity was taken to install wrought-iron gates in the porch. These were made locally, at Franchise Forge, and are inscribed with the words, "Enter into His gates with thanksgiving and into His courts with praise".

For centuries Burwash was at the forefront of the Sussex iron industry. Evidence of this can be found in the earliest known cast-iron sepulchral slab, dated 1343, now on the wall of the Lady Chapel. Originally on the floor, it marked the last resting place of John Collins, member of the ironmaster family who owned a forge at Socknersh, near Brightling. In addition there are several unusual cast-iron headstones in the churchyard and a memorial inside the church to an Elizabethan ironmaster's daughter, Obedience Nevitt, who died in 1619.

The stained-glass triple lancet window at the east end of the chancel depicts St Bartholomew, the Blessed Virgin Mary and St Richard, patron saint of Chichester cathedral, a model of which he is holding in his hand. Another distinguishing feature is the intricate oak carving of the low chancel screen which adjoins the pulpit. The choir stalls are carved to match.

To the left of the altar is a memorial to Cecil Cooper, who became Bishop of Korea in 1930 and suffered great hardship at the hands of the Chinese communists in the 1950-53 war. On return to England he became chaplain to the nearby Anglican convent at Dudwell St Mary. Also of interest is the octagonal post-Reformation font, on which is carved the Pelham Buckle, one of the most famous Sussex heraldic signs. In addition there is a rare sixteenth century bible which was discovered in 1954 amongst a collection of old books in the vestry.

No mention of Burwash would be complete without reference to the writer and poet, Rudyard Kipling, who lived at Bateman's, an ironmaster's house built in 1634 by John Brittan. Once described as "the loveliest small house in Sussex", it is now owned by the National Trust. Kipling worshipped at St Bartholomew's and an oval bronze plaque by the south door commemorates the death of his son, John, a lieutenant in the Irish Guards who was killed at the Battle of Loos in August 1915, six weeks after his eighteenth birthday. This memorial, which includes a Latin inscription meaning "Who died too soon", was the first commercial work of the sculptor Charles Wheeler, who was later knighted and became President of the Royal Academy.

Kipling visited the battlefields of Flanders after the First World War and was instrumental in bringing back 12 wooden crosses that originally marked the temporary graves of Burwash men buried where they had fallen, before they were later permanently recognised by engraved headstones provided by the War Graves Commission. These simple crosses, crudely painted or stencilled with names and service numbers, now hang on the walls in the church porch and provide a focus for quiet reflection before entering. In addition, the village has an unusual war memorial opposite the gates of the church. This was unveiled by Kipling after World War I and now records the names of nearly 100 soldiers, sailors and airmen from Burwash killed in action during two world wars. To ensure that the names of the men who never came home are not forgotten, a light at the top of the memorial is turned on in the evening of the anniversary of each death.

Ships and Sealing Wax

For many years the village was notorious for being on a route used by smugglers going to and from the coast near Beachy Head. In 1892 the Reverend John Coker Egerton wrote that he knew parishioners who remembered "the Trade", as it was known, and that one of his predecessors had taken to his bed, giving out that he was too ill to take the Sunday service, because he knew the church tower was stuffed with contraband! Small headstones in the churchyard, engraved only with a skull and crossbones, mark the last resting place of known smugglers.

This fine church with its many memorials, Victorian wooden pews and timeless views from the churchyard across the valley of the River Dudwell is open every day of the year in order that visitors "can experience that sense of peace in a place where Christian worship has been celebrated for nearly one thousand years".

Chapter 35

BUXTED CHURCH

When entering beautiful Buxted Park, near Uckfield, many visitors will be heading for the popular Buxted Park Country House Hotel or, perhaps, preparing to play cricket on the idyllic ground where Buxted Park Cricket Club play their home matches. Those more familiar with the area are likely to be going, especially on Sunday mornings, to the parish church of St Margaret the Queen, situated inside the park only a few hundred yards from the hotel.

The church now stands alone, but this has not always been the case. Until the early nineteenth century the village of Buxted surrounded the church but the Earl of Liverpool, then Prime Minister and owner of the land, who lived at the nearby manor house, set about extending the park. He also wanted more privacy, so the houses and cottages were demolished and the village was moved to its present location nearly a mile away where, with the arrival of the railway, it continued to flourish. But the history of the church goes back many hundreds of years before this.

Ships and Sealing Wax

The manor of Buxted was given by Caedwalla, King of Wessex, to the Archbishopric of Canterbury in AD 680 and the patronage of the living is still within the Archbishop's gift. The dedication of the church, to St Margaret the Queen of Scotland, is rare, and only one of less than a dozen in the British Isles. In the entrance porch is a delightful stained glass window with her image. Margaret, Queen of Scots (1045 -1093), was the niece of Edward the Confessor, and the wife of King Malcolm III of Scotland by whom she had eight children, six sons and two daughters. She is the only saint who was canonized for domestic virtues, being an exemplary and most pious wife and mother.

The church, in classic Early English style, was built in 1250, almost certainly on the site of an earlier church. It has changed little over the past eight centuries. An oak vestment chest at the rear of the north aisle has been in the church for a similar period. The nave has a magnificent barrel-vaulted roof with the original main beams; it is unusual that two of the pillars are octagonal whilst the remaining six are circular. The chancel was built by Sir John de Lewes, Rector of Buxted, in 1281. Particularly noteworthy is the impressive east window, epitomising the architecture of the decorated period. The embossed plaster roof—the original vaulted roof is still above it—dates from the last days of the reign of Queen Elizabeth I. Amazingly, the plaster remains in almost perfect condition. The frieze along the sides includes urns out of which appear hop flowers, believed to be in gratitude for a particularly fine harvest of hops in the parish at the time, surmounted by stylized marguerite daisies in honour of St Margaret. Under the chancel carpet is a memorial brass dating from 1426, with an inscription in Medieval English.

Roger Paine

The oak pulpit, beautifully carved and decorated with marguerite daisies, is Jacobean. The names of those who have preached from this pulpit include Christopher Wordsworth, rector from 1820 to 1846. He was the brother of the renowned Victorian poet, William Wordsworth. It is on record that he, too, preached at St Margaret's on several occasions. Christopher Wordsworth is buried close to the perimeter wall at the eastern end of the churchyard.

On the south side of the chancel is an enclosed chapel formerly known as Park Pew, as it contained seating for the family and staff of Lord Liverpool when he lived in the manor house, known as Park House. Today it is called the Chapel of the Ascension, the scene depicted in the chapel's stained glass window. Beneath the chapel is the Liverpool family vault. The lectern is unusual, being carved not in the shape of an eagle, as is often customary, but in the form of an imposing Liver bird!

St George's Chapel in the north transept is a war memorial chapel dedicated to those of the parish who lost their lives in battle. The Roll of Honour for the First World War includes the name of Fergus Bowes-Lyon, elder brother of the late Queen Elizabeth, The Queen Mother. She was a bridesmaid at his wedding on 17th September 1914, when he married the Countess of Portarlington who lived at Park House. He was killed in action a year later. Along the altar rail is a beautifully hand-embroidered kneeler made by members of Buxted's Womens Institute. Known as the Millennium Kneeler, it depicts the history of the village over the last thousand years.

High on the west wall of the nave are five lozenge-shaped funeral hatchments relating to the Liverpool family. Behind is the belfry, with eight bells. The three oldest were cast in

1636, with the heaviest weighing three quarters of a ton (760kg). There is more living history in the form of two iron cannonballs cast in the parish nearly five hundred years ago. Buxted owed its early prosperity to the Wealden iron-making industry and the first cast-iron cannon made in England was forged in 1543 by Ralf Hogge, employed by the then rector, William Levett.

A giant yew tree, believed to be one thousand years older than the church, stands in the churchyard. Still flourishing today, the massive overhanging branches are supported by telegraph poles, a living symbol and a reminder of Buxted's history.

Chapter 36

CHALVINGTON CHURCH

The expression "small but perfectly formed" could easily have been coined to describe the church of St Bartholomew in the village of Chalvington, some fifteen miles north-west of Eastbourne. Bartholomew was one of the twelve apostles and a missionary saint who, in the first century AD, having converted the King of Armenia (now southern Turkey) to Christianity, became a martyr when he was crucified upside down and flayed alive on the orders of the king's brother.

The church's original dedication is believed, however, to have been to St Thomas à Becket. A small panel of stained glass, dating from the late thirteenth century and possibly the oldest in East Sussex, portraying the figure of an archbishop holding a crozier and his right hand raised in blessing, with the inscription "S.TH/OM/AS", is at the head of a window in the north wall of the nave. There is also, in the Rolls of the Manor of Chalvington, a record of a Court held on "Saturday next before the Feast of the Translation of St Thomas the Martyr" in 1364, which may imply the

179

church's connection, at that time, to Becket, murdered in Canterbury Cathedral two hundred years earlier.

The parish, originally known as Calvintone or Caveltone, is mentioned in the Domesday Book of 1086. There is no record of a church, but it is known that the church was amongst those taxed by the Pope in 1291. Today it is recognized as an almost perfect miniature example of the late thirteenth century Decorated style. Only 37 feet long and 27 feet wide, it consists of a simple chancel and nave, with a wooden bell turret and shingled spire. Constructed of flint with stone quoins rendered in plaster, its external appearance has altered little since medieval times.

The imposing iron-studded oak door which gives access to the church on the north side is believed to date from the thirteenth century and originally hung in the blocked up, but still clearly visible, pointed-arch doorway in the south wall. The entrance now has a modern wooden porch, although an ancient holy water stoup can be seen set into the wall to the west of the door.

The nave, with six timber tie-beams and supported by king-posts, is higher and wider than the chancel, the walls of which project into it and are overlapped by the nave roof. The large east window with three lights was added around the beginning of the fifteenth century. The stained glass depicts the archangels Gabriel and Michael flanking the figure of Our Lord. The window also contains an inscription in medieval Lombardic writing indicating that "John Diliwyt, rector of this church, caused me to be made". As Diliwyt was rector from 1388 to 1409, it is likely that some of this glass is original. Above, in the decorated tracery, is the coat of arms of Canterbury. A list of Rectors, the first named as Thomas de Escrick in 1319, is displayed on the west wall.

On the north wall of the chancel is a marble monument in memory of The Honourable Ann Fuller. Brass plaques at the rear of the nave, underneath the stained-glass windows in the north and south walls, record that both windows were the gift of Sir Thomas Trayton Fuller, Bart, Rector of Chalvington from 1854 to 1875. One is in memory of his father, John, and his mother, the Hon Ann Fuller; the other commemorates his sister, Sarah. The Hon Ann Fuller was daughter of Lieutenant General George Elliot, who purchased what is now Heathfield Park and later achieved fame as the Governor who withstood the four-year siege of Gibraltar. He was raised to the peerage as Baron Heathfield of Gibraltar in 1787. The magnificent funeral hatchment on the west wall is that of the Hon Ann Fuller.

Despite the small size of the church, there is a feeling of light and space which is enhanced by the choir stalls having been removed from the chancel at the time the sanctuary was extended, some forty years ago. The pews on both sides of the aisle have striking fleur-de-lys decoration dating from the Victorian era. The font, which is square, is fifteenth century, with a wooden cover decorated with eighteenth century ironwork. Perhaps surprisingly for such a tiny church, St Bartholomew's has three bells, each originally cast in the early 1600s.

The wrought-iron gates at the entrance to the churchyard are a memorial to all who gave their lives in World War II, and those at the rear are in memory of Sub-Lt Trevor Bayley RN, aged 21, who was lost when the destroyer HMS *Martin* was sunk on 10th November 1942. A weathered tombstone erected in memory of Job, son of Benjamin and Elizabeth Guy, records that he "departed this life by a kick from a horse 17th April 1878, aged 8 years and 2 weeks". The inclusion of the exact length of his short life provides a poignant reminder of heartfelt grief experienced by loving parents.

The view to the South Downs from the churchyard of St Bartholomew is breathtaking. As timeless as the spirit that this Tom Thumb of a church continues to generate in a scattered but thriving rural community after more than eight centuries.

Chapter 37

CLIFFE CHURCH

William Morris (1834-1896), whose designs generated the Arts and Crafts movement, wrote "You can see the town of Lewes lying like a box of toys under a great amphitheatre of chalk hills...On the whole it is set down better than any town I have ever seen in England." It could also be an accurate description of the view from the top of the tower of St Thomas à Becket church in Cliffe.

Situated in a gap in the South Downs, Lewes is cut through by the River Ouse, with cliffs that rise steeply on both sides of its banks. On the eastern bank is a large chalk cliff, Cliffe Hill, which gives its name to the former village of Cliffe, originally separated from the town by the river. Today it forms part of Lewes and is joined by Cliffe Bridge, an eighteenth century replacement of the medieval crossing, which was later widened and more recently pedestrianised. The church is located at the eastern end of Cliffe High Street.

On 27th December 1836, only a few hundred yards away, vast amounts of snow which had gradually built up on the overhanging cliffs crashed down onto a row of cottages, shattering them by sheer weight. Eight inhabitants were killed. It remains the worst avalanche ever recorded in Britain. In 2000, Cliffe was again the victim of a natural disaster when the River Ouse burst its banks and large parts of the town were flooded, including the church of St Thomas where the floodwaters reached a height of over five feet. Devastation was widespread but the church reopened for worship ten days later.

A chapel of ease, originally attached to the Benedictine college in nearby South Malling, had been built in the village of Cliffe in the twelfth century. Parts of this building can still be seen in today's church, dedicated to St Thomas à Becket, Archbishop of Canterbury, who was murdered in his cathedral in 1170. Between 1576 and 1690 the living was in the gift of the Archbishop; after that time it passed to the Crown, which still holds it today. On the south wall inside the west door hangs a framed copy of the Cliffe Charter, granting permission to hold "a Market and two fayres in ye cliffe". Dated 1410, it is sealed with the great seal of Henry IV. The original is in the county archives. On the north wall, above an eighteenth century oak coffer, is a list of Vicars and Rectors. The first vicar, John de Arundel, held office from 1320 to 1349.

In the chancel, the original Norman chapel, there is a rare double lepers' squint hole. Although this now looks into the chancel from the south aisle, originally it would have been through the external wall so that lepers from the hospital in Lewes could witness the celebration of Mass without entering the church from which they were excluded. The four nave pillars are Norman, as is the west wall of the north aisle. In this wall is a blocked up window with an oil painting on wood of the patron saint, shown as "Sanct. Thomas

Cantuar". On the north wall is an impressive oil painting of the Ascension, by an unknown artist, dated 1645.

The carved oak pulpit is Victorian and has four distinctive painted panels, depicting Our Lord, John the Baptist, David, and Moses, although it is likely these were added at a later date. In the wall close to the door in the south aisle is a fine fourteenth century foliated stoup for holy water. At the top of the right-hand panel of the stained glass window in this wall is a miniature painting of the church. On the west wall are two decorated Royal Coats of Arms; the upper, modelled in hard plaster, is Elizabethan, dated 1598, the other, painted on wood, is early Georgian.

At the entrance to the church, in the fifteenth century tower, a narrow door gives access to a stone spiral staircase leading up to the chamber with the mechanism of the church clock. Made in 1670 by James Looker, a Ditchling blacksmith, this magnificent example of handcrafted seventeenth century engineering is wound daily and remains in perfect working order. After three hundred and forty years it needs only fractional adjustment to keep accurate time. The stairs then lead to the belfry with four bells, the oldest dating from 1619, another from 1649. Going upwards again, the top of the tower affords panoramic views of Lewes. The weather vane has the year 1756 recorded on the tail and the letters "AT/IB", the initials of the churchwardens at the time, on the vane itself.

St Thomas has an unusual distinction in that it is the place of worship for the Russian Orthodox community in the town. Officially authorised by the Archdiocese of Orthodox Parishes of Russian Tradition in Western Europe, services in the traditional manner are held every week on completion of the regular Anglican Sunday morning service.

Ships and Sealing Wax

In the entrance to the church is a handwritten notice, in careful calligraphy, "As you look around this Church you should find yourself moved by a sense of tradition. The contemplation of relics and records of the past moves us to a realization that we are not the first to live on this planet, in this country, or in this place. We, perhaps, have more to learn from those who have gone before than we should have to teach them were they to walk this earth again."

Chapter 38

ETCHINGHAM CHURCH

When standing in the church of The Assumption of the Blessed Mary and St Nicholas, Etchingham, a village on the A265 between Hurst Green and Heathfield, you can sometimes hear a South Eastern commuter train from London Bridge or Hastings coming to a halt at Etchingham station beyond the eastern end of the churchyard. The station is built on the site of a fortified manor house and today's church is where, centuries ago, the manor's chapel once stood. Both buildings, adjacent to the confluence of the Rivers Rother and Dudwell, were originally surrounded by the same moat, traces of which can still be seen. During the disastrous floods of 2000, Etchingham church was under three feet of water. Even the wooden lectern was floating!

Today's church was conceived and built in the decorated style by Sir William de Echyngham, probably to the design of a French architect, between 1363 and 1369. It remains almost unchanged to this day. The first rector is shown as Adam de Foxle in 1362. It seems likely that Sir William originally intended it should be the family necropolis as his son, another William, his grandson, Thomas, and great grandson, also Thomas, were all buried beneath the chancel. At the same time it is evident from the size of the chancel, only slightly smaller in size than the nave, that it was intended to service the spiritual needs of the larger community. This can be seen in the three sedilia seats, unchanged from the time priests first sat in them, and the choir stalls behind the carved oak screen, which remain sturdy enough to last another seven hundred years.

In the choir stalls—nine on each side, three of which are returned—are eighteen misericords. Their intricate carvings, one of the treasures of Etchingham church, include dolphins, keys, birds, quadrangular headdresses of fourteenth century women and, most unusually, a fox preaching to a congregation of six geese. On the reverse side of the screen, in the corners, two small, carved wooden faces gaze impudently down on this unique seating.

The church is entered through a porch on the south side, arched with the upturned trunks of an ancient oak. A sense of the church's history is immediately apparent. Unlike the majority of churches built in the fourteenth century, when towers were normally situated at the west end, Etchingham has an axial tower located between the chancel and the nave. The north and south aisles, too, were part of de Echyngham's original plan and not added later as was commonplace in many early churches. At the east end of the south aisle there would most likely have been a chapel, and the same on the north side.

The space under the tower is treated as part of the nave, but this does nothing to dispel the impression, when passing into the chancel, that you could almost be entering another church. The massive arches supporting the tower to the east and west are higher than those to the north and south. Eighty years ago the tower was underpinned using piles sunk into the ground and jacked upright to correct subsidence which had occurred over the centuries. Other measures included filling the crypt under the nave with concrete, after the coffins in them had been reburied in the churchyard, and adding strengthening braces to the church tower.

The sandstone font, adjacent to the south door, rests on a single column of Purbeck marble, and it, together with the small door in the south wall of the chancel, constitutes all that remains of the original church. An especially noteworthy feature is the memorial brasses, untouched by the Victorian restoration sympathetically executed under architect William Slater in 1857. One, directly in front of the high altar, made by Henry de Lakenham in London, commemorates Sir William de Echyngham, and although his head has long since disappeared it is the oldest brass in Sussex and a fine example of fourteenth century craftsmanship. An inscription, in Norman French, includes "Of earth was I made and formed, And to earth I have returned, 18th January in the year of our Lord 1388". A second inscription, in Latin, reminds that Sir William "built this church anew".

Adjacent is another outstanding brass from the same workshop. Dated 1444, it depicts Lady Joan Echyngham between her husband and her son under a triple canopy. Each knight has a lion at his feet; the lady's rest on a dog. In the south aisle are two further historic brasses both commemorating women dressed in flowing kirtles, Elizabeth Echyngham, who died in 1452, and Agnes Oxenrigg, who died in 1480.

On the floor beneath the tower, adjacent to the chancel, is a small area of fourteenth century encaustic tiles. Well worn and weathered, they are in stark contrast to the more brightly coloured ones which, although similar in design, replaced most of the originals during the Victorian restoration. Medieval stained glass, depicting the coats of arms of Sussex landed families, has been preserved high up in the tracery of the aisles and clerestory windows. The east window in the chancel, too, has original glass with the coats of arms of the Plantagenets, John of Brittany, John of Gaunt, Edward III, and Edward the Black Prince. The remaining glass in this window, with striking blues, greens and reds, was designed by eminent Victorian J R Clayton to represent the five stages in the life of Christ. The tracery in this window is characterized by flame-shaped lozenges which have been appropriately termed "flamboyant". More medieval glass is preserved in the east window of the north aisle where broken fragments were brought together in 1934 to make roundels commemorating the four gospel writers.

The impressive oak pulpit, with exquisite miniature heads and an intricate panel with Christ in the centre and a figure of a knight in chain mail, was carved by James Forsyth in 1857. On the wall of the south aisle is a memorial tablet to Henry Corbould who is buried in the churchyard. Of special interest to philatelists, it commemorates the man responsible in 1840 for the design of the world's first postage stamp, the Penny Black. To celebrate the 150th anniversary of the postage stamp, the village produced two limited edition First Day Covers to recognize the Corbould connection.

On the north wall hangs a large reproduction of the triptych "Descent from the Cross" painted by Rubens in 1612. The original is in Antwerp cathedral in Belgium. The church's imposing central tower contains a solitary bell dated 1632 and is inscribed "John Wilmer made me". Even older, and believed to be oldest church weathervane in the country, is the brass vane designed to represent Sir William de Echyngham's heraldic arms, described as *"azure fretty argent"*, silver criss-crossing fretwork on a blue background. This vane, still in its original position on the church tower, has been blowing in the wind over Sussex for nearly six hundred and fifty years. At the west end of the churchyard is an historic, gnarled yew tree. Still flourishing, it is worth taking a moment to reflect that it would most likely have been growing there when masons were fashioning stones to build the church.

Over the centuries the de Echyngham family was well known for loyalty to the Crown. Queen Elizabeth II, through the Bowes-Lyon branch of her family, is descended from Anne de Etchyngham. On April 13th 2013 the Queen's cousin, HRH Prince Richard, Duke of Gloucester, made an unscheduled stop at the church while visiting the village as part of his work connected with conservation and the environment. This royal visitor to Etchingham church, steeped as it is in history, is now recorded for posterity in a beautifully handwritten page, in the form of a traditional scroll, in the visitor's book.

Chapter 39

FLETCHING CHURCH

Heading east from Haywards Heath on the A272—the ancient Pilgrim's Way between Winchester and Canterbury—you pass through the village of Piltdown (once famous for the discovery of bone fragments believed to be those of a prehistoric man but subsequently exposed as a hoax), before turning down a country lane leading to the historic village of Fletching. Adjacent to Sheffield Park, and near the popular Bluebell Railway, Fletching, with its main street of half-timbered houses, old inns and cottages, is one of the most picturesque villages in East Sussex. The Church of St Andrew and St Mary the Virgin, sited on raised ground, is impressively grand for a small rural community.

Fletching, then called Flescinge, is mentioned in the Domesday Book, although there is no record of the church, which was undoubtedly in existence before that time. This can be detected in the present building, which shows traces of work dating from the late Saxon or early Norman period. Built in Early English cruciform style, the church was completed around 1230 and the first incumbent is recorded as William de Perpund in 1249. In the reign of Richard II the advowson was held by Philip and Joan Sinclair, until it was confirmed to the Priory of Michelham in 1398. At the Dissolution of the Monasteries the patronage was granted to Anne of Cleeves, and afterwards passed to the Dorset family from whom it was purchased by the first Earl of Sheffield. It remained with successive owners of Sheffield Park until 1956 when it passed to the Archbishop of Canterbury. The church has not always had dual dedication; prior to the Reformation it was simply the Church of Our Lady St Mary.

Fletching has strong links with a pivotal event in British history. On the eve of the Battle of Lewes in 1264 Simon de Montfort and his followers came to the village. They received the Holy Sacrament from the Bishop of Worcester in the church, and de Montfort is believed to have held an all-night vigil before leading his troops into battle the next day. The defeat he inflicted on the army of King Henry III led directly to the establishment of a Parliament and sowed the seeds for our present House of Commons. Legend relates that a number of de Montfort's knights, killed in the battle, were carried back to the church the following day and hurriedly buried in full armour beneath the nave.

The church tower, except for its spire and buttresses, is a good example of the Saxon merging into Norman. There is a shallow Norman buttress still in perfect condition on the north side where it has been incorporated into the wall of the aisle. The large buttresses on the west side of the tower were added around 1340. The octagonal broached spire, not especially high but perfectly proportioned, is believed to have been added at about the same time. The English oak shingles on the tower were renewed in May 2008 with funds generously provided by Sir Hugh Collum and a donation by the Friends of Fletching Parish Church.

The Perpendicular porch is early fifteenth century and has a Horsham stone roof and small square-headed windows on each side. It also contains a small holy water stoup. The magnificent oak door, although restored, is over five hundred years old and hung on Sussex wrought-iron hinges. As you turn the engraved iron handle it is worth pausing to reflect that this same door was in place before Queen Elizabeth I ascended the throne. The original Norman church was probably only the length of the existing nave and as wide as the area between the present columns. The north and south transepts are part of the general rebuilding and enlargement in Early English style in the thirteenth century. An unusual feature of the church is that the chancel is four feet wider than the nave and is exceptionally long for a parish church, over fifty feet.

In the north wall of the north transept is the mausoleum for the Earls of Sheffield which was built by John Baker Holroyd, first Earl of Sheffield, in the late eighteenth century. It contains his own monument and those to members of his family in succeeding decades. Also buried here is Edward Gibbon, a good friend of Lord Sheffield. Renowned as the author of *The Decline and Fall of the Roman Empire*, completed in1787, his tomb records "He was buried by the willing assent of John, Lord Sheffield, who caused this memorial to be erected to his faithful friend and learned companion". A further tribute to Gibbon reveals him as "One who has told The Truth despite the prevailing orthodoxies. An Inspiration to All".

The south transept has several fascinating monuments. These include wall tablets to members of the Maryon-Wilson family who, apart from the Sheffield's, were the other landed family in the parish. The imposing alabaster tomb, with full-size recumbent figures of Richard Leche, High Sherriff of Sussex and Surrey, who died in 1596, and his wife, Charitye, remains in almost perfect condition. His widow afterwards married the Earl of Nottingham who, apparently, was as unkind to her as her first husband had been kind. To ensure that posterity might associate her with her first husband, rather than her second, she had her effigy placed alongside his during her own lifetime. The small skull between them indicates the death of their child. There is also the church's quaintest possession, a simple pair of brass gloves mounted on a stone slab in memory of Peter Denot c.1450. As well as being pardoned with other Fletching men who had taken part in Jack Cade's rebellion against the policies of Henry IV, he chose this unique way of recording his business as a glover.

There is also an extremely fine brass memorial of a knight and his lady. This is believed to be Sir Walter Dalyngrygge, and dates from around 1380. He is depicted in full armour, mixed mail and plate, hands clasped together in prayer and his feet resting on a lion. She wears a long kirtle under a mantle and has a small dog at her feet. The large stone family crest, in the form of a unicorn's head surmounting a helmet over a shield, is positioned above the brass. The family built Bodiam Castle in Kent, and a unicorn's head is also over the castle gateway.

In addition, there is a tombstone which commemorates Daniel Hattrell, 1795-1874, a Fletching parishioner who served in the 3rd Foot Guards, now the Scots Guards, and fought at the Battle of Waterloo. He later became a Chelsea pensioner and his family, although poor, were extremely

Ships and Sealing Wax

proud of his achievements and when he died provided money for the stone. But due to deterioration it has been removed from the churchyard to the transept and, with funds raised by the local branch of The Royal British Legion, a new memorial now marks the place of his burial.

Another notable memorial reflects an important episode in the village's history. This is a plaque, dated "1941-1944" with the Maple Leaf emblem of Canada, "In Grateful Memory and Appreciation of the 6,000 Canadian soldiers who were stationed in Fletching Parish before seeing action in the Mediterranean and North West Europe". In the nave, above both the north and south transept arches, hangs the funerary armour of the Nevill family, the Earls of Abergavenny, who were once Lords of the Manor. They comprise helmet, sword, gauntlet and spurs. Dating from around 1720 they were restored by the Master of Armouries of the Tower of London in 1965.

There is much beautiful stained glass throughout the church. The unusual east window is of geometrical design, dating from the latter years of the thirteenth century. It was carefully restored in 1880 and closely follows the original. The Victorian glass is by Charles Kempe. The stained glass in the lancet windows on the south side of the chancel depicts the Apostles. The Early English windows in the east wall of the south transept contain ancient fourteenth century glass which was found in the churchyard about 1880, where it had probably been buried to escape the vandalism of the seventeenth century. In the north transept, the north light contains modern glass designed and made by Alan Younger. Its theme is St Francis of Assisi's "The Song of Brother Sun", which celebrates and praises God for all things, the sun, the

Roger Paine

moon, day and night, the earth, wind, water, fire, flowers and
stars.

Chapter 40

FOLKINGTON CHURCH

If the giant Long Man of Wilmington, cut into the chalk of the South Downs, were able to cast his shadow onto the valley below, it might well include the village of Folkington, tucked away in the hills behind Eastbourne. The Downland church of St Peter ad Vincula, meaning "St Peter in Chains", to whom only a handful of churches in England are dedicated, is at the end of a narrow country lane which, almost unnoticed, leads off the main Polegate to Lewes road.

Surrounded by woods and fields, this simple church, stone-faced with flint, seems hardly to belong in the twenty-first century. Yet in the same way that the tiny flowers which flourish on the Downs in the summer deserve closer study, so does St Peter's church where Christians have worshipped for over eight hundred years.

The history of the Manor of Folkington can be traced back to the pre-Conquest era and it is evident there was a church on the existing site at least from Norman times. The present church was built in the thirteenth century and the list of rectors records the first incumbent as Gervase, in

Roger Paine

1226. This list also reveals a small piece of English history in that Thomas Brett (1678-1689), is shown to have been "Deprived as Non-Juror". The Non-Jurors were a group of Anglican clergy who, after the "Glorious Revolution" of 1688, refused to take the oath of allegiance to William and Mary, and were relieved of their "livings" or positions.

St Peter's, with dimensions of only 67 feet by 24 feet, is smaller than many village halls. Nevertheless, the original tie-beam and crown post roof gives a feeling of light and space to the interior, accentuated by there being no visible division between the chancel and nave, although this separation is clearly evident from the outside. Because of the stresses caused by the high roof, the external walls are heavily buttressed.

Four lancet windows in the chancel and a blocked door in the north wall date from the Early English period. Further additions, including two windows in the Perpendicular style in the nave and a wooden broached-spire bell tower, recently re-shingled, date from around 1400. A single bell which also dates from this time, originally one of three, is still rung on special occasions. It is inscribed *"Vox Augustini Sonet in Aure Dei"*, "The Voice of St Augustine Sounds in God's Ear".

Particularly interesting, and typifying the close-knit manorial community of Folkington, are the late Georgian box-pews on each side of the nave. Originally for personal use by the major families in the village, they are now part of general seating for the congregation. The unadorned wooden pulpit is in the centre of the church, almost within touching distance of the historic box-pews. The substantial stone-built, octagonal font with wood-panelled and decorated arches on the pedestal, dates from the mid-fifteenth century.

Ships and Sealing Wax

A major restoration of the church was carried out in 1870. This included the addition of the vestry on the south side, rebuilding the chancel roof and new stained pressed glass by James Powell in the east window. The church's long association with prominent local families is evident from two beautifully conserved marble memorials in the sanctuary. Both display the coat of arms of the Thomas family whose descendants lived in the village for nearly two hundred years from 1652. One is dedicated to the Honourable Sir William Thomas Bt. and was erected by his nephew and heir, William Dobell; the other is to "Pious and Virtuous" Lady Barbara Thomas, wife of Sir William, who died in 1697. The inscription, "She was one of the Best of wives, her Devotion was constant and regular...Godlyness was her imployment and Heaven is her Reward," is surely an epitaph any married woman might be flattered to receive.

Among several plaques on the north wall are those commemorating Rupert Gywnne, MP for Eastbourne 1910-1924, who lived at Wootton Manor, and his sister, the acclaimed musician Violet Gordon Woodhouse (1871-1948), with words by the poet Sacheverell Sitwell, "Echoes of her music will sound forever in the hearts of those that loved her"; and Viscount Monkton of Brenchley (1891-1965), Attorney General and adviser to King Edward VIII during the abdication crisis, who lived at The Old Rectory. On the wall, close to the thirteenth century doorway into the church, is a contemporary carving of Christ by John Skelton, the celebrated Sussex sculptor whose work is also in Chichester Cathedral.

The organ, made by renowned organ builder Henry Speechly, is, in itself, a memorial. Presented to the church by May Gwynne, a brass plaque records, "This organ is offered in deep thankfulness for the love that saved the life of her beloved son Lieut Colonel Roland Vaughan Gwynne DSO in the Battle of 31st July 1917 on the Western Front in Flanders". The nearby war memorial, also the gift of May Gwynne, besides recording the names of five men from Folkington who fell in the First World War, lists those "to whom was granted a safe return". Such heart-warming sentiments are seldom found on similar memorials.

In the south-west corner of the churchyard, in an area set aside for the Gwynne family, is the grave of Elizabeth David CBE (1913-1992), daughter of Rupert Gwynne. World famous for her cookery books which transformed British eating habits in the post-War era, her headstone depicts a large French cook pot and sundry ingredients. The church visitors' book records that today's "foodies" come to Folkington to pay homage to this celebrated "kitchen goddess". Likewise, early music enthusiasts visit as a tribute to Violet Woodhouse.

The words of Rudyard Kipling, in his poem "Sussex", quoted on a prominent churchyard gravestone, encapsulate the feelings few can fail to experience when visiting St Peter's:

Here through the strong unhampered days
The tinkling silence thrills;
Or little, lost, Down churches praise
The Lord who made the hills.

Chapter 41

FRISTON CHURCH

When heading out of Eastbourne towards Seaford in East Sussex, the road winds up a steep hill after leaving East Dean, so that Friston's tiny church of St Mary the Virgin may not be immediately noticeable. But this unpretentious church, adjacent to the lane leading to Crowlink, is majestically sited and commands far-reaching views to Birling Gap and the Seven Sisters.

A place of worship is known to have existed on the site for a thousand years, but all that is visible of the original Saxon church are a blocked up doorway and window in the south wall. These also indicate that the oldest part of the church is the nave. This, together with the chancel, the porch and Selwyn transept, comprise the entire church. Although simple in origin and small in size, the church has much of interest, not least its name and dedication. For four hundred years it was known as the Church of St James until it reverted to its original, current name in 1957.

There are two Norman doorways, one inside the porch on the south side, the other forming the entrance to the vestry on the north. But the most impressive feature is the massive timber framing of the nave, with tie-beam roof, crown posts, wall plates and struts. The timber, which dates from around 1450, remains in a remarkable state of preservation and almost certainly came from Friston Forest, less than a mile away. The timelessness of the wood fills this historic church with a sense of strength and quiet dignity.

The porch over the entrance is of pre-Reformation origin. Of special interest are the historic graffiti markings, particularly a mutilated carving of Christ on the cross. It has been done, very roughly, on a piece of hard chalk—perhaps by a medieval traveller—with the point of a knife. In the corner of the porch is the broken half of a holy water stoup, and next to the doorway, buried in the wall, can be seen a fragment of a medieval coffin lid.

The chancel dates from the early fourteenth century. On either side of the altar are two projecting slabs, which in medieval times would most likely have supported figures of Christ and the church's patron saint. There is also an aumbry, where the sacraments would have been kept, and a recessed piscina, although the basin has long gone. In the south wall is a Norman lancet window with stained glass donated by Lord Liverpool, one-time resident at Friston Place. This depicts St James the Apostle dressed as a pilgrim with staff, water bottle and scallop shell. As the chancel's single south-facing window it captures whatever sunlight is available, providing exquisite fragments of colour wholly proportionate to the size of the sanctuary.

In the east wall is a magnificent, award-winning stained-glass window designed, cut and painted by local artist Jane Patterson. Dedicated in September 2002, it consists of two windows describing an interpretation of the story of the

Ships and Sealing Wax

Ascension of Christ witnessed by Mary, his Mother, and an angel. The windows also depict local landmarks, including, in the left window, the ancient church pond opposite the entrance to the church, complete with lily, dragonfly and a frog.

On the north side of the church is the Selwyn transept. Constructed in the nineteenth century, it was the gift of Miss Anne Gilbert who lived at Birling Manor House, intended not only to provide additional seating but also as a permanent place for two large Selwyn monuments previously in the chancel. These impressive memorials commemorate the Selwyn family, who lived at Friston Place for more than two hundred years from 1500. The memorial in alabaster on the west wall is to Thomas Selwyn, who died in 1613, and his wife, Elizabeth. Their effigies and those of their six daughters, in ruffs and wimples, are next to those of their newborn babies, indicating the high infant mortality rate that existed in those times. On the opposite wall there is an imposing marble memorial recording the family of Sir Francis Selwyn who had fifteen children, eight daughters and seven sons. It also notes the death in 1704 of his eldest son and heir, William Thomas, the last of the family, *ultimus Selwynorum*. On the death of William, despite the size of the family, there was no one to continue the family name, recorded as *nunc extincta*.

At the west end of the church is a memorial in recognition of RAF Friston, an operational Fighter Command airfield from 1942 until 1946, situated on land belonging to nearby Gayles Farm. During World War II the population of East Dean and Friston doubled with an additional 1,200 RAF and 120 WAAF personnel. The parish registers record that RAF church services were held in the church and that there was more than one wedding. A former RAF pilot, who returned in 1988 after more than forty years, recorded in the visitor's book, "Here is something that hasn't changed." He would probably say the same about the church if he visited it again today.

Outside, the well-maintained cemetery is entered through a rare example of a wooden Sussex tapsell gate, which pivots on a stanchion and was designed to prevent cattle from entering the churchyard. Several headstones record simply, "A Sailor, Merchant Navy, 1939-45, Known unto God". These, and even more poignantly, a simple wooden cross with the words "Washed Ashore", all reflect the dangers faced by those who go down to the sea in ships. The English Channel is only a mile away. Another noteworthy headstone, with the words "Blessed are the Meek at Heart", marks the last resting place of distinguished composer Frank Bridge (1879-1941), who lived in Friston for the last seventeen years of his life. He was a teacher of Benjamin Britten, and deputized for Sir Henry Wood at the legendary "Proms" concerts in London.

When the Diocesan Advisory Committee visited St Mary the Virgin it was described as "The Jewel of Sussex". The adage "The best things come in small packages" seems particularly appropriate to Friston Church.

Chapter 42

HARTFIELD CHURCH

The village of Hartfield was once, as its name suggests, a major centre for hunting in the extensive forests which covered a large proportion of the Weald of Sussex. In the heart of the Ashdown Forest, designated an Area of Outstanding Natural Beauty, Hartfield now straddles the B2110 between Tunbridge Wells and East Grinstead. It is also well known as the home of A A Milne, author of Winnie the Pooh, who would take his son, Christopher Robin, walking in the local countryside. The famous "pooh-sticks" bridge is here, and the village has become a place of pilgrimage for devotees of the iconic little bear from around the world.

The parish church of St Mary the Virgin is located close to the school, with which it has always had strong ties. Although the village is mentioned in the Domesday Book of 1085, there is no mention of the church. Records indicate, however, that the first Rector of Hartfield, named Walter, was instituted in 1263. It seems likely, therefore, that there would have been a place of worship on the raised ground where today's church is situated for some considerable time before this. Evidence points to the present church being constructed in the middle of the thirteenth century, a period of extensive building in the Chichester Diocese.

The only remaining part of the original church is the rough built stonework of the north wall, with one blocked up lancet widow clearly visible from the outside. The church would have been much smaller than it is today, with the nave ending where the double timber tie-beams are now. The chancel and the sanctuary would then have been about the same length as the nave. The tall arched recess in the north wall is thought to have been the way into the stairway up to the rood loft. In the north wall there are three different styles of arches in close proximity, each reflecting the distinct styles of the century in which they were built, namely the thirteenth, fourteenth and fifteenth.

The south side of the church, including windows in decorated style and the chapel, dates from the fourteenth century. The church tower, with its impressive shingled broached spire, is in Perpendicular style and dates from the fifteenth century. The church spire is currently in need of re-shingling and shingles, similar to small wooden tiles, can be purchased for £5 each.

As in many parish churches, there was extensive restoration during the Victorian era. In St Mary's this started in 1864. The roof inside was restored with many new timbers, and much other woodwork, including the pews, was renewed. The priest's vestry with the chamber for the organ, by Walker & Sons, donated in 1892, was rebuilt, as was the porch. The six bells, still in regular use, were cast a century earlier, in 1782, by Chapman and Mears of London.

Ships and Sealing Wax

The church is approached up a narrow street of attractive white weather-boarded cottages, above which can be glimpsed the spire. A lychgate gives access to the churchyard and is probably one of the most unusual in the country. It is an integral part of the half-timbered Lych Gate Cottage which was originally connected to its next-door neighbour, thus forming an arch. A gravestone nearby recalls a nineteenth century couple who lived in the tiny cottage for over sixty years—it was even smaller in those days—and brought up seven children there. The date 1520 is inscribed on one of the external walls. The churchyard is extensive and well populated. With paths flanked by yew hedges it slopes gently down to two lower areas. A majestic tulip tree adds grandeur to the west end of the churchyard.

St Mary's has an interesting history of involvement with local charities. One of these is the Nicholas Smith Charity or, as he is sometimes known, "Beggarman Smith". In the seventeenth century Mr Smith, a wealthy man, disguised himself as a beggar and went around the county seeking somewhere to live and where he would be made welcome. He was frequently turned away, until he came to Hartfield, where he was warmly received. He was so grateful that he bought a house in the village and in his will made provision for the poor of Hartfield by stating that annually on Good Friday £10 should be distributed from beside the place where he is buried to forty "poor and indigent people". Every year deserving villagers gather around his grave to receive his bounty.

A brass memorial inside the church commemorates the Coyfe & Hooker Fund, endowed by John Hooker of Court House, Hartfield, who died in 1900. He left a sum of £1,000 "upon trust invested" to the Rector and Churchwardens for

Roger Paine

"...bread, coals, fuel and other such things as they may think expedient for gratuitous distribution amongst such poor and deserving persons being inhabitants of Hartfield at Christmas". Once again the benefactor's wishes are carried out annually.

Churches and churchyards have a reputation for unusual words on memorials. The oldest memorial in St Mary's, an alabaster tablet with black marble columns on the north wall of the south chapel, written by the person who it commemorates but without mentioning his name, follows in this tradition. He was the Rev Richard Randes, Rector 1622-1640, a scholar and fellow of Trinity College, Oxford, who in spite of fondness for drink was a humble man who understood his own frailties. His memorial is written entirely in Latin and explains "Here lies one unworthy even of a name, since while he was in the light, he did nothing worthy of a name. I now, poor wretch, trust wholly in Thee, oh light of the world, my hope, my life and my salvation. I sleep until the last trump shall sound."

In the chancel, on the south wall, is a marble memorial to the Rev Henry Stedman Polehampton, brother of Rev Edward Polehampton, Rector 1859-1891. This vividly recalls that he was Chaplain to the East India Company stationed at Lucknow in 1856 and wounded at the Garrison Hospital in 1857. "On the 9th day of the siege died of cholera, July 20th, aged 33, was buried in the Residency by those to whom in a strange and fiery trial he had fearlessly ministered." The desperate times of the Indian Mutiny are remembered in a parish church in the Ashdown Forest.

Also in the chancel are several memorials to generations of the Maitland family. A watercolour sketch of the chancel and sanctuary, showing what it was like in 1874 before the east end of the church was altered, hangs on a pillar in the nave. It was painted by Colonel F T Maitland, whose father, General Frederick Maitland, and his wife, Catherine, are commemorated in stained glass in the east window. The impressively carved wooden lectern, in the shape of an eagle, is inscribed "In loving memory of our parents, George Carnac Fisher DD, Bishop of Southampton, and his wife Mary Penelope, married in this church 28th April 1870". A charming additional inscription reads "He was a man of quick sympathies."

But Hartfield church is far from being solely about looking back. Recently over one hundred local people of all ages from the village and surrounding areas collaborated in a specially written community play, *Parallel Lives*. This told the story of the lives of real people who have lived in Hartfield and its partner parish of Coleman's Hatch during the past century. It was performed over a period of two weeks in the church which, according to the writer and director, provided a setting "greater than any set you'd find in the West End of London".

Chapter 43

HERSTMONCEUX CHURCH

The village of Herstmonceux is a busy rural community between Battle and Hailsham in East Sussex. With a quirkiness often to be found in the English countryside, the parish church is two miles away, down a country lane appropriately named Chapel Row leading to Church Road.

To find All Saints Church you pass through the hamlet of Flowers Green, with its barely noticeable roadside sign, go past the former pub The Welcome Stranger—known locally as The Nodding Donkey, but which has not been a hostelry for years although it still retains its sign and car park—and pass Herstmonceux Chapel, the Free Church which celebrated its 200th anniversary in 2011, until you can go no further. The church is nearer to Herstmonceux Castle than it is to the village, although it has been in existence for much longer than the medieval castle.

All Saints Church stands on an area of raised ground, thought to be an early sacred site, and commands unrivalled views across the Pevensey levels to the South Downs. The Manor of Herste is mentioned in the Domesday Book, which also notes "There is a church." The original village, which probably surrounded the church, was moved northwards, possibly at the time of the plague in the fourteenth century, or a century later when Sir Roger Fiennes, a veteran of the Battle of Agincourt and builder of the nearby castle, received permission to enclose 600 acres, which would have included any houses and the church.

Whilst there is little doubt that a place of worship has existed since Saxon times, the oldest parts of the present church are the tower and the west wall, together with square-edged pillars in the north aisle, which date from the twelfth century. The nave, chancel and aisles were added over the next two hundred years, whilst the north, or Dacre, chapel was built in the fifteenth century. These additions reflect the importance of the church and its ever-increasing links with the castle. This is especially evident in the east wall, and the north wall of the chapel, which are built of red Flemish brick in exactly the same manner as those used for the castle. It is one of the earliest uses of this building material to be found in a church in Sussex.

The church presents unusually varying appearances due to the tower with its shingled spire being offset from the nave, the Dacre chapel having been added, and two large dormer windows above the north and south aisles added in Victorian times. When viewed from the south, with prominent buttresses supporting the walls and a porch, the former church entrance, you could be forgiven for thinking that you were looking at a country manor house rather then a rural parish church. Internally, the trussed medieval roof with tie beams over the nave and the curved timber panelling of the chancel roof provide a sense of height and space. The north porch, added in the eighteenth century but replaced in 1874, is now the main entrance to the church.

Between the chancel and the chapel is the church's greatest treasure, the Dacre tomb. Erected in 1534, this magnificent tomb chest with canopy is built of Caen and Bonchurch stone and Purbeck marble. It is probably the finest of its type in Sussex. The north side shows more signs of wear than the chancel side, which seems to indicate that it may have been exposed to the weather and formed part of the outside wall of the church until enclosed by the chapel in the fifteenth century.

On the tomb lie the effigies of Thomas, 8th Lord Dacre (1470-1533), and his son Sir Thomas Fiennes, who pre-deceased his father in 1528. Both wear Milanese armour, their hands in an attitude of prayer. Their feet lie on animals representing the bull of the Dacres and the wolfhound of the Fiennes. It is thought that the figures may have been brought from nearby Battle Abbey when it was dissolved by Henry VIII, and that they originally depicted the brothers Hooe until they were later altered to represent Dacre and Fiennes. Above the canopy on the chancel side is an ornately carved cornice of shields and helmets. The middle shield bears the arms and eagle crest of the Fiennes family, builders of Herstmonceux castle in 1440 and Lords of the Manor for nearly 300 years. The tomb was restored and repainted in 1970 with the advice of the College of Arms. Although to modern eyes it might appear gaudy, it is believed to be accurate.

A further memorial to a member of the Fiennes family, Sir William Fiennes, father of the builder of Herstmonceux Castle, lies on the floor of the chancel. This memorial brass, dated 18th January 1402, is in almost perfect condition. It shows the knight in full armour wearing a sword, with his feet resting on a lion. The inscription is in medieval French. Another distinctive memorial in the chancel is the plaque commemorating Douglas McGarel Hogg, 1st Viscount Hailsham, who "Served God and The King Truly, as soldier, lawyer and statesman". A former Lord Chancellor, he worshipped in the church for many years and died in 1950.

On the west wall of the south aisle is a memorial to Lieutenant Colonel Claude William Henry Lowther, erected by his two sisters. He was Lord of the Manor of Herstmonceux in 1911, after the castle had become a ruin and been demolished, and was responsible for initiating its repair and restoration. In 1914, at the outbreak of war, he raised and equipped three battalions of the Royal Sussex Regiment whose soldiers became known as Lowther's Lambs.

The stained glass in the east window of the south aisle commemorates the five sons and two daughters of William and Anne Hooper Greenaway. On the south wall of the tower there is a brass plaque commemorating one of their sons, Major Henry Greenaway (1840-1879), "In affectionate remembrance of an honoured comrade and true friend" which includes the regimental badge of the 10th Bengal Lancers, Hodson's Horse, inscribed with the battle honours "Abyssinia, Delhi and Lucknow", a far cry from the rolling meadows and woods of Sussex.

The font, of light-coloured sandstone with a square bowl supported on a circular stem and four octagonal pillars, dates from the late fourteenth century and is covered by a distinctive wooden carved lid, probably of Victorian origin. Next to this, in the north aisle, stands a marble sculpture of a small child known as "the cherub". It is thought to be the

Roger Paine

work of the celebrated sixteenth century French sculptor Jean Goujon, and was presented to the church by Colonel Lowther.

The exceptionally fine pipe organ, installed in 1878, was made by Henry Bevington. The organ in St Martin-in-the-Fields church in London is by the same distinguished firm. The All Saints organ was restored to its original condition in 1997. Dark oak box pews, some with doors and tall brass candleholders at the aisle ends, add a Dickensian touch and remind one of the church's nineteenth century restoration.

In the early hours of the morning of 3rd July 1944 the church suffered damage from an enemy bomb, which demolished three windows and damaged the roof, spire and other windows. Much of the stained glass was smashed, but the oldest fragments that remain are the fifteenth century yellow and white glass in the upper lights of the east window in the north chapel. Three months later, after urgent repairs, the church reopened.

The main entrance to the church from Church Road is directly opposite the gateway leading to Herstmonceux Castle. This highlights the historic bonds that have linked the buildings and the communities associated with them for nearly six hundred years. A well worn mounting block stands hard against the church wall outside the gate. It is not difficult to imagine, in centuries past, members of the congregation after morning service on Sundays walking through the churchyard and then mounting their horses for the long ride back to the village, or the shorter distance to the castle. In view of the location of All Saints Church, these sturdy stone steps tell their own story.

Chapter 44

HYTHE CHURCH

The imposing parish church of St Leonard's in Hythe, which means "haven", one of Kent's historic Cinque Ports, stands high and proud at the rear of the town. With a view from the churchyard across the Channel, on a fine day you can see the coast of France; links with the sea have helped to shape its history. The church is reached by steep alleyways and winding roads that lead up from the town's High Street which, at one time, was the quayside of a busy seaport. It was also the landing place for pilgrims who would visit the church to give thanks for safe arrival before continuing their journey to the shrine of St Thomas à Becket in Canterbury Cathedral.

St Leonard's Church was built by the Normans around 1080 adjacent to an existing stone Saxon church. The entrance arch in the choir vestry, which leads into the former St Edmund's chapel, now the north transept, was part of the ancient church, thus providing a continuity of worship on the site for over a thousand years. The dedication to St Leonard can be seen in the stained glass window in the south porch. A hermit monk, he founded a monastery in France in the sixteenth century. Returning crusaders are said to have regarded him as the patron saint of prisoners and the window depicts a prisoner in chains at the saint's feet.

The size of the original Norman church would have been that of the nave which exists today, finishing at what are now the chancel steps. But as the fortunes of Hythe flourished, the church was extended between 1120 and 1220, with north and south aisles being added, together with the magnificent three-storied chancel. This has been described by Professor Francis Bond, a renowned authority on medieval church architecture, as "the finest chancel of any church in England, not to say Europe". It is reminiscent of a cathedral and the light which pours through the chancel's clerestory windows enhances this sense of grandeur.

It was at this time, too, that the chancel floor was raised to its present height, reached by nine wide stone steps, in order to accommodate a vaulted ambulatory beneath the sanctuary. This enabled church processions carrying St Leonard's relic to remain on consecrated ground when circulating the church on holy days.

In the fourteenth century the west tower and the south porch were added, with a parvis above for the priest. Used by the town council for meetings until the Town Hall was built in 1794, it is now the parish office. But in 1580 a severe earth tremor "shook the tower of St Leonard's so violently that the bells sounded". And over the next two hundred years the character of Hythe changed: the harbour silted up, the flow of pilgrims ceased, and there was a plague as well as a great storm and losses at sea. All took their toll, leading to a lack of maintenance. This and the earlier tremor were the most likely reasons for the collapse of the tower in 1739. "At eleven o'clock, the steeple of their church fell down, and they have been busy digging out the bells," reported a local newspaper. "About ten persons were present when it fell, waiting for the keys to go up the steeple for a view. But some delay being made in bringing them, they all happily saved their lives, and no other damage than being terribly frightened." A truly providential escape. The tower was rebuilt in 1750 using some of the original materials, and is twelve feet lower than the one it replaced.

For many visitors to Hythe Church the most fascinating feature is the collection of skulls and bones in the crypt, although it is not, strictly speaking, a crypt, as it is accessible from ground level and forms part of the ambulatory which passes below the east end of the chancel. There are some 1,200 skulls and 8,000 thigh bones. , with just over 1,000 of the skulls on four shelves; the rest are stacked in neat piles which also contain some smaller bones. The collection is believed to have been in the church since earliest times, certainly from the thirteenth century.

Despite many theories about victims of battles and the plague there is now little doubt that the bones are churchyard remains, although not all are necessarily from St Leonard's. It is especially notable that, as can be seen from the collection of jawbones, the general standard of teeth was good, although they are well worn, and holes which today would involve filling were non-existent, indicating a sugar-free diet. Recently the collection has been studied by postgraduates from Bournemouth University, and by St Leonard's Osteological Research Group, an independent group of forensic scientists who worked voluntarily in the crypt for two weeks a year. These studies, using the latest analysis, profiling and measuring techniques, have overturned some long-held arguments as to the reasons for the cause of death of particular individuals. A computer database record of the completed research has also been compiled.

As well as its remarkable history in many areas, St Leonard's is a vibrant and thriving church with a particularly fine musical tradition. The present organ console is now in the south transept and mobile for concerts. Built by Harrison & Harrison in 1936, some of the pipework is from the previous organ, which was situated at the west end of the nave.

St Leonard's is also keen to be recognised as an "open and inclusive church" and one that believes "the way we treat one another is far more important than the beliefs that we hold." This is surely a statement which has relevance far beyond Hythe's parish boundaries.

Chapter 45

MAYFIELD CHURCH

Mayfield, set on a hilly ridge between Heathfield and Tunbridge Wells, is one of the most charming of many historic villages in Sussex. With its long high street, dominated by The Middle House, a timber-framed Elizabethan building dating back to 1575 and now a hotel and restaurant, it was described by the Victorian writer Coventry Patmore as "the sweetest village in Sussex".

Originally known as Maid's Field, which is depicted on the village sign by a young woman dancing with children in a flower-covered meadow, the imposing parish church is dedicated to St Dunstan, the great Saxon Archbishop of Canterbury, who built a wooden church on the present site in AD 960. He was also a skilled metal craftsman who, according to legend, was working at his forge when the devil, disguised as a woman, appeared. Noticing a cloven hoof peeping from beneath her skirt, St Dunstan realised it was the devil and immediately clamped his red-hot tongs on the devil's nose. Letting out a blood-curdling screech, the devil resumed his proper form and flew away to cool his inflamed organ in a nearby stream!

This story, often related to visitors, remains a staple ingredient of Mayfield folklore. A stained-glass window, in the original Norman lancet window in the north-west corner of the church, has a design taken from an ancient drawing in the British Museum depicting the redoubtable St Dunstan.

In the twelfth century the Normans replaced the wooden church with one of stone, but a fire swept through the village in 1389 and almost completely destroyed the church. Only the tower, a small part of the west wall and the footings of the north wall remain from the original building. The church was then rebuilt in the fifteenth century in the Perpendicular style. The battlemented, quadrangular porch which forms the south entrance has a vaulted roof with a carved dragon, or serpent, curled round the central boss. There is also some eighteenth century graffiti on the entrance columns, indicating that nothing is new when it comes to carving your initials and a date...!

Inside the church are many features of historical interest. The sandstone font is clearly dated 1666 and is carved with the initials of the vicar of Mayfield at the time, Robert Peck, as well as those of his two churchwardens. Dominating the nave are two elaborate chandeliers, with weighted balancing devices enabling them to be lowered for cleaning. The chandelier at the west end is dated 1773 and bears the monogram of Thomas Baker (1728-1782), and the larger one, at the east end, is dated 1737 and was given by Thomas's father, George Baker (1679-1756). The chandeliers are believed to have been placed in the church to provide candlelight at funerals which, in the eighteenth century, often took place after dark.

Ships and Sealing Wax

On the interior west wall is an unusual, diamond-shaped clock face known as a preacher's dial. The purpose was to keep the preacher informed about the length of his sermon in order that a full quota of instruction was imparted. As only hours are measured, no plans have been made to restore it to working order.

In addition to several noteworthy memorials there are two cast-iron tomb slabs set in the floor of the nave. The rougher one was probably the work of an unskilled moulder, as the number "7" and the letters "N" and "S" are reversed. There is also some intricate wood carving in the church. The strapwork pulpit and the remains of the rood screen on either side of the chancel steps originate from the seventeenth century and are carved in oak. On the wall either side of the main altar are two commandment table boards, painted around 1750 with the Ten Commandments, the Lord's Prayer and the Creed; they are the work of village schoolmaster Walter Gale.

On the south wall, near the entrance, is a twentieth century memorial to the commanding officer and crew of HM Submarine *Tetrarch*. The ship had been adopted by Mayfield's Women's Institute in the early years of World War II and had presented the village with a ship's crest, which is also displayed. The submarine, alas, was sunk by a mine in the Mediterranean on 2nd November 1941. There were no survivors.

There is also an interesting modern stained glass window in the south chapel in memory of General Sir John Glubb (Glubb Pasha) who commanded the Arab legion and later the Jordan Army. He retired to Mayfield and was a churchwarden for fifteen years. The dedication of this window, which includes the figure of Sir John wearing the traditional Arab *shemagh*, was attended by King Hussein and Queen Noor of Jordan in 1993.

A list of vicars, dating back to 1270, indicates the extraordinary record of Mayfield having had four father-son vicars for an unbroken period of one hundred and thirty-two years between 1780 and 1912. The son of the second Reverend Kirby, Henry Thomas Murdoch Kirby, was vicar for fifty two years.

The present vicar has masterminded opening up the west end of the chancel to create a flexible space for meetings, learning and socializing. The last part of the project was uncovering the top portion of the Saxon arch separating the nave from the vestry and creating a glass partition to the bell-ringing chamber, letting light in from the ancient west window, which had not been seen from inside the church for 150 years.

Chapter 46

PEVENSEY CHURCH

The village of Pevensey was once surrounded on three sides by a vast natural seawater harbour which stretched five miles inland from the present coastline. On this major defensive neck of land the Romans built a stone fortress, which was enlarged by the Normans after William the Conqueror landed there in 1066.

Over the next two hundred years the settlement grew in importance, and in 1207 King John granted a Royal Charter which brought Pevensey into the prestigious Cinque Ports system with its own powers and privileges. Between 1200 and 1216 Pevensey church was built. The overall construction was carried out using flint boulders readily available on the nearby seashore. Large quantities of greensand stone were also used, having been brought by ship from a quarry at the western end of Eastbourne's seafront. On completion, it was dedicated to St Nicolas, patron saint of seafarers, a permanent reminder today of Pevensey's once-important role as a flourishing seaport.

Roger Paine

The church is now the oldest building in the village still used for its original purpose and is a fine, almost untouched, example of Early English architecture. The sharp pointed arches of the aisles and chancel are typical of this style, and the three large lancet windows above the altar at the east end remain in near-perfect condition. The view from the west end of the nave gives an excellent idea of the overall layout and it is immediately apparent that the centreline deviates markedly to the left. This is not an error of design or construction, nor does it indicate that you are in need of an eyesight test, but a deliberate attempt—not unusual in churches of this era—to create either an illusion of greater length, or, according to legend, to depict the drooping of Christ's head on the cross. However, in St Nicolas the nave is, in fact, only 5 feet longer than the chancel, whereas in most churches it is significantly longer.

The cradle roof at the east end of the chancel is a splendid example of medieval craftsmanship. Made of hand-sawn and hand-jointed Sussex oak, it is almost entirely as originally constructed circa AD 1205. For many years the chancel and the nave were closed off from each other by a crude stone wall some nine feet high, built under the chancel arch. The only part of the church then used for worship was the nave. The chancel was used as a stable for cattle and as storage for farm implements and sacks of coal, together with kegs of brandy and spirits landed by smugglers, who used Pevensey as a major unloading point for contraband brought over from France!

By the end of the nineteenth century, however, the church had become seriously dilapidated and was in urgent need of repair. The Reverend Robert Sutton was appointed vicar in 1875 and almost immediately initiated a programme of essential restoration and extensive additions. He also obtained the services of George Gilbert Scott Jnr, an ecclesiastical architect from London and son of Eminent Victorian architect Sir George Gilbert Scott, to oversee the works. Particularly noteworthy was the building in 1887 of the vestry on the site adjoining the tower to the east, almost certainly the foundations of a former chapel or chantry.

During this time, too, the church tower was taken down to first storey level and then built up by two storeys before a shingled steeple, higher than the original, was constructed on top. This steeple, in distinctive "witch's-hat" style, is the one that exists today. The additional storey means there is an unusually long "draught" (length of pull) of some 40 feet between ringers and bells. In the north-west corner of the bell tower is a magnificent cast-iron spiral staircase leading up to the bell-chamber. Still in regular use, it is much admired, and coveted, by visitors.

Amongst many interesting artefacts is a rough-crafted wooden muniment chest dating from 1664, once used for storing church silver and valuables. The chest had three locks each, with different keys which would have been held by the vicar and the two churchwardens so it could not be opened without all three being present! The font is made of Caen stone and was most likely installed when the church was built 800 years ago. The retractable, ornate canopy was carved by a local man in 1890. Close by is a large and heavy stone ball of the type used as ammunition for massive siege catapults prior to the invention of cannons as weapons of war. Many of these stone balls can still be seen in Pevensey Castle. On the stone frame of the door, under the porch on the north side, are three crosses dating from the thirteenth century, etched when crusaders and pilgrims set out for their distant destinations from the port of Pevensey. Some of the crosses depict only the downstroke, as it was customary to do this before departure, and add the crosspiece on safe return. Those without these additions tell their own story.

Travel and history are inseparable in Pevensey, which now welcomes 200,000 visitors every year. Many take time out to visit the parish church, and their donations, together with the hugely successful fundraising efforts of local people, have helped to raise over £100,000 for the ongoing restoration of this historic church. As the Reverend Alfred Evans, curate for six years at the beginning of the twentieth century remarked, "The grey walls and ancient stillness should remind one of the peace and presence of God, and before leaving let a prayer be offered, 'Lord, I have loved the habitation of Thy House and the place where Thine honour dwelleth.'" Visitors to St Nicolas today will surely echo his words.

Chapter 47

PIDDINGHOE CHURCH

Dating back over nine hundred years, and standing high on the banks of the River Ouse as it sweeps in a majestic curve on its way to the sea, two miles away at Newhaven, is the church of St John the Evangelist, Piddinghoe. Particularly impressive is the flint-built round tower, one of only three such towers in Sussex. The others are in the nearby village of Southease, and at St Michael's in Lewes. Originally they may have served as watchtowers to warn of invaders approaching from the sea.

At St John's, the tower is surmounted by a wooden-shingled, octagonal spire topped with an unusual weathervane. This is in the form of a large gilded salmon-trout, a fish often caught in the fast-flowing Ouse. The vane has adorned the tower for over a century, and was immortalized by Rudyard Kipling in his 1902 poem "Sussex": "where windy Piddinghoe's begilded dolphin veers". A classic example of either poetic licence or Kipling's extremely poor eyesight, as it bears little resemblance to a dolphin and was modeled on a salmon trout seen on a fishmonger's slab in Lewes! It was repaired and re-gilded in 1980.

Piddinghoe, long bypassed by the Newhaven to Lewes road, has a tradition of independence. Enshrined in a local saying, "Englishmen fight, French 'uns too; We don't, we live in Piddinghoe", which identifies, through rhyming, the correct pronunciation of the village's name. St John's church, surprisingly cavernous and somewhat dark, can give the impression of a medieval monastery. Since the church was known to be thriving in 1121 when it was ceded to the Priory of St Pancras at Lewes, the first house that the Cluniac monks established in England, this is understandable. One of the founders of the order was William de Warenne, who in 1095, following the Norman Conquest, was responsible for building St John's. Originally the church consisted of only the nave and tower.

By the middle of the twelfth century the nave had been enlarged by building the north and south aisles; by the early thirteenth century the chancel, and chancel aisles, had been added. The arches to the north aisle are rounded in Norman style, while those to the south aisle are in pointed Gothic fashion. The finely proportioned arch of the Early English chancel is considered an outstanding example of an arch from this period.

There are two small carved stone heads on each side of the arch. It is believed that these could be Simon de Harpetyng and his wife. As a wealthy local landowner in the early thirteenth century he may have contributed to the arch's construction, seeking eternal salvation by leaving these likenesses before God in perpetuity. Another ancient carved head on the north wall of the nave has been likened to that of a man preaching a lengthy sermon. The craftsman has shut the eyes and opened the mouth so that the man seems to be saying too much but seeing nothing! The font is near the south entrance but was formerly adjacent to the "devil's door", now blocked up but still visible in the north wall. It is made from green Eastbourne sandstone and dates from the late thirteenth century. The cover was given by the Sunday school in 1905.

By the late nineteenth century St John's was reported to be in such a dilapidated state as to preclude the holding of services. The south aisle had collapsed and been demolished. In February 1882 a major programme of restoration, including essential repairs to the existing fabric and expansion of the building to its former size, was commenced. This required the church to be closed and the congregation moved to the adjacent village school. The aisle was rebuilt (including the removal of the west end gallery), the tower repointed, the spire re-shingled and the chancel and part of the nave re-roofed. Today's entrance porch on the south side was added, Victorian encaustic tiles were laid to cover the original flagstones, new pinewood pews replaced the old box-pews, and a new pulpit, lectern and organ were installed. After only nine months, the work was completed, and the church was re-consecrated on 24th November 1882. The maintenance of the church continues to be an enormous burden and fundraising an ongoing necessity. The Friends of St John's was formed for this purpose in 1998.

There is much fine stained glass, the majority of which was installed during the 1882 restoration. The Pre-Raphaelite design of the glass in the circular (oculus) window high in the east wall depicts "The Recording Angels". In the south aisle there are a series of windows showing the twelve apostles, whilst in the north aisle they display events in the life of Christ. In the west end of the north aisle there is a striking stained-glass window donated in 1983 in memory of Dr Elizabeth Holmes who lived in the village. Designed by Marguerite Douglas-Thompson, inspired by "The light of God shines on us without evening", it depicts the movement from darkness to light around a jewel-like centre. It is regarded as one of the most attractive modern stained-glass windows in Sussex. Behind the lectern, a beautiful circular mosaic plaque, crafted by Ann Clark of Lewes, commemorates the 2000 Millennium.

The large churchyard, which slopes down almost to the bank of the Ouse, allows a view of the proud expanse of church roof, from the nave ridge right down to within a few feet of the ground, in one magnificent uninterrupted sweep. Also in the churchyard are the ancient village stocks, originally used for imprisoning miscreant local inhabitants. Although the wooden hand and leg "cuffs" have decayed, the stone supports are original. They serve as a reminder that "God's little acre" had many uses in years gone by and, like the church, was the focal point of village life.

Chapter 48

RODMELL CHURCH

Rodmell is probably best known for Monks House, where the famous novelist and literary critic Virginia Woolf lived for more that twenty years. Sadly, in 1941, suffering from severe depression, she walked down to the River Ouse and, with her pockets filled with large stones, drowned herself. Adjacent to the house is St Peter's Church, one of several medieval churches along the Ouse valley.

To find the church, turn off the Lewes road to the Newhaven road at the Abergavenny Arms and you are immediately into the village, with its cluster of flint cottages and half-timbered and thatched houses flanking narrow streets. There has been a settlement here since Saxon times. The entrance to St Peter's, with its pyramid shingled spire, is at the end of a path leading to the local primary school. You have to cross the school playground to reach the church.

At the time of the Domesday Survey of 1086 the manor of Rodmell was held by William de Warenne, founder of Lewes Priory. His son granted the church to the monks there, and it seems probable that they would have been involved in building the church in the early years of the twelfth century. The church's external appearance remains largely unchanged from this time.

Surviving internal features are the nave, chancel and south chapel, originally the private chapel for the lord of the manor. To the left of the entrance is the baptistery, with a magnificent square twelfth century font and central supporting pillar made from Sussex marble. The four corner legs are later additions. The wooden cover dates from Tudor times. On the wall is part of the fifteenth century carved wooden screen, which would have been located between the chapel and the chancel. There is also the church's original weathervane, in the form of a large fish, removed from the steeple in 1930. A replica was made by the village blacksmith, Christopher Dean. Over sixty years later this vane was taken down and renovated by his son, Frank, also the blacksmith. At the age of eighty, using scaffolding erected for re-shingling the spire, Frank climbed to the top to restore it.

The church's early origins can also be seen in the narrow lancet windows, one on the north side of the chancel, two in the porch and, most unusually, one lancet and two roundel windows high above the chancel arch. Above the pulpit is a small quatrefoil window containing an enchanting fragment of medieval stained glass depicting Christ crucified. The square church tower was added in the late twelfth century. Also dating from this time are two robust central pillars between the south aisle and the nave, and the chancel. Both feature impressively decorated square capitals. The east window, in Perpendicular style, was added in the fifteenth century. The stained glass, depicting events in the life of St Peter, is Victorian.

Ships and Sealing Wax

By the nineteenth century the fabric of St Peter's was in urgent need of repair. For thirty-three years the Reverend Pierre du Putron, Rector until he died in 1891, oversaw extensive restoration. His achievements are recorded on a brass plaque beneath the Norman window in the chancel: "He was permitted to see in the restoration of this Church the fulfilment of his earnest desire". The chancel arch, pulpit and lectern date from this restoration. The arch replaces an earlier one with similar distinctive dog-tooth carved blocks. The chancel floor has several well preserved memorial tablets, complemented by colourful Victorian encaustic tiles.

Colour is also provided by the woven tapestry kneelers. Freddie Bleach, churchwarden, began work on these in 1975. His interest in spinning, weaving and dyeing had been aroused when serving in the Shetlands with the Royal Navy in World War I. A pen and ink illustration shows Freddie at work on his three-hundred-year-old spinning wheel. After he died, in 1977, the work was continued by nimble-fingered local ladies. More decorative work is on the panels at the front of the altar. These designs were painted by members of the Bloomsbury Group who lived at nearby Charleston Manor. Their numbers included Leonard and Virginia Woolf.

Of particular interest is a rare palimpsest, a brass memorial which has a different inscription on each side. Nearly six centuries old, this ancient brass is believed to have been removed from the church before being returned in 1859. One side, inscribed in Latin, reads "Near this, John Broke and Agatha, his wife, daughter of John de Radmeld and his wife, died April 1434 who gave many gifts to this church, and on whose soul may God have mercy". This refers to the ancient De Rodmell family who for centuries lived in the old manor house, Rodmell Place. The manor was later given by Henry VIII to Anne Boleyn. The inscription on the palimpsest's reverse side reads "Here lies the body of John de la Chambre who departed this life 4th December 1673". Using the same piece of brass, two hundred years after its first use, may have been a sign of difficult economic times!

In the churchyard is a beautiful sundial. The slate dial, mounted on a stone plinth detailing its installation in 1876, has been painstakingly restored following severe storm damage in 1987. Near the base of the dial is inscribed "50° 51' North", the exact location of St Peter's. Outside the central circle are the names of sixty-five cities and countries around the world, from Antwerp to Washington, each positioned on its longitude so the time there can also be calculated.

This historic timepiece and the view from the churchyard, across the Ouse valley to the South Downs, seems to symbolise the quintessential timelessness of the church and its surroundings.

Chapter 49

ROTHERFIELD CHURCH

Set high on a ridge above the Ashdown Forest, just a mile or so from the town of Crowborough and seven miles from Tunbridge Wells, is the village of Rotherfield. It is believed to be one of the oldest Saxon settlements in what was originally a vast area of oak forest. The parish church of St Denys, on raised ground flanking the main street, dominates the village.

A church on this site can be traced back over 1,200 years to when Duke Bertoald, the local Saxon lord whose estates included the village of Rotherfield and who after falling seriously ill was unable to find a cure at home, made a pilgrimage to the Benedictine Abbey of St Denys in France. Here were kept the holy relics of St Denys which were said to work miracles and the monks had become well known for their prayers for the sick. After several days of prayer, Bertoald recovered from his illness and returned to Rotherfield, where in AD 792 he built a church as a thank-offering. He also gave it the same name as that of the abbey where he had been healed. A translation of the Duke's will, threatening eternal punishment for anyone attempting to usurp his gift, hangs in the church.

Apart from the present site and dedication nothing now remains of Bertoald's original eighth century church. Almost certainly it would have been built of wood from the surrounding forest and may have been burned by the invading Danes before their eventual defeat by King Alfred. In the churchyard is a giant yew tree supported by posts and certified by the Conservation Foundation to be at least 1,500 years old. It is worth taking a moment to reflect that this tree, now practically hollow, would have been well established when the present sandstone church was built around 1060.

The church is impressively large for a village and externally somewhat austere, with a heavily buttressed and battlemented tower. But the immaculately maintained interior, comprising eleventh, twelfth and thirteenth century parts, with fifteenth century additions, has numerous interesting features. The oldest areas are the nave, chancel and Nevill Chapel on the north-east corner. Although this 900-year-old chapel has been much altered, there is evidence of Saxon stonework on the external walls and a Tudor fireplace was uncovered during alterations in 2001. The chapel, named after the Nevill branch of the Abergavenny family, local lords of the manor from 1450, may have been built on the site of the early wooden church. There are two imposing wooden beams across the roof, and the ceiling displays carved bosses including two "green men" and other grotesque heads.

The twelfth century nave was originally rectangular with a flat roof—the recesses for the beams are still visible above the magnificent chancel arch—but this was later extended upwards, and the arched rafters now provide a lasting tribute to the skill of medieval craftsmen. The north aisle, with circular pillars, dates from the thirteenth century, and the south aisle, with octagonal pillars, from the fourteenth.

One of the most remarkable features of St Denys is the wall paintings. All are over six hundred years old. For several centuries they were completely covered, but despite the ravages of time they provide a fascinating example of the early paintings which at one time would have decorated every available surface. First exposed in 1893, many have since faded, but the fifteenth century Doom painting above the chancel arch facing the nave, showing Christ seated on a rainbow with his feet on an orb and his forearms raised, can be clearly seen. Below Him are the heads of two monks, which are thought to refer to the church's early foundation. On the left of the arch is a winged St Michael, weighing on a balance the souls of the departed, a reminder to the congregation as they look upwards that everyone's life may, at the last, be found wanting.

Among several treasures is the exquisitely carved oak pulpit, with winged lions around the edge and a decorated canopy supported by two eagles. Originally in the Archbishop of York's palace at Bishopsthorpe, it was made four hundred years ago, in the days of Oliver Cromwell, by Francis Gunby of Leeds. Archbishop William Thomson's daughter married Canon Goodwyn, Rector of Rotherfield from 1889 to 1898, and the pulpit was installed in 1896 as a memorial to the archbishop.

The octagonal carved oak font cover, near the south door, was made in 1533 and includes the coat of arms of the Nevill family. This depicts the ship in which the ancestors of George Nevill, then Lord of the Manor of Rotherfield and a friend of

Roger Paine

Henry VIII, accompanied William the Conqueror to England. The original Norman stone font stands close by. It went missing for a number of years until found in a local field, being used as a cattle trough. How it came to be there has never been satisfactorily explained, although when discovered in 1816 a churchwarden, Samuel Wickens, was the tenant of the farm!

Beneath the engraved brass First World War memorial, listing the names of those Rotherfield men who were killed in action, is an unadorned wooden table. This was used by Archbishop Randall of Canterbury when he held a field service at Hesdin in Northern France on Sunday 21st May 1916. Some of the soldiers who received Holy Communion from the Head of the Anglican Church on that day were surely destined to die in the trenches. The Battle of the Somme, which started on 1st July 1916, resulted in the loss of 58,000 British lives.

A notable feature of St Denys is the stained glass, the earliest being fragments of fourteenth century glass at the top of the east window in the Nevill Chapel and believed to be some of the earliest in Sussex. The five-light Perpendicular east window of the chancel has stained glass made in 1878 by the eminent Victorian William Morris. This window, which depicts the *Te Deum*, was designed by the artist Sir Edward Burne-Jones. The delicately drawn figures and foliage springing from a single root, although partially obscured by the intricate alabaster reredos, form a unique and outstanding example of Pre-Raphaelite art.

The church's original timber-framed spire was destroyed in the hurricane of October 1987. On the east wall of the south aisle hangs a wooden cross, dedicated by the Bishop of Chichester on 15th October 1989 and made from one of the original beams supporting the spire. Nearby is all that remains of the original gilded cross from the top of the spire. The new spire, which rises to a height of 165 feet, was lowered into position in sections from a helicopter. It is now supported by steel beams and has chestnut shingles.

Rotherfield Church has been eulogized by a parishioner in a charming poem "My Village". The verse

> The church five centuries strong within the village,
> Its Norman font beneath the stair,
> It has withstood both fire and pillage,
> Its Eucharist bells still pierce the air"

seems to sum up, in a few simple words, the beautiful and historic church of St Denys.

Chapter 50

SALEHURST CHURCH

The church of St Mary The Virgin, Salehurst, also the parish church of Robertsbridge, is separated from Robertsbridge by the busy A21 bypass where the road crosses the River Rother. The two villages would, at one time, have seemed closer together, but dual carriageways and roundabouts have now forced them apart, and whilst there are a few farms, a dozen or so houses and The Salehurst Halt public house nearby, St Mary's, the largest parish church in East Sussex, can appear almost isolated in the countryside.

The reason this magnificent church is some distance from the local centre of population is that when it was built, some eight hundred years ago, the main road from London, now Beech House Lane, went through Salehurst, past the church, and across the river to Robertsbridge Abbey, founded as a Cistercian monastery in 1176. For centuries Salehurst held an important position in the Wealden iron industry and was the centre of the agricultural community on the Sussex/Kent border until, in the nineteenth century, the railway from London arrived in Robertsbridge.

Ships and Sealing Wax

In the Domesday Book the entry for Salhert (Salehurst) records "there is a church and sixteen acres of meadow". While no evidence of this Saxon church still exists, it is likely the present church occupies the same site. The church is built of Hastings sandstone and the masonry is mainly in irregular shaped blocks. The chancel, the nave and the lower stages of the tower were built between 1220 and 1250 AD. Much of the building's fabric owes its existence to the influence of Robertsbridge Abbey and it is probable the monks were involved in its construction. Between 1176 and 1538, when the Abbey was dissolved, it received several royal visitors, including King Henry III in 1225 and 1264, and his son, Edward I, in 1295.

After the first stage of building the church had been completed, in Early English style, the north and south aisles were added towards the end of the fourteenth century, together with the upper portion of the tower, in decorated style. The massive tower is one of the most remarkable features. Structurally it is built inside the church but has no solid support walls. The whole weight is carried by four huge pillars enclosing three lofty arches which extend up to the level of the floor of the ringing chamber. After seven centuries this remarkable feat of engineering shows no sign of settlement or stress. The walls of the battlemented tower are several feet thick, comprising varying sizes of sandstone blocks, and there is a peal of eight bells, mostly dating from the late eighteenth century. Although the bell ringers have reported that the tower sometimes "rocks" when they are ringing, the stonework appears as robust as ever.

Like the tower, the nave is an enormous structure. It is eighty-five feet long with strikingly imposing arcades separating it from the side aisles. For a parish church, serving two rural villages, it has almost cathedral-like proportions and the large clerestory windows provide much natural light. The chancel is at a slightly higher level than the nave, having been raised at some stage, which accounts for the low position of the piscina in the south wall. The stone which forms the pedestal of the altar is thought to be one of the altar stones of Robertsbridge Abbey, now in ruins, which was recovered from a nearby farm at the beginning of the last century.

One of the treasures of the church is the medieval stone font in the tower atrium. Known as the "salamander font" it depicts carved salamanders, creatures which mythology claims to be the symbol of the virtuous man who can pass through the fires of temptation. It was also the emblem adopted by the Crusaders, and legend relates the font was given by King Richard I, "Richard the Lionheart", in gratitude to Abbot William of Robertsbridge Abbey who led the expedition to rescue the ransomed king after he had been imprisoned in Bavaria when returning to England after the third Crusade. On the wall next to the font hang the words of a song written in 1193 by the king to his sister, Mary of Champagne, during his imprisonment.

At the east end of the south aisle is the Lady Chapel. Above the altar is a beautiful stained glass window made by the renowned Pre-Raphaelite designer Charles Kempe, whose work can be seen in several English cathedrals. It includes his signature motif, a golden wheat sheaf. On the north side is the Wigsell Chapel, built around 1350 by Sir John Culpeper, owner of the nearby Wigsell estate. On a corbel is an unusual carving of a cowled monk holding a hare or rabbit. The only grotesque in the church, it may have connections with the pagan fertility goddess Eostre. Her name provides the word for Easter and she was traditionally shown with a rabbit, the source of the "Easter bunny" so familiar today.

Four well-preserved funeral hatchments are sited on the west wall of the nave. These emblematic representations of the coats of arms of local landowners or nobility were displayed outside the deceased's house from the time of death until they accompanied the funeral cortege to the church. The Salehurst hatchments date from 1779 to 1824. The one for Jane Micklethwait of Iridge, who died in 1819, includes a skull, which indicates she died without issue.

Portions of exquisite smokey-green "Griselle" glass, depicting foliage and various birds, are in the upper lights in the north and south aisles, and date from the fourteenth century. There is a seventeenth century oak poor box with iron strapwork, and a parish chest dated 1678, with carved initials: "CW"(Churchwardens), "JC" (John Chambers) and "JS" (John Sivier), the names of the holders of the post at that time. Both the box and chest remain in use today. In the chancel is an oil painting, dated 1649, of the Reverend John Lord, Vicar of Salehurst from 1640 until his death in 1681. Lord was recognized as a Royalist sympathiser, which may account for his absence from the parish for three and a half years during the Civil War when the area was known to support Parliament.

On the wall of the south aisle is a memorial to Private Henry Osborne, aged 39, killed at the Battle of Loos in Flanders in 1915. The inscription reads "Erected as a mark of respect by the Directors & Staff of the Kent & Sussex Railway upon which undertaking he was employed in the Engineers Dept." At the time this railway ran from Robertsbridge past the church. Inside the west entrance, beneath the bell-ringing chamber, is a painted sign in the shape of a bell, recalling "On Tuesday October 29th 1919 in three hours and ten minutes A Peal of Grandsire Triples, 5040 changes, was rung on the Bells of this Church". The names of the eight local bell ringers who performed this feat are recorded for posterity.

Like many medieval parish churches, in the nineteenth century St Mary's underwent extensive restoration which transformed the interior. Completed in 1861, this included removal of the western gallery, repaving the floors with tiles, re-timbering the chancel roof and that of the nave with new rafters and iron ties, and replacing the old family pews in the nave and aisles to allow a large congregation to be seated at ground level. It is also likely that at this time the six iron tomb slabs dating from 1661 to 1714, commemorating members of the Peckham family, local ironmasters, were removed from their original positions and placed on the floor of the tower atrium. The extensive and rambling churchyard contains a variety of interesting headstones and table tombs, including several with fine Harmer terracotta decorations.

Of more recent vintage is the stained glass in two lights of a memorial window in the wall of the south aisle. Installed in 2001, it depicts in rainbow colours the Cross in Light and was inspired by the words shown at the foot of the windows: "Life Is Eternal and Love Is Immortal, Death Is But A Horizon and The Horizon Is But The Limit Of Our Sight." These words, attributed to Abraham Lincoln, are derived from a prayer by William Penn. Apart from this striking nod to modernity, and today's enthusiastic congregation, St Mary's medieval vastness remains a lasting testament to changed times.

Chapter 51

TICEHURST CHURCH

In the High Weald, close to Bewl Water in East Sussex, is the historic village of Ticehurst. Its early growth was due to the fourteenth century iron industry that flourished in the area. The imposing church of St Mary the Virgin dominates the village and is a lasting reminder of Ticehurst's original prosperity.

A wooden church is thought to have stood on the existing site, and the first mention of a priest in the parish, "Adam, Presbyter de Tychenherste", is contained in a deed relating to Combwell Priory dated 1180. Although no records of building the present church can be traced, it is believed that William de Echyngham, who completed rebuilding the church in nearby Etchingham in 1363, and whose family coat of arms appears in a stained glass window and in stonework on the ceiling of the porch, was also responsible for similar rebuilding work at St Mary's.

The size of the church is emphasized by the huge arch in the tower, which is mainly of thirteenth century origin. The tower also contains the vast west window, one of the church's most beautiful features; like the arch of the west door, it is in fourteenth century decorated style. Above the tower's ringing platform are six bells made by Thomas Jannaway of Chelsea in 1771. They are rung every Sunday. The tower is topped by a short shingled broach spire and has a battlemented turret at its north-east corner.

At the east end is another large window, in Perpendicular style, with stonework which was restored in 1856. Some of the original medieval glass was reused in the window in the north wall of the sanctuary, where there is a rare fourteenth century "Doom" or "Last Judgment" picture. This shows naked people, sinners, in a cart being pulled by devils and taken down to hell. One of them wears a crown, another a bishop's mitre, most likely to remind that in the eyes of God everyone is equal when penance is due.

Up a wooden staircase adjacent to the entrance door is the old "priest's room". It also served as a Sunday school and a prison. The inner door to the chamber is made from fourteenth century oak planking. High on the left chancel arch is an opening in the wall. This was the entrance to the "rood loft" from where the priest would read the gospel. The present rood screen and cross were carved locally in Frant and erected in 1916. The oak lectern and choir stalls were made in the early 1960s by the Yorkshire wood carver Robert Thompson. They bear his trademark signature, a mouse. This can be found carved into the base of the lectern and on the brackets under the choir seats. There is intricate oak carving dating from the sixteenth century on the cover and sides of the font.

On the south side of the chancel is the clergy vestry, formerly the Pashley Chapel. This contains a "squint" set into the wall dividing the sanctuary from the chapel so that worshippers there could see the altar. On the wall of the chapel is an iron tombstone, dating from the time when the local iron industry was at its peak. It has no writing but bears the arms of the May family who, from the sixteenth century, lived at nearby Pashley Manor.

To the north of the chancel is the Courthorpe Chapel. Many members of the Courthorpe family, who lived for over four hundred years at Whiligh, an estate near Wadhurst, are buried in a vault beneath the chapel. On the wall, in a glass case, is an example of a Sussex smock worn by farmworkers until the early twentieth century. There is also an original black-painted Victorian funeral bier with adjustable brass rails to ensure that coffins did not slide off when being taken to their final resting place.

On the north wall is a brass plaque and a window in memory of Reverend Arthur Eden, much loved Vicar of Ticehurst for fifty-seven years, 1851-1908. His achievements in rebuilding the church remain in evidence today. An image of his bearded face was used to replace that of the badly faded face of St Mark when the stained glass in the west window was repaired in 1985. His memory also lives on in the name "Eden Court", given to a new housing development built in the village in 2004.

In the entrance porch are Rolls of Honour with the names of all those from Ticehurst who served in the armed forces in two world wars. Inside, on the north and south pillars of the chancel, are memorials listing those who died in these conflicts. A project to re-cover the prayer kneelers in needlepoint, depicting a range of colourful scenes, was started in 1982 and completed when the fifty-second kneeler was finished in 2007. All were designed, stitched and fitted by people of the village.

Roger Paine

The churchyard, with its yew-canopied entrance path, probably dates back to before the Norman Conquest. But St Mary's is not solely about looking back. A new extension designed to match the existing church was officially opened by the Bishop of Chichester in 2010.

Reverend Francis Pott was appointed curate in 1861. A prolific hymn writer, he is best remembered for the beautiful "Angel Voices, Ever Singing..." written in the year he came to Ticehurst. This hymn's rousing words, "Can we know that Thou art near us, And will hear us? Yes, we can!" appear particularly apt for St Mary's in the twenty-first century.

Chapter 52

WADHURST CHURCH

Standing high on the East Sussex/Kent border, some seven miles south-east of Tunbridge Wells and over five hundred feet above sea level, is the town of Wadhurst. The name, of Saxon origin, means "Wada's settlement in the clearing in a wood".

The parish church, dedicated to St Peter and St Paul, has an elegant if slightly crooked broached spire which rises to 124 feet, making it a landmark that is easily recognizable from many parts of the surrounding countryside. It was added to the tower in the fourteenth century, and its great height has resulted in six lightning strikes over the centuries. The first was in 1575, the last in 1873. It survived the great storm of 1987 without major damage. The weathervane is dated 1699.

The first Vicar of Wadhurst is recorded as Walter de Otiugeton, who was the vicar from 1313-14, although it is believed that a church had existed on the present site for at least three hundred years prior to that. Apart from the tower, which dates from the twelfth century, little of the early church remains. It has been constantly added to and improved over succeeding centuries. The large and clear-glass windows give the church an immediate sense of light and space. The fifteenth century clerestory windows, high above the arches on the north and south sides, enhance this effect.

The immense oak beams supporting the roof of the nave are over five hundred years old and would almost certainly have come from the forests which at one time surrounded Wadhurst. The oak from this area was always regarded as being of the highest quality, and wood from the nearby estate of Whiligh has been used for decades for reconstruction and repairs to the magnificent roof of Westminster Hall in London. The spaciousness of the church is sustained by both the chancel and the nave being of almost the same width.

The church was enlarged eastwards from the tower in the thirteenth and fourteenth centuries when the side aisles and north transept were added. In the fifteenth century the vaulted entrance porch was built. In the centre of the ribbed ceiling is the inscription "IHS", the first three letters of the Greek word for Jesus. A narrow door inside the church gives access to a parvis, the upper room above the porch. Adjacent is the thirteenth century stone font which has been used for baptisms for nearly eight hundred years.

In the middle clerestory window on the north side is a single light of fine stained glass, given in 1903 in memory of a former curate and his wife. It depicts Pope Gregory I with his emblem, a dove, symbolizing the Holy Spirit. A small window on the north side of the tower dating from Norman times, only about a foot high and three inches wide, provides a few shafts of light to the belfry. In the west wall of the south aisle is an attractive stained glass window depicting Christ among the children. It was made, possibly by William Morris, from a design by the eminent Victorian and Pre-Raphaelite artist Sir Edward Burne-Jones. The east window of the chancel is a memorial to Reverend John Foley, Vicar of Wadhurst for over forty years, 1846-87. Other windows nearby commemorate the deaths of six of his children, all at a young age, in the mid-nineteenth century.

The fifteenth century window at the east end of the south aisle also contains impressive stained glass. This shows Christ in Glory and was installed in memory of the 114 men of the parish who died in the First World War. Their names are recorded on brass panels. Look carefully and it will soon be apparent that 9th May 1915 was an especially tragic day for the town. At the Battle of Aubers Ridge, twenty-five men from Wadhurst—all but one serving in the Royal Sussex Regiment, and including two sets of brothers—lost their lives, almost an entire generation of young men from one rural community killed in action on a single day. It was a day when British troops suffered 11,000 casualties taking part in an attack which was a complete failure and epitomized the carnage and futility of much of the fighting on the Western Front. Wadhurst is now twinned with the French village of Aubers in the Lille district of Northern France.

Given Wealden's pre-eminence in the early iron industry, which flourished in the sixteenth century and continued right up into the early years of the nineteenth, several churches in the area have iron memorial slabs set into the floor. But none has as many as the thirty to be found in Wadhurst, more than are found in any other location in England, for which the church is justly famous. Mainly dating from the seventeenth century, a period which saw a huge increase in the iron industry locally, all are in excellent condition. They were made by preparing a bed of sand and pressing into it a block of wood already carved with the names, dates, inscriptions or coats of arms. This was then lifted off and molten iron was poured over the sand, filling the indentations made by the carvings. When the iron had cooled and solidified it was turned over, any sand adhering was brushed off, and the slab was ready to be taken to the church and lowered into place. However, some cruder slabs were made by pressing individual letters into the sand mould back to front. Perhaps it should be no surprise that some words are misspelt or the letters are the wrong way round.

Every landowner whose estates lay near deposits of ore became an ironmaster, and rectors received their tithes from iron, as from corn. Small families grew to wealth and power on the iron beneath their fields. Eight of Wadhurst's memorial slabs commemorate the Barham family, considered pre-eminent among local ironmasters. One, in the chancel, commemorating William Barham who died aged 80 in 1701, includes his coat of arms showing three muzzled bears, a pun on the family's original name of Berham.

In the Norman tower are eight bells, all in regular use. Originally there was a ringing gallery, but the bells are now rung from the ground floor, and each has a bell rope of 75 feet. The oldest bell was cast by John Hodson in 1670 at the Whitechapel Foundry in London; his name is inscribed on the bell. The unique wrought-iron screen separating the nave from the tower was designed by Duncan Wilson and erected in 1957. The floral decoration includes lambs and hops, representing local farming activities, together with the county emblem, the Sussex martlet. On the front of the altar, dating from 1932, is a wooden screen featuring vine leaves, exquisitely hand carved by a local craftsman, Frank Rosier.

Ships and Sealing Wax

As you leave the church, pause for a moment to sit on one of the two wooden seats in the porch. Both are inscribed "In loving memory of Annora Violet Watson Smyth of this parish, born October 23 1901, died April 29 1912". Given by her mother, it adds, "These seats—her own wish". A carving of the ten-year-old's face adorns the ends of the seats. A nearby message from Wadhurst's vicar reads, "Whatever aspect of church life you would like to take part in, we can assure you of a very warm welcome", and has poignant echoes of a young girl's wish exactly one hundred years ago.

Chapter 53

WARBLETON CHURCH

The parish church of St Mary the Virgin, half a dozen cottages and a traditional country pub, The Black Duck, comprise the hamlet of Warbleton, some two and half miles southeast of Heathfield, deep in the unspoilt East Sussex countryside. For nearly two centuries, from 1540, it was at the heart of the Sussex iron industry. Narrow winding lanes, Hammer Lane and Furnace Lane, serve as a reminder of those times.

St Mary's Church is sited on raised ground, believed to be a Neolithic mound, with far-reaching views to the South Downs. Much larger than might be expected for a small rural community, the church's chancel and nave were built in the thirteenth century, with the porch and north aisle added a century later. All were built of local sandstone, which can be clearly seen in the east wall of the chancel behind the altar. The tall tower, built in Perpendicular style and added in the fifteenth century, has a large number of grotesque heads protruding from beneath the battlements. Entry is through the south door, which, unusually for a church, is made in two halves. Outside the church on the south wall of the chancel is an arched recess of the decorated period, which is probably a canopied tomb or an Easter sepulchre.

There is a four-bay arcade on the north side of the nave, which has octagonal pillars with square bases. On the south side of the chancel are two Early English lancet windows, one having been made later into a larger window. Behind the pulpit, south of the chancel arch, is the lower entrance to an early sixteenth century rood stairway. The most impressive feature of the interior is the massive oak manorial pew, built in 1722, which stands high on legs and is reached by a stairway, akin to climbing up the companionway of a ship onto the bridge. It dominates the interior and had a long association with the Roberts and Dunn families, local lords of the manor. It also provides a fascinating insight into the class structure of English country life in the eighteenth century, when the local squire and his family would be sitting higher than everyone else in the church, including the vicar. Although not unique, such pews rarely exist today, most having been removed from village churches during the nineteenth century. Fortunately, St Mary's is an exception.

The church has a number of interesting memorials, although two are not immediately visible. Firstly, beneath the carpet in the chancel there is a fine canopied brass effigy commemorating William Prestwyck, rector of the church from 1414 until his death in 1436. He was also Dean of the Collegiate Chapel, Hastings. Wearing vestments for administering mass, he lies under an ogee-headed canopy depicting a pelican, the bird representing Christian piety. An inscription in Medieval English forms the borders of the memorial, and a translation, or metrical interpretation, is shown nearby. This includes the poetical words, "When fourteen hundred years their course had gone about, And three times twelve, may Christ his every sin blot out".

Secondly, on the north wall of the north chapel, hidden by the pipe organ, is a magnificent marble monument with Corinthian columns, the work of renowned Flemish sculptor John Michael Rysbrack. It contains the bust of Sir John Lade, who lived at Cralle Place from 1718 to 1740. A native of the parish who became an MP and leased the manor of Warbleton in 1717, he is also believed to be responsible for installing the manorial pew. Inscribed on his monument, one of the finest examples of its kind, are Sir John's views on religious and political issues of the day.

At the bottom of the stairs to the manorial pew is an imposing studded iron-bound chest, probably made in one of the local forges, dating from the fourteenth century. Used for the storage of parochial and manorial records, money and other valuables, it had three different locks. One key was held by the vicar and one by each of the two churchwardens so it could only be opened when all three were present. Two wooden funeral hatchments high on the north wall of the chancel commemorate Henry Harcourt, a former rector, and his wife. They bear his coat of arms and a crest. At the west end of the south wall is a wooden reredos painted in 1890 in the then-fashionable early Italian Renaissance style. It depicts Christ in majesty with attendant saints and angels beneath on a gold background. It may once have hung on the chancel arch.

The impressive moulded stone font, adjacent to the south door, dates from the building of the church in the thirteenth century. Most of the stained glass is nineteenth century. The west window of the tower (1882), although partially obscured by the bell-ringing ropes, is the work of Charles

Ships and Sealing Wax

Kempe, the celebrated stained glass designer whose work can be found in many English cathedrals. There are several fragments of glass dating from earlier times including the heraldic shields of the Pelham and Lewknor families in the north chancel window.

The church has been long associated with Richard Woodman, burned alive for his Protestant faith, together with nine other martyrs, in Lewes on 22nd June 1557. A highly respected ironmaster and farmer, he was also a churchwarden of St Mary's and lived in a house close to the church. His alleged "crime" was his outspoken objection to the parish priest (named Fairbanke) "for turning head to tail" and preaching "clean contrary to that which he had before taught". This outspoken criticism of the Roman Catholic form of worship, imposed by Queen Mary throughout the country, led first to his arrest and appearance in court, and then imprisonment. Although initially released, after numerous cross-examinations during which he continued to robustly defend his beliefs, he was condemned by the Bishop of Winchester and executed. It is thought that at one time he may have been imprisoned in a cell in the church tower.

A memorial in the churchyard, adjacent to the south wall, records "Close by in the meadow behind stood the abode of Richard Woodman", and on the north wall of the nave there is a framed print captioned, "The burning of Richard Woodman and Nine Other Protestant Martyrs before the Star Inn, Lewes". This dramatic engraving captures the horror of the execution and the eagerness of the crowds who had gathered to watch. Nearby is a harrowing extract from the Book of Martyrs (1842 edition) in which Woodman vividly describes his capture. So I took down a lane that was

Roger Paine

full of sharp cinders and they came running after with a great cry, with their swords drawn, crying "Strike him, Strike him!" which words made me look back....I stepped into a great miry hole and fell down withal, and before I could arise and get away, he was come up to me. His name is Parker the Wild as his is counted in all Sussex".

Each year, on 5th November, the martyrdom of Richard Woodman and his fellow Protestants is commemorated with the slogan "No Popery" by members of Bonfire Societies. Parades take place in Lewes and in many other towns and villages throughout East Sussex.

Chapter 54

WARTLING CHURCH

Walk westwards through the gently sloping churchyard of St Mary Magdalene Church in Wartling, a village on the road between Pevensey and Windmill Hill in East Sussex, and the view towards the Downs and the Channel is one which has changed little in a thousand years. One exception is that the salt marshes, now the Pevensey levels, would once have been covered by the sea, with waves lapping the raised ground on which there was a small wooden chapel, known to have been in existence before the Domesday Book. This had been attached to the College of St Mary in Hastings Castle by Robert, the Count of Eu. Henry, Robert's grandson, reorganised the college, and the tenure of Wartling was granted to one of its senior officials, known as a prebend.

The earliest parts of today's church, believed to have been built on the site of the earlier structure, date from the thirteenth century. The first vicar is recorded as having been appointed in 1373. The church consists of a variety of different building materials, including medieval sandstone blocks, decorated Victorian brickwork and a shingled broach spire. There is a feeling of quiet, unadorned space, indicative, perhaps, of the timeless agricultural nature of the village and surrounding countryside. The walls of a timber-framed barn, belonging to neighbouring Court Lodge Farm, form part of the southern boundary of the churchyard.

On the north side of the church, the Victorian porch leads through a fifteenth century doorway into an area under the belfry. Originally this stood on oak posts which came down inside and rested on stone benches on each side of the font. One of these benches still exists on the north wall. The belfry is now supported by timber struts hidden in the arch, which is also wooden, although it gives the appearance of stone. The church once had four bells, but these were melted down and re-cast to make one bell, which is used today for summoning parishioners to worship.

At one time, too, there was a gallery above the rear pews, but all that remains are some filled holes indicating the position of the supporting posts. The church is one of very few which has a full set of box pews. The high, dark wood sides and well-fitting doors, to keep out draughts, enclose you as you step inside. With heating pipes running along the footings in the aisle, they may not be as comfortable as their modern counterparts but are warm and welcoming in winter.

High on the wall above the fourteenth century chancel arch is a square painted board with the date 1731 and the coat of arms of George II. Royal coats of arms had originally been ordered to be displayed in all parish churches by Henry VIII but most were removed or destroyed during Cromwell's constitutional reforms. It is likely that the existence of such overt loyalty to the King, as Head of the Established Church, is also an indication of support for the monarchy, which was traditionally strong in country communities. In the east window of the south aisle, now the vestry, a copperplate signature, "Georg Dawes, Glazier, Boreham Street", can be seen engraved on one of the diamond-shaped panes, recognizing the work of this local craftsman when the window was re-glazed in October 1786.

In the chancel are a number of elaborate memorials and wall tablets commemorating members of the Curteis family, local landowners in the late eighteenth and nineteenth centuries, who lived at Windmill Hill Place.

At the east end of the north aisle is an impressive oak war memorial, screening the vicar's vestry. The names of six men of the parish, all with well known Sussex family names—Dawes, Haffenden, Jarvis, Luck, Peerless, and Shelley—who gave their lives in World War I, are commemorated here. On the north wall is a plaque in recognition of the personnel who were stationed at RAF Wartling. This was one of two radar stations established during the Second World War on the levels below the church. The other was RAF Pevensey, well known for its towering radio masts. Both played a significant role in the wartime defence of Britain, and RAF Wartling remained operational during the Cold War until decommissioned in 1964. The plaque has a crest which depicts a wildcat, reminding one that the station was on constant alert, along with the Latin inscription "Detecta Destruantur", meaning "Let that which is found be destroyed".

On the outside of the buttressed south wall at the rear of the church are a small embossed Catherine wheel and a carved Pelham buckle, the badge of honour of the once powerful Pelham family. Sir John Pelham's daughter, Katherine, died in 1459 and it is believed that the south aisle,

Roger Paine

known as the Catherine chapel, may have been built in her memory,

An unusual feature of the church is the lectern. In many parish churches this is often in the form of an eagle, but here it is in the shape of a heron. With a five-foot wingspan and made of elm wood from the nearby Glynde estate, it was designed and carved by Martin Wynn Pierce in 1978. This unique work of art acknowledges that there have been heronries near the church in Wartling for over three hundred years.

The simple and unpretentious church of St Mary Magdalene, adjacent to a building which dates back to 1534, now the popular Lamb Inn, is not only a place of worship in this historic village but also serves as a timely reminder of the unchanging values and immutable heritage of rural England.

Chapter 55

WILLINGDON CHURCH

The village of Willingdon, nestling in the shelter of the Downs, now forms part of the town of Eastbourne. But as you walk down narrow Church Street from the parish church of St Mary the Virgin you will be following in the footsteps of Romans, Saxons and Normans who walked this way centuries earlier.

There has been a Christian presence in Willingdon since before the Norman Conquest and the manor of "Willendone" is referred to in the Domesday Book. The first Vicar of Willingdon is recorded as Godfrey the Priest in 1086. In the thirteenth century, Simon, Bishop of Chichester, granted lands at Willingdon to Robert, Abbot of the Benedictine monastery at Grestain in Normandy, and this French connection lasted until 1413 when the abbots were disenfranchised and Henry V returned the patronage to Chichester.

In the sixteenth and seventeenth centuries the patronage was leased to the Parker family of Ratton Manor, and in 1750 the Freeman-Thomas family became the lords of the manor.

Roger Paine

The influence of these ancient families remains an important feature of the church and the fourteenth century Ratton Chapel, a small, self-contained chapel still used regularly for worship, occupies the entire north-east corner.

The church has a shingled spire in "witch's-hat" style with five buttresses, and dates from the thirteenth century. This is all that remains of the original church, which must have stood where the north aisle is now, and means that the tower is offset, standing a little behind and separate from the present church. Before being enlarged in the fourteenth century to appear as it is today, the nave is believed to have originally been another type of building, possibly a priest's house. The entrance porch has a fine barrel-vaulted ceiling and is constructed, like the majority of the church, from grey sandstone blocks mixed with local flints.

The high ceiling of the chancel, added in the fifteenth century, is supported by a magnificent arrangement of wooden beams. These, and those in the nave and north aisle, are a particularly striking feature, and when looking upwards you could be forgiven for imagining they are the timber-framed ribs of a wooden ship under construction. Dominating the chancel is a rood of three carved and gilded figures portraying the Virgin Mary, Christ Crucified and the Apostle John. Designed by Sir Ninian Comper, it is a copy of the rood in Wakefield Cathedral.

In the Ratton Chapel there are many memorials to the Parker family in the form of wall plaques, alabaster tombs, floor brasses and heraldic shields. The first owner of Ratton Manor, John Parker, is depicted in a brass portrait on the sanctuary floor, which shows him as he was in 1558. A medieval coffin lid with a foliated cross is also embedded in the floor, possibly from a stone coffin of the kind which can be seen in the churchyard to the west of the porch. This very rare example of a complete medieval stone coffin had formerly been used as a cattle trough at the summit of the Downs.

On the Chapel's north wall is a recessed alabaster monument to Sir Nicholas Parker who died in 1619. In this coloured, life-size effigy the Elizabethan knight lies with his head on a cushion, his hands clasped in prayer. His three wives, dressed in farthingales and mantles, are depicted on the side of his tomb. The Freeman-Thomases, to whom the Ratton estate passed through marriage, are most notably represented by a framed banner with the coat of arms of Freeman Freeman-Thomas, 1st Marquess of Willingdon, former Governor General of Canada and Viceroy of India. His elder son, Lieutenant Gerard Freeman-Thomas, Coldstream Guards, was killed in action in 1914, and his name, together with all those from the parish who died in two world wars, is engraved on the chancel war memorial.

In 1944 the church was damaged by flying bombs. The vicar at the time, Reverend Harry Copsey, wrote, "The bombs started to fall on a Sunday morning.... Fortunately no one was hurt but we could not see the church for dust. Soldiers passing by came in and swept up the centre aisle, and we carried on with Matins with a congregation of about 100." The east window behind the altar and the windows in the south wall were blown out in the blast. All were replaced with new stained-glass designs. Particularly impressive is the war memorial window with four lights, one of which depicts a South Downs scene, with the figures of a soldier, a sailor and an airman looking on from the side.

At a service on 1st December 1946, following refurbishment works to the chancel and altar, the Bishop of

Roger Paine

Lewes formally adopted patronage of the church and decreed that in future it should be officially recognized as "St Mary the Virgin, Willingdon". Today, St Mary's is the parish church for almost 12,000 local residents, as the boundaries extend east across the main Eastbourne Road to include the large housing estate of Willingdon Trees. Although the church is justly proud of its many memorials and architectural features, history and the twenty-first century still manage to co-exist at St Mary's as seamlessly as they have for the best part of a thousand years.

Chapter 56

WILMINGTON CHURCH

On the northern slopes of Windover Hill, which rises six hundred feet above the sea just below the South Downs Way, a remarkable example of ancient craftsmanship looks down on the Church of Saint Mary and Saint Peter, Wilmington. This unusual figure, holding a staff longer than himself in each hand, is known as the Long Man of Wilmington.

Cut into the chalk, he stands two hundred and thirty feet high and is now made of hundreds of whitewashed stone blocks set into the grass. But his origins remain a mystery. Although many theories have been put forward, there seems little doubt he was here before Saxon times and may have been a pagan symbol of a god flinging open the gates of Dawn. It is significant that the location of the Long Man means the hillside is in shadow for five months each year and the giant only emerges into the sunlight with the coming of Spring. This unique figure undoubtedly pre-dates Wilmington church and adjacent Wilmington Priory, and probably the attractive village of Wilmington, too.

Roger Paine

It is believed the church was founded around AD 1000 to serve the Saxon settlement of Wineltone, the name by which Wilmington is recorded in the Domesday Book of 1086, although there is no specific reference to a church. It seems likely, however, that some form of wooden church existed on the current site, either at that time or beforehand. After the Norman Conquest, the Benedictine Abbey of Grestain in Normandy acquired property across South-east England, including Wilmington, and it was at the beginning of the twelfth century that Wilmington Priory was built, to accommodate the monks as the Abbey's representatives in England. But as it seemed unnecessary to construct a chapel solely for such a small community, a church that could be used by both monks and parishioners was built next to the priory. This is the Norman church of Saint Mary and Saint Peter which exists today. The chancel was used as the choir for the monks, and its nave as the parish church.

The priory, although ruined but partially restored and now occupied by the Landmark Trust, was originally connected to the church by a covered cloister walk, which is now the south aisle. In the west wall is a blocked-up arch, which may once have led down to a short tunnel to the priory crypt. This entrance to the church would have been well used by the monks in view of the number of services Benedictines were required to attend each day, several of which were in the early hours of the morning. A list of Vicars of Wilmington indicates the first as "Master Samson, Prior and Rector", in AD 1206, followed by Geoffrey de Caz in 1208. There was a prior in charge of the church for two hundred years until the priory ceased to be a religious establishment in 1413.

The church, like the priory, is built of flint, the stone most easily obtained locally. Only the arches and pillars are constructed of imported stone. The central pillar supporting the arches separating the nave from the south aisle is made of chalk, material rarely used in construction. During the fourteenth century the nave was rebuilt and remains unchanged to this day. The church has natural light—often lacking in medieval churches—provided by its magnificent high trussed rafter roof with tie-beams and king posts, four two-light Early English style windows, and the large east and west windows. The chancel is surprisingly long, and its huge sidewalls date from the time when the church was first built, as do the narrow round-headed windows of Caen limestone and the stone seats used by the monks, which now have the appearance of narrow ledges. On the floor, two large memorial tablets with elaborate family crests commemorate long-serving eighteenth century parish priests.

High on the north wall is a peculiar carved stone figure, removed in 1948 from a corresponding position on the exterior wall. Some believe this may have been a form of gargoyle; others suggest it could be a Norman representation of the Madonna. Another theory is that it might have been associated with pagan fertility rites. The shape and form is similar to that found in Romanseque churches in parts of Europe. It has attracted the sobriquet of "The Wilmington Madonna".

In the thirteenth century the north chapel was built onto the church. It is entered through an arch which leads from the nave into the north transept. In July 2002 a devastating fire, believed to be an act of arson, virtually destroyed the entire area then used as the vestry. This included the Bevington pipe organ, and the beautiful "Bee & Butterfly" stained-glass window. Smoke and water damage extended to the whole church and necessitated a daunting repair programme, including careful cleaning of all the surfaces. The ceiling between the rafters was replaced by traditional plasterwork, and within the north transept stonework was rebuilt and the burned timber ceiling was replaced in oak. A Bevington organ of similar vintage was tracked down, overhauled and sited at the west end of the church. This change of location for the organ is considered to have improved the proportions of the church.

In common with many other churches, Saint Mary and Saint Paul underwent extensive restoration during the Victorian era when the Lady Chapel at the east end of the south transept was consecrated, and the two windows in the south wall also date from this time. In 1883 the box pews in the nave were replaced by the existing pews, the western gallery was demolished, stalls were erected in the chancel to accommodate the choir, and the Gothic chancel arch was erected to replace the original, which had been destroyed some three hundred years earlier. Two fine stained glass windows in the Sanctuary, depicting Moses and Aaron, were installed around 1845.

The impressive carved oak pulpit with sounding board is Jacobean and was placed in the church in 1610. The stone font inside the north door dates from the fourteenth century and is large enough to allow baptism by total immersion. The porch was built in the fifteenth century and has been used for a variety of purposes, including the calling of marriage banns, holding coroner's courts and displaying public notices. The imposing oak door has given access to the church for over seven hundred years.

To commemorate the millennium in 2000, new stained glass for the west window beneath the tower was specially commissioned. Designed by Paul San Casciani, it was

Ships and Sealing Wax

inspired by the centuries-old yew tree in the churchyard, and is symbolic of the tree of life and a reminder that Christ died on a cross made of wood. A description of the design—based on the rings seen in the transverse section of the trunk—and of the techniques employed, has been placed nearby.

The same artist was responsible for the new "Bee & Butterfly" stained glass window installed in the north transept following the destructive fire. This outstanding replacement window depicts a phoenix, symbolic of the church rising again from the ashes, and like the original window includes a centre panel with Saint Peter surrounded by beautiful butterflies, moths and a bee. Salvaged pieces of the old stained glass are set at the bottom below the rising phoenix. In recognition of the restoration work carried out in the church following the fire, on the north wall of the nave there is a stone carving in the shape of a heraldic shield, the work of Geoffrey Aldred of Lewes, inscribed "In Gratitude to Almighty God for the restoration of this church AD 2004".

The extensive churchyard has been in continual use since Norman—and probably since Saxon—times. The most enduring feature is the ancient yew tree, with a girth in excess of twenty-three feet, which almost overshadows the church. It has been authenticated as being over 1,600 years old. Although now supported by props and chains, it continues to produce new growth every year. It is not difficult to imagine that this same yew, whose life has spread across the millennia, could have been seen by those, whoever they were, who first carved the mysterious Long Man into the chalk of the South Downs. This carefully maintained and active church surely reflects the words, attributed to Christ and quoted in the millennium window, "Raise the Stone and thou shalt find Me, Cleave the Wood and I am there.".

Chapter 57

WITHYHAM CHURCH

The parish church of St Michael and All Angels in the village of Withyham in East Sussex, between Groombridge and Hartfield north of Crowborough, is on top of a small hill overlooking a lake and the rolling pastures of Buckhurst Park.

Withyham was placed under the patronage of St Michael shortly after the Norman Conquest, although the first recorded mention of a church was not until in 1291 when Edward I required monies to be paid to the Pope to help fund a crusade. Withyham's contribution was valued at 45 marks, about £30. At the outbreak of war with France in 1324, Edward II sequestered all property belonging to foreign religious orders. This included Withyham, which was then attached to a Benedictine Priory at Morteyn in France. A list of rectors and patrons of St Michael's stretching back to 1328 is displayed in the church.

During rebuilding of the church in the fourteenth century, the Sackville Chapel at the east end of the north aisle was added. The connection with the Sackville family goes back over 800 years. Jordan, grandson of Herbrand de Sauqueville, who took his name from the village of Sauqueville near Dieppe, married an heiress, Ela Dene, whose land in Sussex included the manor of Buckhurst in Withyham. Centuries later Lady Elizabeth Sackville, daughter of the 3rd Duke of Dorset, married George West, 5th Earl De La Warr, another Sussex family of great antiquity and prestige. Today, William, 11th Earl De La Warr, is Patron of St Michael's. He and his wife Anne, Countess De La Warr, live in nearby Buckhurst House and regularly worship in the church.

In 1663 a thunderbolt struck the church spire, melting the bells in the belfry and almost destroying the entire building by fire. The only parts of the original church remaining are the north wall, south chancel wall, and the lower part of the tower. Rebuilding work was not completed for almost ten years. A sundial above the porch of the south door with the initials "IB", Isaac Burgess, rector at the time, with the date 1672, commemorates the reopening of the church. The opportunity was also taken to enlarge the Sackville Chapel which fills the north-east corner of the church. The chapel is still privately owned by the Sackville family and does not come under the jurisdiction of the bishop. The bells were also recast, and again in 1908 when a further two were added. These provide today's magnificent eight-bell peal.

Amongst many fine stained-glass windows are several in mosaic pattern made from fragments of medieval glass which survived the fire. The impressive east window above the altar was put in during the early nineteenth century and consists of ten panels which relate the story of the New Testament. Four paintings depicting the Passion of Christ,

Roger Paine

understood to be by Niccolo Di Pietro Gerini, the Florentine painter, were donated to the church in 1849. Now, because of their value, only facsimiles are displayed. The originals can be seen at Leeds Castle in Kent. The arch over the nave is dominated by a mural of The Last Judgement painted by Reverend The Hon Reginald Sackville-West, later to become 7th Earl De La Warr, when he was rector from 1841 to 1865.

The Sackville Chapel, with a vault beneath and enclosed by seventeenth century iron railings, contains many memorials to the Sackville and De La Warr families. An armorial stained-glass window illuminates the east wall. With funeral hatchments and ancient banners, the chapel could be the setting for one of Shakespeare's great English-monarch plays. The altar tomb, the work of Danish sculptor Caius Cibber, is that of young Thomas Sackville. At the side kneel marble life-size figures of his grief-stricken parents, the 5th Earl and Countess of Dorset. The poignant inscription includes, "Here Lyes The Thirteeneth Child And Seventh Son, Who Died In His Thirteenth Yeare His Race Had Run". Other memorials record that Gilbert, 8th Earl De La Warr, was killed in action in World War I, and Flying Officer Thomas Henry Jordan Sackville, second son of the 9th Earl De La Warr, died in air operations during World War II, six months before his 21st birthday.

Today, the Rector of St Michael's oversees a vibrant church community in Withyham and the surrounding area. In the churchyard, outside the south entrance, is a rosemary bush. Rosemary, the traditional symbol of remembrance, reaffirms that it is better to embrace the future rather than the past. Pluck a sprig as you enter the church for a wedding or a funeral. The weight of history is inescapable at St

Ships and Sealing Wax

Michael and All Angels but this timelessness also generates a feeling of enlightenment.

Chapter 58

SPRINGTIME WITH ROBERT BROWNING

Oh, to be in England
Now that April 's there,
And whoever wakes in England
Sees, some morning, unaware,
That the lowest boughs and the brushwood sheaf
Round the elm-tree bole are in tiny leaf,
While the chaffinch sings on the orchard bough
In England—now!

And after April, when May follows,
And the whitethroat builds, and all the swallows!
Hark, where my blossom'd pear-tree in the hedge
Leans to the field and scatters on the clover
Blossoms and dewdrops—at the bent spray's edge
—
That 's the wise thrush; he sings each song twice
over,
Lest you should think he never could recapture
The first fine careless rapture!

Ships and Sealing Wax

And though the fields look rough with hoary dew,
All will be gay when noontide wakes anew
The buttercups, the little children's dower
—Far brighter than this gaudy melon-flower!

This enchanting poem, entitled "Home-thoughts, from Abroad", the classic description of Springtime in England, was written by Robert Browning, the prolific Victorian poet more usually associated with lengthy philosophical and narrative works. It was written in Italy where Browning lived with his wife, Elizabeth Barrett Browning, in the mid-nineteenth century. The fifteen years they spent there, first in Pisa, then at Casa Guidi in Florence, were probably the happiest of their lives. Their son, Robert "Pen" Browning, was born in Florence in 1849.

It might seem odd, therefore, to find the poet casting himself in the role of a homesick traveller recalling the songs of native English birds, "the chaffinch sings on the orchard bough" and "the wise thrush, he sings each song twice over", or comparing indigenous flowers, "The buttercups, the little children's dower" with the colourful Mediterranean "gaudy melon-flower". Yet by using a few simple but well chosen images and rhymes the poet manages to exquisitely encapsulate, if not an expression of desire to return to the land of his birth, then those "home thoughts" which all of us have, at one time or another, when we are abroad. In this case, Browning sublimely evokes the unequalled freshness of an English spring morning.

Robert Browning was born in Camberwell, south-east London, on 7th May 1812, becoming proficient at reading and writing at the age of five and going on to learn Latin, Greek,

Roger Paine

French and Italian by the time he was 14. He attended the newly established London University when he was 16 but left after one year, anxious to pursue further learning at his own pace. By the time he was 20 he was convinced he would become a great poet, although his early published works achieved little success and he was fortunate that his family had sufficient money to support his literary endeavours. He also tried his hand at writing verse drama for the stage, but these plays are now all but forgotten.

In 1845, Robert arranged to meet the poet Elizabeth Barrett, who had mentioned his work in one of her poems, and, expressing immediate and undying love, they married in secret a year later. He was 34, she was 40. Elizabeth was one of the "Barretts of Wimpole Street" and her domineering father had convinced his daughter that due to her constant ill health she should be treated as an invalid. But, undeterred, and against her father's wishes, the couple eloped to Italy, accompanied by Elizabeth's much-cherished spaniel, Flush, whom she immortalized in her poem "To Flush—My Dog". Happy years of writing poetry followed, including many love poems, with both Robert and Elizabeth achieving success through their published works. When she died, in 1861, a grief-stricken Robert returned with their son to England.

The next twenty-seven years of Browning's life were spent writing and establishing himself as one of the great British poets, which he had always yearned to be. Although never a "vox pop" poet like Tennyson, his admired contemporary, Browning became a cult figure in his own lifetime. The two poets are buried in Poet's Corner in Westminster Abbey, where Browning was given a grandiose funeral on 12th December 1889.

Chapter 59

"TRANSITION" WITH ERNEST DOWSON

A little while to walk with thee, dear child;
To lean on thee my weak and weary head;
Then evening comes: the winter sky is wild,
The leafless trees are black, the leaves long dead.

A little while to hold thee and to stand,
By harvest-fields of bending golden corn;
Then the predestined silence, and thine hand,
Lost in the night, long and weary and forlorn.

A little while to love thee, scarcely time
To love thee well enough; then time to part,
To fare through wintry fields alone and climb
The frozen hills, not knowing where thou art.

Short summer-time and then, my heart's desire,
The winter and the darkness: one by one
The roses fall, the pale roses expire
Beneath the slow decadence of the sun.

Roger Paine

As soon as the Christmas decorations have been put away for another year, and festive indulgences subjected to a regime of New Year resolutions, you know that the gloom-laden days of January have arrived. These dog days at the beginning of each year have, over the centuries, inspired poets to express wistfulness for happier times.

Ernest Dowson, a contemporary of Oscar Wilde, W B Yeats and Aubrey Beardsley, was no exception. Yet this little known—and even less understood—poet was a major figure in the romantic late Victorian literary world. Writer of many poems, novels and short stories, he can also be credited with introducing into the English language such well known expressions as "gone with the wind" and "days of wine and roses".

Ernest Christopher Dowson was born into a comfortably well off, middle-class family in Lee, south-east London, on 2nd August 1867. Alfred, his father, had inherited the family dry-dock and ship repair business known as Dowson's, or Bridge, Dock on the River Thames. His mother, Annie Swan, described as a hauntingly lovely, fragile woman, gave birth to Ernest when she was 18 years old. Within a few years, however, Alfred had developed the first signs of consumption, or tuberculosis, as it is more commonly known today. For the sake of his health, the family moved to the warmer climate of the south of France.

It was here, and in Italy, that young Ernest received his education from a variety of tutors. Although woefully ignorant of subjects such as geography and mathematics, he became highly proficient in languages, especially French and Latin, and developed a deep love of literature. He entered Queen's College, Oxford, in 1886 but left after two years

Ships and Sealing Wax

without obtaining his degree. Many friendships he made there were to last throughout his life.

On leaving university, he joined his father in the dry dock business. But the new shipyards in the north of England were beginning to take over from the Thames, and smaller docks, like Dowson's, were finding it increasingly difficult to compete. As Alfred's health deteriorated, money dwindled and the business was eventually declared bankrupt.

Ernest had begun to successfully write poetry whilst at Oxford, but rather than spending time in the squalid surroundings of Bridge Dock, Limehouse, he preferred frequenting the theatres and bright lights of the West End with his friends. It was at this time that Dowson met Adelaide, the eleven-year-old daughter of a Polish tailor and his wife, who ran a small restaurant in Soho. His all-consuming passion for this young girl, who epitomized purity and beauty, was to remain the love of his life.

There has never been any suggestion of a relationship between the pair. She later married a tailor and lived above the restaurant, but Ernest's total infatuation never waned and surfaced in probably his best known poem, "Cynara", in which the last line of each of the four stanzas is "I have been faithful to thee, Cynara! in my fashion". These words became the inspiration for Cole Porter when writing "I'm always true to you, darlin', in my fashion" in the musical *Kiss Me Kate*.

By 1890, Dowson was one of a small group of poets and writers who had formed the Rhymers' Club. They met every month in the Cheshire Cheese, a long-established inn in Fleet Street. These bohemian characters, Oscar Wilde amongst them, gave rise to a movement known as "The Decadents", whose hedonistic lifestyle at the end of the nineteenth century was eventually to be shattered forever by

Roger Paine

the carnage of the First World War. Ernest, now living a life of late nights, heavy drinking and sexual excesses in the company of various women, also suffered his first attack of tuberculosis. In 1894 his father, by now in an advanced stage of the disease, died of an overdose of chloral hydrate, prescribed to cure insomnia.

Six months later, severely depressed by her husband's death and, probably, Ernest's dissolute lifestyle, his mother was found hanged in the bedroom of her home. The coroner's verdict was "suicide whilst temporarily insane".

Dowson's life began to go rapidly downhill. Although he continued to write, and spent two years traveling in France, his tuberculosis, exacerbated by alcoholism and depression, became steadily worse. Returning to London, almost penniless and living as a vagrant, carrying nothing more than his tattered book of verse, he finally found shelter with friends, Robert Sherard and his wife, who took him into their home. He spent the last six weeks of his life there before he died, aged 32, on 23rd February 1900. Ernest Dowson is buried in the Catholic section of Ladywell cemetery—he had converted to the religion ten years earlier—less than two miles from where he was born.

In spite of his tragic life, Dowson was a brilliant craftsman of English verse who left behind an inimitable legacy of enchanting words and phrases. Published posthumously in *Decorations* in 1900, his evocative poem "Transition", with its wintry starkness, sense of longing and images of a countryside changing inexorably with the seasons, shows that for all his personal torment and unrequited love he was always conscious of beauty. Not simply in his surroundings, but also in human nature.

Chapter 60

SPRINGTIME WITH ROBERT HERRICK

First, April, she with mellow showers
Opens the way for early flowers;
Then after her comes smiling May,
In a more rich and sweet array;

Next enters June, and brings us more
Gems than those two, that went before;
Then, lastly, July comes, and she
More wealth brings in, than all those three.

This charming poem, "The Succession of Foure Sweet Months", by clergyman and poet Robert Herrick, was first published in 1648. Yet Herrick was largely unknown in the seventeenth century and forgotten in the eighteenth—and it was not until the nineteenth and twentieth centuries that his name became more widely recognised. The simple lyricism of his poems led to him becoming one of the most accomplished non-dramatic poets of his age, one whom the Victorian poet, Charles Swinburne, described as "the greatest

Roger Paine

songwriter...ever born of the English race". His poems are easier for modern readers to understand than many of those of his contemporaries.

Robert Herrick was baptised on 24th August 1591 in Cheapside, London, the seventh child and fourth son of Nicholas and Julia Herrick. He was only just over a year old when his father, a prosperous goldsmith, died falling from the window of the fourth floor of their house. Whether this was suicide remains unknown, but the Queen's Almoner did not, as was usually the case for suicides in those days, confiscate Herrick's estate for the crown.

His mother never remarried and Robert, educated at the Merchant Taylors School, left at the age of sixteen to become apprenticed to his uncle, Sir Willam Herrick, also a goldsmith, and jeweller to the king. After six years of the goldsmith's trade, he terminated his apprenticeship and at the comparatively advanced age of twenty-two entered St John's College, Cambridge. He subsequently transferred to a less expensive college, Trinity Hall, from where he graduated in 1617.

Little is known of his activities after leaving Cambridge except that in 1623 he took holy orders, although he was not assigned to a parish. During this period in London he continued with writing poetry, which he had started at university. He also became acquainted with Ben Jonson, the eminent dramatist, poet, actor and man of letters, then doyen of London's cultural scene. In the absence of a father, Robert had at last found someone who could live up to his expectations, and he became a member of the "Sons of Ben", a group centred on admiration for Jonson's works. Herrick dedicated at least five of his poems to Jonson.

Ships and Sealing Wax

In 1627, Herrick became a chaplain to George Villiers, the first Duke of Buckingham, when he led an expedition to liberate French Protestants besieged in Saint-Martin-de-Ré. But due to a combination of illness amongst the troops, effective action by the French and a fierce storm at sea when Buckingham's ships were returning to England, two-thirds of the force perished. It is was no surprise that in 1629, at the age of thirty-eight, Herrick should exchange a life of danger and uncertainty for one of comfort and routine by taking up the appointment as Vicar of St George the Martyr, the parish church of Dean Prior, near Buckfastleigh in Devon. The church still exists today. In the seventeenth century it would have been a five-day journey from London. Here, on the edge of Dartmoor, living the secluded life of a country parson, Herrick wrote some of his most memorable poems.

Although his stipend was small, he took his duties seriously and local people described him as "much beloved by the gentry in those parts for his florid and witty discourse". His poems often describe this idyllic and placid life, surrounded by the ever-changing pastoral scene. Cared for by his devoted maid, Prudence Baldwin, Herrick never married, and none of his poems refer directly to loving one woman, although some of his early works make references to the female body and lovemaking. Many of the women he names in his poems are thought to be fictional. It was the richness of sensuality and the variety of life that he loved most and this is repeatedly apparent in his work.

In 1647, in the wake of the Civil War, Herrick, a devoted Royalist, refused to make pledge to the Solemn League and Covenant, and his position as vicar was revoked. He returned to London where, dependant on the charity of friends and family, he prepared his poems for publication. There were

Roger Paine

1,402 of them, including "The Succession of Foure Sweet Months", which were published under the title *Hesperides; or the Works both Human and Divine of Robert Herrick.* Although he wrote over 2,500 poems, including such engaging monometers as "Thus I/ Pass By/ And Die/ As One/ Unknown/ And Gone", *Hesperides* remains his greatest work.

When King Charles II was restored to the throne in 1660, Herrick petitioned to be restored to his living. Perhaps the monarch felt well disposed to him on account of his verses celebrating the births of both King Charles and his brother James before the Civil War, and in the summer of 1662 Herrick once again became the Vicar of Dean Prior. He lived there until his death in October 1674 at the age of 83. He and his maid lie in unmarked graves in the churchyard.

The overriding message of Herrick's work is that life is short, the world is beautiful, love is splendid, and in the short time we have we must make the most of it. The poem on the passing of the months is one of this *carpe diem* genre. In another poem he included the well-known words "gather ye rosebuds while ye may". Both are examples of "seize the day" and in today's uncertain world seem as poignantly relevant as when Herrick wrote them nearly 400 years ago.

Chapter 61

SPRINGTIME WITH WILLIAM WORDSWORTH

I wandered lonely as a cloud
That floats on high o'er vales and hills,
When all at once I saw a crowd,
A host, of golden daffodils;
Beside the lake, beneath the trees,
Fluttering and dancing in the breeze.

Continuous as the stars that shine
And twinkle on the Milky Way,
They stretched in never-ending line
Along the margin of the bay:
Ten thousand saw I at a glance,
Tossing their heads in sprightly dance.

The waves beside them danced, but they
Out-did the sparkling waves in glee:
A poet could not but be gay,
In such a jocund company:
I gazed—and gazed—but little thought

Roger Paine

What wealth the show to me had brought.

For oft, when on my couch I lie
In vacant or in pensive mood,
They flash upon that inward eye
Which is the bliss of solitude;
And then my heart with pleasure fills,
And dances with the daffodils.

This much-loved poem, "I Wandered Lonely as a Cloud", also called "Daffodils", by William Wordsworth, has achieved lasting fame throughout the English-speaking world. Since the mid-sixteenth century these bright yellow flowers have been recognized as the first true indicator of the arrival of spring. Shakespeare writes in *The Winter's Tale*, "When daffodils begin to peer... Why, then comes in the sweet o' the year."

This simple poem, one of the loveliest of all Wordsworth's works—although describing a familiar subject from nature, and despite the sometimes hackneyed opening lines—has lost none of its freshness since it was written over two hundred years ago. The musical eloquence of the words instils the reader with the feelings the poet himself is experiencing.

William Wordsworth was born on 7th April 1770 in Cockermouth in Cumbria, in the heart of the Lake District, the second of the five children of John and Ann Wordsworth. His sister, Dorothy, was born the following year; they were baptised together and were inseparable companions throughout their lives. His father was a legal representative of the Earl of Lonsdale, which allowed the Wordsworths to live in a fine Georgian mansion in the town. His mother died

289

Ships and Sealing Wax

when he was eight years old. Young William went to the local Hawkshead Grammar School, and Dorothy was sent to live with relations in Yorkshire. He later attended school in Penrith, where he was to meet his future wife, Mary Hutchinson.

At the age of eighteen William went to St John's College, Cambridge, returning to the Lake District in the holidays, where he began walking in the fells and absorbing the unique beauty of the local landscape. Whilst visiting France in 1791 he fell in love with a Frenchwoman, Annette Vallon, by whom he had a daughter, Caroline. Although the revolutionary years were to keep them apart, he managed occasional visits, usually with his sister, and provided them with financial support. In 1793 his first published work, *Descriptive Sketches*, achieved some success, and in 1795, having inherited a substantial legacy, he was able to pursue a career writing poetry. In 1802 he married his childhood sweetheart, Mary. William and Dorothy lived at Dove Cottage in Grasmere, where Mary also moved after the marriage. Mary and William had five children, three of whom pre-deceased their parents. The couple later moved to Rydal Mount, Ambleside, where, in 1829, Dorothy suffered a severe illness, which rendered her an invalid for the rest of her life.

The poem "I Wandered Lonely as a Cloud" is believed to have been inspired after William and Dorothy had been walking together near Glendale not far from where they lived. Composed by Wordsworth in 1804, his sister wrote later, in reference to their walk: When we were in the woods beyond Gowbarrow Park, we saw a few daffodils close to the waterside. But as we went along there were more and more and at last under the boughs of the trees, we saw that there

Roger Paine

was a long belt of them along the shore. I never saw daffodils so beautiful they grew among the mossy stones, some rested their heads upon these stones as on a pillow for weariness and the rest tossed and reeled and danced and seemed as if they verily laughed with the wind that blew upon them over the lake.

In 1795, Wordsworth had become close friends with the poet Samuel Taylor Coleridge, later famous for writing *The Rime of the Ancient Mariner* which was published in *Lyrical Ballads* with another of Wordworth's well-known poems, "Tintern Abbey". This enhanced Wordsworth's reputation as a major poet and, with Coleridge's work, helped to launch the Romantic Age in English Literature. With fellow poet, Richard Southey, who also lived in the Lake District, the three men became known as the Lake Poets.

With Southey's death in 1843, Wordworth became Poet Laureate, which he remained until he died on 23rd April 1850. He is buried in St Oswald's church in Grasmere. His wife, three of his children, and his sister are also buried there. There is a monument to Wordsworth in Poet's Corner in Westminster Abbey. Although "Daffodils" is not regarded as Wordworth's masterpiece—this accolade is reserved for "The Prelude"—the wistful thoughts of the author, so imaginatively expressed, will forever encapsulate the joy experienced every year at the coming of spring.

Chapter 62

SUMMER WITH WILLIAM MORRIS

Now came fulfillment of the year's desire,
The tall wheat, coloured by the August fire
Grew heavy-headed, dreading its decay,
And blacker grew the elm-trees day by day.
About the edges of the yellow corn,
And o'er the gardens grown somewhat outworn
The bees went hurrying to fill up their store;
The apple-boughs bent over more and more;
With peach and apricot the garden wall,
Was odorous, and the pears began to fall
From off the high tree with each freshening breeze.

This poem is an extract from *August*, part of William Morris's monumental epic *The Earthly Paradise*, published in four parts between 1868 and 1870. The work is a sequence of episodes, two per month, each with its own story. Writing in colloquial English, Morris imbues his poem with a mystical quality, not simply describing the changes taking place in the countryside in August but also reminding of the coming of autumn.

Today, William Morris's poetry is little known, and he is probably most famous for his interior designs, especially textiles and wallpaper which, at the beginning of the twenty-first century, have become synonymous with his name and the Arts & Crafts revival. However, this multi-talented Victorian was a man of many parts: artist, novelist, poet, designer, translator, champion of free speech and a campaigning Socialist. Aptly summed up by a biographer, "The fame of Morris during his lifetime was probably somewhat obscured by the variety of his accomplishments."

Born on 24th March 1834, in Walthamstow, East London, he was the eldest son of nine children of William and Emma Morris. The family was comfortably well-off, and young William had a happy childhood, culminating in receiving a substantial legacy which provided him with an annual income when he reached the age of twenty-one. Educated at home, and at Marlborough College after his father died, he went to Exeter College, Oxford, in 1853, intent on becoming a clergyman.

There he met Edward Burne-Jones, who had similar intentions. They became life-long friends. At Oxford Morris became a member of an undergraduate aesthetic circle which idealized medieval art and chivalry. He also began writing poetry which was heavily indebted to the works of Keats, Browning and, most of all, Chaucer.

In 1855, Morris and Burne-Jones went on a walking tour of the great Gothic cathedrals of Northern France and were so overcome by the grandeur that they decided to abandon their clerical studies and become artists. Morris left Oxford without graduating and soon afterwards, much to his

Ships and Sealing Wax

parent's dismay, began working in an architect's office in London. There he met Philip Webb, who became another close friend and associate and later designed many landmark buildings, including Standen House in West Sussex, now owned by the National Trust and decorated with Morris ceramics, carpets and fabrics.

But architecture failed to sustain Morris's interest and he turned to art. Through Burne-Jones, now well established as a successful painter, he met Dante Gabriel Rossetti, already leader of the fledgling Pre-Raphaelite Movement. In 1857 the three men painted the frescoes in the Oxford Union. It was at this time that they met Jane Burden and Elizabeth Siddal, both from working-class backgrounds, who were acting as models for Rossetti. Each epitomised the Pre-Raphaelite ideal of beauty. Morris married Jane in 1859 and they had two daughters. Two years after marrying Rossetti, Elizabeth committed suicide. Jane, frequently ill and moody, within a few years embarked on a lifelong love affair with Rossetti, one of her husband's closest friends.

This put a great strain on Morris, but he never sought a divorce, immersing himself instead in the design partnership he founded in 1861, and, in an emotional sense, withdrawing into his poetry. In the extract from "August" there is a real sense of sadness for what once was, but is now no more. In 1892, after the death of Tennyson, Morris was offered, but declined, the highest honour that can be bestowed upon a poet, that of Poet Laureate.

William Morris died aged sixty-two, on 3rd October 1896 at his home, Kelmscott Manor, Hammersmith, West London.

Chapter 63

"IN FLANDERS FIELDS" WITH JOHN McCRAE

In Flanders fields the poppies blow
Between the crosses, row on row,
That mark our place; and in the sky
The larks, still bravely singing, fly
Scarce heard amid the guns below.

We are the Dead. Short days ago
We lived, felt dawn, saw sunset glow,
Loved and were loved, and now we lie
In Flanders fields.

Take up our quarrel with the foe:
To you from failing hands we throw
The torch; be yours to hold it high,
If ye break faith with us who die

We shall not sleep, though poppies grow
In Flanders fields.

Ships and Sealing Wax

This short poem by John McCrae, written during World War I and epitomising the poignancy of sudden death in battle, also established the poppy as being forever associated with Armistice Day, the eleventh day of the eleventh month of every year. The flower is now recognised as an international symbol of pride and respect.

McCrae, a major and a military doctor, wrote the poem on 3rd May 1915 during the second week of the Second Battle of Ypres, when he was second in command of the 1st Brigade Canadian Field Artillery. The field guns of his brigade's batteries were in position on the west bank of the Ypres-Yser canal, having arrived there on 23rd April. It is believed that the death of a good friend, a former student of McCrae's, Lieutenant Alexis Helmer, was the inspiration for "In Flanders Fields".

On the morning of 2nd May, Helmer had left his dugout and was killed instantly by a direct hit from a German shell. Body parts that could be found were later gathered into sandbags and laid in an army blanket for burial that evening. Alexis was twenty-two years old and a popular young officer. In the absence of a chaplain, Major McCrae conducted a simple service at the graveside, reciting from memory passages from the Church of England's Burial Service. A wooden cross marked the burial place. Lieutenant Helmer is now commemorated on the Menin Gate Memorial in Ypres.

Although the precise details of when McCrae first drafted the poem may never be known, he was seen writing a poem the day after Helmer's death, using the pages of his despatch book, sitting on the rear step of a field ambulance while looking at his comrade's grave and the vivid red poppies that were springing up in a small burial ground established during the First Battle of Ypres the previous year. Poppy

296

seeds are known to lie in the ground for many years, and only when the ground is churned up do they sprout and flower. There was an abundance of churned-up soil on the battlefields of the Western Front. When McCrae wrote his poem, poppies had blossomed around him in a manner never previously seen.

Lieutenant Colonel Morrison, McCrae's commanding officer, later wrote: The rows of crosses increased day after day, until in no time at all it had become quite a sizeable cemetery. Just as John described it, it was not uncommon early in the morning to hear the larks singing in the brief silences between the bursts of the shells and the returning salvos of our own nearby guns. Some time later that year, McCrae sent "In Flanders Fields" to *Punch* magazine, where it was published, anonymously, on 8th December 1915. The identity of the author, however, soon became well known and the verses were one of the most popular poems of the war, used in countless fund-raising campaigns and frequently translated. According to his biographer, McCrae, although astonished by his sudden fame, "was satisfied if the poem enabled men to see where their duty lay". The phrase, "To you from failing hands, we throw the torch", has since been used in countless exhortations to greater endeavour in many different contexts.

John McCrae, grandson of Scottish immigrants, was born on 30th November 1872 to David and Janet McCrae in Guelph, Ontario, Canada. Although from a military family, he studied medicine at the University of Toronto, and it was there he published his first poem. In 1902, having qualified as a doctor, he was appointed resident pathologist at Montreal General Hospital. Two years later he went to England, where he became a member of the Royal College of

Ships and Sealing Wax

Physicians. He served in the Canadian Artillery in South Africa in the Second Boer War and on return was appointed Professor of Pathology at the University of Vermont. He also taught at McGill University in Montreal.

When Great Britain declared war on Germany in 1914 McCrae became a field surgeon in the Canadian Army. Much to his intense disappointment, as he wanted to remain in the front line, shortly after writing his poem in 1915 McCrae was ordered to set up No 3 Canadian General Hospital at Boulougne-sur-Mer in Northern France. Promoted to Lieutenant Colonel and Commandant of the Hospital, he contracted meningitis and died of pneumonia there on 28th January 1918. The following day he was buried, with full military honours, in the Commonwealth War Graves Commission section of nearby Wimereux Cemetery.

His name is commemorated in many public institutions throughout Canada. In addition, there is the In Flanders Fields Museum in the town of "Ieper" (Ypres) in Belgium. The impressive Roll of Honour of Clan McCrae's dead of World War I, in the grounds of picturesque Eilean Donan Castle in the Western Highlands of Scotland, prominently features John McCrae's haunting poem.

Chapter 64

SUMMER WITH STEPHEN SPENDER

The Chalk Blue (clinging to
A harebell stem, its loop,
From which there hangs the flower
Shaken by the wind that shakes
The butterfly also)—
Opens now, now shuts, its wings,
Opening, closing, like a hinge,
Sprung at touch of sun or shadow.
Open, the wings mirror
All the cloudless sky.
Shut, the milky underwing
Cloud-mirroring, is bordered by
Orange spots nailed there
By a pigmy hammering.

Stephen Spender, the author of this poem, "Chalk Blue", is remembered by many as belonging to the generation that, disillusioned by the horrors of World War I, went up to Oxford and Cambridge in the late 1920s to indulge in a

Ships and Sealing Wax

hedonistic lifestyle while embracing hopes of a better world by joining the Communist Party. It was the era of successful poets and writers such as W H Auden, Christopher Isherwood, Cecil Day Lewis and Louis MacNiece, all friends of Spender, as well as the infamous Russian agents, Guy Burgess and Donald Maclean.

Much of Spender's best poetry was written during this time. It also saw him begin work on his novel *The Temple*, which was not published until nearly sixty years later, in 1988. It tells the story of a young man who travels to Germany and finds a culture more open than in England, particularly about relationships between men, despite the frightening anticipation of Nazism. In the introduction he writes: In the late twenties young English writers were more concerned with censorship than with politics. 1929 was the last year of that strange Indian Summer—the Weimar republic. For many of my friends and for myself, Germany seemed a paradise where there was no censorship and young Germans experienced extraordinary freedom in their lives."

His autobiography, *World Within World* contains portraits of Virginia Woolf, W B Yeats, and T. S. Eliot in addition to those of Spender's Oxford contemporaries. First published in 1951, it vividly describes the political and social atmosphere in the decades before the Second World War and is recognized as one of the great illuminating literary biographies,

Stephen Harold Spender was born in Kensington, London, on 28th February 1909. His father, Edward, was a journalist, and his mother, Violet Schuster, a poet and painter. He was educated at Gresham's School, Holt in Norfolk and, after the death of his mother, at University College School, Hampstead. Subsequently he went to

Roger Paine

University College, Oxford, although he left without finishing his degree. It was from there that Spender first visited Germany. Relishing the cultural and personal freedom he experienced, he began an affair with Tony Hyndman with whom he lived for two years.

At the end of this relationship, in 1936, he met and married Inez Pearn. Their marriage, however, lasted only three years, ending when she left him to marry another poet, Charles Madge. During the Spanish Civil War, Spender went to Spain and joined the International Brigade fighting Franco's fascists. He was told by the head of the Communist Party in Great Britain "go and get yourself killed. We need a Byron in the movement." But like many left-wing idealists at the time, he became disillusioned and when the pact between Germany and Russia was signed he felt his beliefs had been betrayed.

Declared unfit for military service in the Second World War, due to poor eyesight and the effects of a childhood illness, he joined the London Auxiliary Fire Service. For two years, from 1939, he edited the magazine *Horizon* which he had co-founded with another poet and author, Cyril Connolly. In 1941 he married again. This time his wife was the beautiful concert pianist Natasha Litvin, ten years his junior. Although his ex-boyfriend Hyndman was a witness at their wedding, it was an extremely happy marriage, which lasted the rest of his life and produced a son and a daughter. His daughter, Lizzie, married the Australian comedian Barry Humphries. Although marriage ostensibly marked the end of his romantic associations with men, his sexuality remained a topic of debate.

His post-war work took him again to Germany, where he was a member of the Allied Control Commission tasked with restoring civil authority. He then carved out a career as an international man of letters. He attended intellectual conferences to discuss issues such as free speech, became a counsellor to UNESCO, and taught English at many institutions in the USA, where in 1965 he was appointed the seventeenth Poet Laureate Consultant in Poetry to the United States Library of Congress. He eventually became Professor of English at University College, London, from 1971-1977. His achievements were officially recognised when he was made CBE in 1962, and knighted in 1983.

Although Spender said of himself that he lacked "the stillness of attention necessary for creative work", he continued to write extensively whilst maintaining his globetrotting lifestyle. His last book of poems, *Dolphins*, was published the year before he died of a heart attack, aged eighty-six, on 16th July 1995. The Stephen Spender Memorial Trust was founded in 1997 to commemorate Spender's life and works and to encourage some of his principal interests: poetry, poetic translation, and freedom of creative expression. He once remarked, "Great poety is always written by somebody straining to go beyond what he can do."

His poem "Chalk Blue" is not simply a charming description of the tiny Chalk Hill Blue butterfly, at one time as common as the summer sun on the South Downs and as symbolic as the white cliffs of Sussex and Kent, but also a wistful evocation of the much changed English countryside. The butterfly is now a protected species and Spender, for all his recognition of technological changes in the future, described in his much quoted 1930s poem "The Pylons", would just as surely have mourned the lost rural innocence his poem "Chalk Blue" epitomizes.

Chapter 65

AUTUMN WITH JOHN KEATS

Season of mists and mellow fruitfulness,
Close bosom-friend of the maturing sun;
Conspiring with him how to load and bless
With fruit the vines that round the thatch-eves run;
To bend with apples the moss'd cottage-trees,
And fill all fruit with ripeness to the core;
To swell the gourd, and plump the hazel shells
With a sweet kernel; to set budding more,
And still more, later flowers for the bees,
Until they think warm days will never cease,
For Summer has o'er-brimm'd their clammy cells.

Who hath not seen thee oft amid thy store?
Sometimes whoever seeks abroad may find
Thee sitting careless on a granary floor,
Thy hair soft-lifted by the winnowing wind;
Or on a half-reap'd furrow sound asleep,
Drows'd with the fume of poppies, while thy hook
Spares the next swath and all its twined flowers:

Ships and Sealing Wax

And sometimes like a gleaner thou dost keep
Steady thy laden head across a brook;
Or by a cyder-press, with patient look,
Thou watchest the last oozings hours by hours.

Where are the songs of Spring? Ay, where are they?
Think not of them, thou hast thy music too,--
While barred clouds bloom the soft-dying day,
And touch the stubble-plains with rosy hue;
Then in a wailful choir the small gnats mourn
Among the river sallows, borne aloft
Or sinking as the light wind lives or dies;
And full-grown lambs loud bleat from hilly bourn;
Hedge-crickets sing; and now with treble soft
The red-breast whistles from a garden-croft;
And gathering swallows twitter in the skies.

Each year, as the leaves on trees begin to change colour, the days begin to shorten, or on noticing a chill in the air, many will find themselves murmuring, "Season of mists and mellow fruitfulness", the opening line of this immortal poem, "Ode to Autumn", by John Keats. The timeless description of autumn, irredeemably embedded in collective hearts and minds, was written by a youthful Englishman after a Sunday afternoon stroll nearly two hundred years ago.

Keats's literary career amounted to just three and a half years. During this brief time he wrote one hundred and fifty poems, but those on which his reputation rests are the odes and sonnets written in a span of nine months in 1819. This intense flowering of talent remains unparalleled in literary history. Although his work often received critical attacks at the time, Keats's influence on generations of poets since has been immense.

In a letter to a friend on 21 September 1819, following a walk along the River Itchen at Winchester, Keats described the impression the scene had made upon him: How beautiful the season is now, how fine the air. A temperate sharpness about it. Really, without joking, chaste weather. I never lik'd stubble-fields so much as now. Aye, better than the chilly green of the spring. Somehow a stubble-field looks warm in the same way that some pictures look warm. This struck me so much in my Sunday's walk that I composed upon it. What he composed was "Ode to Autumn".

Keats was born on 31 October 1795 to a middle-class family at 85 Moorgate in the City of London, in a tavern where his father was an ostler; he later fell from a horse and died from a fractured skull. Keats had a disrupted childhood, as his mother died from tuberculosis in 1810, leaving him and his siblings in the care of his grandmother. It was then that he attended the school which first instilled in him a love of literature. On leaving school he was apprenticed to an apothecary before moving, in 1815, to become a medical student at Guy's Hospital. During this time he devoted more and more time to studying literature.

Following his grandmother's death, and being forced to care for his younger brother, Tom, who also succumbed to tuberculosis in 1818, he went to live at Wentworth House in Hampstead, the home of his close friend, Charles Armitage Brown. It was there that he fell in love with the girl next door, Fanny Brawne. This short-lived romance was sadly to be cut short when Keats was diagnosed with tuberculosis, the disease which had plagued his family, and in 1820 he went, for the sake of his health, to live in Rome, in a house on the

Ships and Sealing Wax

Spanish Steps. Despite attentive care from friends, he died on 23 February 1821, aged twenty-five. The doomed love of Keats and Brawne, later to be scandalized in Victorian society after the publication of their correspondence, was made into a critically acclaimed film "Bright Star", directed by Jane Campion, in 2009.

Scholarly praise has been unanimous in declaring "To Autumn" one of the most perfect poems in the English language. Of many memorable images created are how autumn has its own sounds: "in a wailful choir the small gnats mourn", "full-grown lambs loud bleat", "hedge-crickets sing", "with treble soft the red-breast whistles", "gathering swallows twitter". As well as describing so evocatively the many characteristics of the season, a deeper reading could suggest the poet is talking about the process of life, autumn symbolizing maturity in human and animal lives. The next season is winter, but Keats relishes the present, hoping "warm days will never cease". His peerless words paint as vivid a picture as any artist with a brush on canvas. No autumn is complete without his poem.

Chapter 66

CHRISTMAS WITH JOHN BETJEMAN

The bells of waiting Advent ring,
The Tortoise stove is lit again
And lamp-oil light across the night
Has caught the streaks of winter rain
In many a stained-glass window sheen
From Crimson Lake to Hooker's Green.
The holly in the windy hedge
And round the Manor House the yew
Will soon be stripped to deck the ledge,
The altar, font and arch and pew,
So that the villagers can say
'The church looks nice' on Christmas Day.

Provincial public houses blaze,
And Corporation tramcars clang,
On lighted tenements I gaze
Where paper decorations hang,
And bunting in the red Town Hall
Says 'Merry Christmas to you all'.

Ships and Sealing Wax

And London shops on Christmas Eve
Are strung with silver bells and flowers
As hurrying clerks the City leave
To pigeon-haunted classic towers,
And marbled clouds go scudding by
The many-steepled London sky.
And girls in slacks remember Dad,
And oafish louts remember Mum,
And sleepless children's hearts are glad,
And Christmas-morning bells say 'Come!'
Even to shining ones who dwell
Safe in the Dorchester Hotel.

And is it true? And is it true,
This most tremendous tale of all,
Seen in a stained-glass window's hue,
A Baby in an ox's stall?
The Maker of the stars and sea
Become a Child on earth for me?
And is it true? For if it is,
No loving fingers tying strings
Around those tissued fripperies,
The sweet and silly Christmas things,
Bath salts and inexpensive scent
And hideous tie so kindly meant,
No love that in a family dwells,
No carolling in frosty air,
Nor all the steeple-shaking bells
Can with this single Truth compare--
That God was Man in Palestine
And lives today in Bread and Wine

Roger Paine

John Betjeman was one of the best known poets, writers and broadcasters of the twentieth century. Born to a middle class family in Hampstead, North London, in 1906, he was knighted in 1969 and held the post of Poet Laureate from 1972 until his death at Trebetherick, Cornwall in 1984.

After school at Marlborough he went to Magdalen College, Oxford, where, despite having immersed himself in books and writing from an early age, he was considered a failure and left without a degree. This rankled with him for the rest of his life, although he retained an enduring love of Oxford and received an honorary doctorate of letters from the university in 1974. His school and college days are movingly recorded in his blank verse autobiography *Summoned by Bells*, published in 1960, and made into a television film in 1976. The book remains a bestseller, thanks to the easy-to-read style and candid observations.

The same might be said about his poetry, much of which is immediately recognizable by its wry humour and quintessential Englishness. Because of its unpretentious rhythms, metres and rhymes (although not as simple as they sometimes appear), Betjeman's work has always captured the imagination of millions of people from all walks of life, many of whom would not normally consider reading a poem.

Betjeman was also a prolific writer on architecture, with a fondness for Victorian buildings, especially churches and railway stations. Active in campaigning to save historic buildings from the bulldozers, he was instrumental in saving St Pancras railway station in London. When plans to demolish the building were announced he is said to have called the intention a "criminal folly". A statue of him, at platform level, commemorating the part he played in successfully ensuring this magnificent building still exists in

Ships and Sealing Wax

its original form, was unveiled when the station reopened as the terminus for Eurostar in November 2007.

During the 1960s and 70s Betjeman made many television appearances, often reading his own work. In his corduroy suit, badly knotted tie, crumpled collar and battered trilby, he portrayed a bumbling and avuncular image. He appeared to be someone who never took himself too seriously, the epitome of the English virtue of understatement. This endeared him to many sections of the public, although his critics alleged he was often out of touch, wallowed in nostalgia and did not want to face up to the realities of modern life. Elements of this are probably true, but he was always respected for being a deeply religious man, a practising Christian and dedicated to the Anglican Church.

In the above poem "Christmas", published in a collection entitled *A Few Late Chrysanthemums* in 1954, John Betjeman openly celebrates the religious as well as the secular significance of the birth of Christ. Using the colours found in an artist's palette to describe a church's stained glass window, and mentioning "inexpensive scent", "bath salts" and "hideous tie" to convey the austerity of Christmas in post-war Britain, he paints a lasting and memorable word picture. Whilst the last three verses proclaim Christ's birth, they do so in the form of a question, "And is it true?" This has sometimes been regarded as Betjeman questioning his own faith, but in view of the poem's final line is more likely to be an affirmation of his piety.

It is worth recalling John Betjeman's own words about poetry: "Too many people in the modern world view poetry as a luxury, not a necessity like petrol. But to me it's the oil of life." This poem surely deserves to be read aloud at Christmas.

Chapter 67

CHRISTMAS with KENNETH GRAHAME

"What's up?" inquired the Rat. "I think it must be the field-mice," replied the Mole, with a touch of pride in his manner. "They go round carol-singing regularly at this time of year. They're quite an institution in these parts." "Let's have a look at them!" cried the Rat, jumping up and running to the door. It was a pretty sight, and a seasonal one, that met their eyes when they flung the door open. Some eight or ten little field mice stood in a semi circle, red worsted comforters round their throats, their fore-paws thrust deep into their pockets, their feet jigging for warmth. One of the elder ones was just saying, "Now then, one two, three!" and forthwith their shrill little voices uprose on the air, singing one of the old-time carols that their forefathers composed in fields that were fallow and held by frost, or when snow-bound in chimney corners, and handed down to be sung in the miry street to lamp-lit windows at Yuletime.

Villagers all, this frosty tide,
Let your doors swing open wide,

Ships and Sealing Wax

Though wind may follow, and snow beside,
Yet draw us in by your fire to bide;
Joy shall be yours in the morning!

Here we stand in the cold and the sleet,
Blowing fingers and stamping feet,
Come from far away you to greet—
You by the fire and we in the street—
Bidding you joy in the morning!

For ere one half of the night was gone,
Sudden a star has led us on,
Raining bliss and benison—
Bliss to-morrow and more anon,
Joy for every morning!

Goodman Joseph toiled through the snow—
Saw the star o'er a stable low;
Mary she might not further go—
Welcome thatch, and litter below!
Joy was hers in the morning!

And then they heard the angels tell
'Who were the first to cry Nowell?
Animals all, as it befell,
In the stable where they did dwell!
Joy shall be theirs in the morning!'

This poem, "Carol", from *Wind in the Willows* by
Kenneth Grahame, one of the most beloved works of
children's literature ever written, is included in the
enchanting episode just before Christmas when Ratty has

Roger Paine

gone to have supper with Mole. Grahame's prose, which introduces the carol sung by the field mice, is as evocative as any in the book. Although the participants are all animals, the dazzlingly well chosen and crafted words of the poem, which has also been set to music, conjure up everyone's Christmas idyll, secular and religious. The gentle sensitivity of Mole, the manic worldliness of Toad, and the bustling domesticity of Rat, has permeated the imaginative lives of generations of children as well as adults.

Kenneth Grahame was born in Edinburgh on 8th March 1859, one of four children. His mother died of scarlet fever when he was five and his lawyer father, no longer able to cope with the growing family, took to drinking heavily, and the children were sent to live with their maternal grandmother in Cookham Dean on the edge of the Berkshire downs. The years Grahame spent there, including boating on the River Thames and jaunts into the surrounding fields and woods with a favourite uncle—who was the curate at nearby Cranbourne church—left a permanent impact, and were to be a major influence on the creativity of his future writing. Grahame became head boy at St Edward's School, Oxford, and, although shy and sensitive, he excelled both academically and at sport. He hoped to go to Oxford University but, due to the financial constraints of his relatives, a position as a gentleman-clerk was found for him at the Bank of England in London.

Finding the routines monotonous, he started to write stories and articles for magazines, publishing several books in the 1890s and becoming a respected member of London's literary scene. In 1899, at the age of forty, he married Elspeth Thomson in Fowey, Cornwall, and less than a year later their son, Alastair, was born. Blind in one eye and with a

Ships and Sealing Wax

pronounced squint in the other, he was nicknamed "Mouse" by his doting parents and heavily indulged throughout childhood.

After twenty years in the City, Grahame was appointed Secretary of the Bank of England, but in 1907, following health problems and a bizarre incident in which he was shot at by a lunatic visitor, he retired and moved with his family back to the countryside in Berkshire. "Mouse" was now about the same age as Grahame had been when he had first moved there, and it was as bedtime stories for his son that *Wind in the Willows* had its beginnings. The book was published in 1908.

Initially it received adverse reviews, and it was not until Grahame sent it to the then President of the United States, Theodore Roosevelt, who had expressed admiration for his earlier books, that sales took off. It has remained a bestseller ever since. Parts of the book were dramatized by A. A. Milne as *Toad of Toad Hall*, and illustrated by Ernest Shepard of *Winnie the Pooh* fame. "Mouse", after disrupted schooling, went to Oxford University, but was found dead on a railway track five days before his twentieth birthday. It is believed he committed suicide, although out of respect for his father it was recorded as an accidental death.

The author died at his home, Church Cottage in Pangbourne, at the age of seventy-three. On his headstone, in the cemetery of St Cross Church, Holywell, Oxford, where he is buried with his wife and son, are the words: "To the beautiful memory of Kenneth Grahame, who passed the River on 6 July 1932, leaving childhood and literature through him more blest for all time".

Chapter 68

THOMAS PAINE

On 8th June 1809, in a small house on Grove Street, Greenwich Village, New York City, Thomas Paine died peacefully in his sleep. In Great Britain many may wonder not only who Thomas Paine was but also question what relevance there can be in recalling his death over two hundred years later.

In spite of Tom Paine being revered in the United States of America, his authorship of the hugely influential pamphlet *Common Sense*, published in Philadelphia in 1776, in which he openly called upon the American colonists to throw off their allegiance to Great Britain, and was considered by George Washington to be the primary force in securing American independence from oppression, it should not be wholly surprising that he remains comparatively unknown in the country of his birth.

Tom Paine was born in Thetford, Norfolk, on 29th January 1737. A statue of him in frock coat, clutching a large book and quill pen, stands in the town centre. The only son of a staymaker, a maker of whalebone or steel stays for

Ships and Sealing Wax

women's corsets, he grew up in modest surroundings and left the local grammar school at the age of twelve to learn the trade of staymaking from his father. However, being disenchanted, he ran away to sea before completing his apprenticeship to serve on board a privateer, to all intents a pirate ship licensed by the government to capture ships belonging to France, with which the country was at war.

At the age of twenty, after two years at sea, Paine came ashore and went back to his old trade of staymaking, this time in London. But finding life in the capital too expensive, he moved, in 1758, to Dover in Kent, where he obtained temporary employment with a staymaker named Benjamin Grace. In the following year, after a loan from Grace, he set up a small staymaking business in the town of Sandwich. A plaque on the seventeenth century cottage at 20 New Street records his residence there.

Through his business dealings with a prominent local draper, Richard Solly, Tom met Mary Lambert, who was employed as a maid in the Solly household. After a brief courtship, the couple married in St Peter's Church, Sandwich, on 27th September 1759. A few months later Paine's staymaking business faltered, and, with Mary pregnant, the newlyweds moved to nearby Margate. For poor, working-class women at that time childbirth was always dangerous, and less than a year after they were married Mary and her baby died during delivery. At the age of twenty-three Paine suddenly found himself alone, a widower in a strange town with no secure means of employment. Although he always kept the tragic details of his loss strictly private, like so much of his personal life, he was to later observe, "There is neither manhood nor policy in grief."

Roger Paine

As Mary's father had been employed as an exciseman in nearby Sittingbourne, it seems likely that her recollections, in conversation with her husband, prompted Paine to consider a new career. In 1761 he returned to his parents' house in Thetford, and began studying for the examination to become an Excise officer.

His first appointment was collecting revenues in the small market town of Alford in Lincolnshire. But after nearly three years he was forced to leave the service under a cloud, having been accused by his senior officer of "stamping", or failing to properly examine goods being produced, imported or exported. Despite this charge, which he always denied, Tom decided to eat humble pie and wrote to the Excise Board in 1766 to seek reinstatement: "I will endeavour that my future conduct shall as much engage your honours' approbation as my former has merited your displeasure."

Whilst awaiting their decision, he went again to live in London, and it was there that he first met Benjamin Franklin, then the agent for the American colony of Pennsylvania. Reinstated to the Excise on 19th February 1768, Tom's first posting, at an annual salary of £50, was to Lewes in Sussex. He was one of six Riding Officers—as excisemen were known—who had responsibility for collecting excise duties from an area, or "ride", which extended south to the coast and west as far as Brighton.

Paine soon found his feet in Lewes. Through well-established connections with the Methodist church—his father was a Quaker—he rented a room from Samuel and Esther Ollive, who lived above the snuff and tobacco shop they owned in Bull House at the upper end of the town. This fifteenth century timbered house, known as "the house with a monkey on it", due to its carved gargoyle, has changed little

Ships and Sealing Wax

since that time. Lewes had a strong Nonconformist population and Samuel Ollive's father had been the minister of the adjoining Westgate Chapel from 1711 to 1740. The tradition of "No Popery" lives on with the historic Bonfire Societies and the procession through the town on 5th November each year.

After Samuel Ollive died, Tom was invited to help run the business, and as Elizabeth, the Ollive's twenty-year-old daughter appeared to get along well with their lodger, Mrs Ollive announced that the couple would marry. They made their vows in Westgate Chapel and were formally married at St Michael's Church, opposite Bull House, on 26th March 1771.

During this period Paine became involved in local activities, foremost of which was his membership in the Headstrong Club. This was an association of public-spirited citizens who met once a week in the White Hart Hotel to debate pressing local, national and international matters. The club continues to thrive, and there seems little doubt that Paine was an active participant and author of several tracts and articles. It seems likely, too, that he first articulated his radicalism here, earning the reputation of being the most "obstinate haranguer". He was also an enthusiastic member of the Lewes Bowling Green Society, where on a sloping green bordered by limes under the shadow of Lewes castle, unchanged to this day, Tom and other Headstrong members would play bowls and socialize long into the summer evenings.

Paine was also responsible for writing a petition, "The Case of the Officers of Excise", seeking to improve the pay and conditions of his fellow excisemen. This was supported by virtually all three thousand excise officers throughout the country. His efforts, however, went unrewarded and the submission fell on deaf ears as parliament refused to acknowledge the claim. It also led to the Board of Excise deciding that because of the time he had taken in writing the pamphlet, and lobbying MPs in London, he was guilty of absence without leave from his duties in Lewes and should be sacked.

Again unemployed, and with his recent marriage having fallen apart, although the reasons for this have never been satisfactorily explained, and with the Ollive's tobacco business in ruins, Paine declared himself bankrupt. The furniture, contents and stock of Bull House were auctioned, and, as eighteenth century custom demanded of a separated woman, Elizabeth was forced to leave Lewes, never to return. Carrying a few personal belongings, she went to live with her brother in Cranbrook, Kent, and for the remainder of her life eked out a living as a dressmaker, before dying thirty-four years later, one year before her estranged husband.

Now age thirty-seven, Paine returned to London, where he renewed acquaintance with Benjamin Franklin, who later became one of the Founding Fathers of the United States of America. Armed with a letter of introduction from Franklin, Tom boarded a ship for Philadelphia. Whatever hopes and aspirations he might have had when he walked up the gangway of the *London Packet*, these were soon dispelled when, like most of the passengers, he was struck down with "ship fever", attributed to the impurity of the air between decks. So seriously was he affected that he was carried ashore on a stretcher when the ship docked in Philadelphia on 30th November 1774.

After six weeks, thanks to the attention of Benjamin Franklin's physician, he made a full recovery. Just as importantly, the letter of introduction from Franklin, in which he wrote, "The bearer, Mr Thomas Paine, is very well recommended to me as an ingenious, worthy young man..." enabled Paine to more easily establish himself in an unfamiliar country than many other immigrants arriving from England at that time.

In January 1775, whilst Paine was browsing in a Philadelphia bookshop, he struck up a conversation with the owner, Robert Aitken, a printer from Aberdeen who had arrived a few years earlier. Aitken was in the process of publishing a new journal on the premises, to be known as *The Pennsylvania Magazine*. Having established a rapport with Paine, and having been shown some of the unpublished manuscripts and pamphlets Tom had brought with him from Lewes, Aitken offered him the post of editor of the new magazine.

This gave Paine the opportunity of serving his literary and political apprenticeship, not least by writing about the growing controversy between the American colonies and the British Empire, which had been gathering pace since the colonists had demonstrated their anger at customs duty imposed on tea at the infamous "Boston Tea Party" twelve months earlier. Although Paine was later to recall "I viewed the dispute as a kind of lawsuit. I had no thoughts of independence or of arms. The world could not then have persuaded me that I should be either a soldier or an author." However, events outside his control were to take a hand not only in shaping his own future but also in changing the world forever.

On April 19th 1775 British troops opened fire without warning on a group of American militiamen in Lexington, Massachusetts. Eight were killed and ten wounded. Although

Roger Paine

the circumstances were different, it is not difficult to detect similarities between this action and the consequences of "Bloody Sunday" in Northern Ireland two hundred years later. When Paine heard the news in Philadelphia he was shocked and angered. He wrote, "When the country, into which I had just set my foot, was set on fire about my ears, it was time to stir." And stir he did, by writing a series of politically inflammatory articles for *The Pennsylvania Magazine*. But Aitken did not share Paine's passionately held views and their collaboration came to an end.

Nevertheless, the tide of revolution was rising. In September 1775, angered by the bloody conflict at Bunker Hill, Paine wrote a pamphlet called *Plain Truth*, later to be re-titled *Common Sense*. On 10th January 1776 *Common Sense,* printed and stitched together, and priced at two shillings, was, as Paine later remarked, "turned upon the world like an orphan to shift for itself".

Pamphlets were the accepted method of imparting news, views and comment, and *Common Sense* soon outpaced all others in terms of sales and demand. No other pamphlet published in America had ever caused such widespread interest. During the spring and summer of 1776 copies poured off the presses in a never-ending stream. It is estimated that in just a few months 150,000 copies were sold. Whilst Paine may have been preaching to the converted, he had the gift of imparting a sense of urgency in his writing and articulating what many had never dared to mention, namely "independence". He attacked monarchical government and the alleged virtues of the British parliament and urged the establishment of a republican constitution.

The pamphlet proved hugely popular, although the number of people who were converted to the cause of

Ships and Sealing Wax

independence as a result is unknown. Thomas Jefferson's historic Declaration of Independence on 4th July 1776 was not written by Paine, but his contribution to initiating public debate about independence was as enormous as it is indisputable.

Thrilled by these events, Tom volunteered for military service. Joining a ragtag band of Pennsylvania citizens he became secretary to the group's commander, General Daniel Roberdeau. Throughout the autumn and into the winter of 1776 Paine wrote a series of eyewitness accounts of the early Revolutionary skirmishes. Although the Continental Army was ill-equipped and poorly organized, Paine remained convinced that his political writing in the *Pennsylvania Journal* could invigorate the war effort and inspire faith in the Revolution.

His next publication, *The American Crisis*, was a turning point. This essay was to be among his most famous, and is sometimes considered to be one of the best pieces of political writing in the English language. Published a week before Christmas 1776, it was, like most of his writing of this period, written to be read aloud to people either unable to read for themselves or unfamiliar with books or pamphlets.

On Christmas Day General Washington ordered the text of *The American Crisis* to be read to his soldiers waiting to cross the Delaware River and attack the British forces camped at Trenton. Paine's famous words immediately passed into folklore and have been quoted on countless occasions since:

> "These are the times that try men's souls: The summer soldier and the sunshine patriot will, in this crisis, shrink from the service of their country; but he

that stands it now, deserves the love and thanks of man and woman [....] the harder the conflict, the more glorious the triumph."

The following day the enemy, mainly thousands of Hessian mercenaries, was defeated and the Revolutionary movement had taken a decisive step towards achieving independence for America.

The following month Paine was recommended by John Adams, one of the most influential Founding Fathers of the United States, for the post of Secretary to the Continental Congress's Committee for Foreign Affairs. But, as on previous occasions, he was not prepared to temper his outspoken views. Living up to his principled commitment to open government, he felt it necessary to call into question the behaviour and hypocrisies of Congress itself. This was his undoing, and early in 1779 he was forced to resign. He remained close to George Washington but his financial position remained precarious, and when the war came to an end he had to campaign to obtain recompense from the government.

Without a role in the new republic, Tom became increasingly restless and left for Europe in 1787. For the next four years he divided his time between Britain and France, busied himself designing an iron bridge, and tried to find financial backing for this innovative project. His passion, however, was again sparked by revolution, this time in France. Angered by the philosopher Edmund Burke, who had strongly supported the American Revolution but now condemned events across the Channel, Paine responded by writing his most influential work, the *Rights of Man*. In this he urged political rights for all men because of their natural

Ships and Sealing Wax

equality in the sight of God. All forms of hereditary government, including the British constitution, were condemned because they were based on farce or force. Only a democratic republic could be trusted to protect the equal political rights of all men.

Accused of sedition and libel, Paine was hounded out of Britain and went to live in France, where he became a French citizen. Here his support for the moderate republicans—he opposed the execution of Louis XVI—made him a target for the leaders of the Reign of Terror, and he was thrown into the Luxembourg prison. It was only an extraordinary twist of fate which saved him from losing his head to the guillotine.

Whilst incarcerated, Paine embarked on another important work, *The Age of Reason*. In this he declared that nature was the only form of divine revelation, and that God had established a uniform, eternal order throughout creation. He rejected Christianity and denied that the Bible was the revealed word of God. The bitterness of Paine's attack ensured that he made more enemies, and although he was welcomed into the new National Convention in Paris, and was co-author of the French Constitution in 1792, his time in France had finally come to an end. He returned to America in October 1802. His *The Rights of Man* and *The Age of Reason* are still bestsellers today.

Increasingly neglected and ostracized, his last years were marked by poverty, poor health and alcoholism. When he died in New York at the age of 72 he was virtually an outcast, a pauper, and only five people attended his funeral. Since he refused to acknowledge that Jesus was the son God, even on his deathbed, he could not be buried in consecrated ground and was laid to rest in a small corner of the farm he had been given at New Rochelle, thirty miles from New York. This had

Roger Paine

been a gift in 1784 from New York City's Legislative in recognition of his "contribution to the freedom, sovereignty and independence of the United States".

President Barrack Obama recognized these same qualities when he quoted, in his inaugural address on 20th January 2009, words written by Paine in *The American Crisis* and read by General Washington to his troops camped by the Delaware River in 1776 at the very lowest point of the Revolutionary War: "Let it be told to the future world [...] that in the depth of winter, when nothing but hope and virtue could survive [...] that the city and the country, alarmed at one common danger, came forth to meet it." The President of the USA continued, "America, in the face of our common dangers, in this winter of our hardship, let us remember these timeless words."

Some years after Paine's funeral, William Cobbett, the radical parliamentary reformer and a long-time admirer of Paine, dug up his bones with the intention of returning them to Britain to give him a heroic burial on his native soil. But the bones were still amongst Cobbett's effects when he died twenty years later. There is no confirmation about what subsequently happened to them, although there have been various claims to having discovered parts of Paine's remains, such as his skull and right hand. A bust of Thomas Paine is in the Hall of Fame of Great Americans in Bronx Community College. In addition to his statue in Thetford, Norfolk, there are ones of him in the Parc Montsouris in Paris, and in Morristown and Bordentown, New Jersey.

An oil painting of Tom Paine, by the artist Julian Bell, is permanently displayed in a niche in the brick wall of Lewes' old market tower. Paine is depicted with the streets of eighteenth century Lewes behind him, and beyond his

Ships and Sealing Wax

outstretched left arm—surely a symbol of his uncompromising and unshakeable convictions—the River Seine can be seen flowing seawards from Paris where the Bastille is burning; and, beyond that, across a vividly blue Atlantic ocean, is the outline of the eastern seaboard of America. "My country," he wrote in *The Rights of Man*, "is the world."

Hero or villain? Patriot or traitor? Revolutionary or radical? Popular journalist or political commentator? Rabble-rouser or erudite philosopher? Barrack-room lawyer or literary genius? The answer is probably that, at different times to different people, Thomas Paine was all of these—an epitaph which he might, over two hundred years after his death and in spite of his reputation for confrontation and argument, be happy to accept.

Chapter 69

GERMAN TROOPS IN BEXHILL-ON-SEA

At first glance "German Troops In Bexhill-on-Sea" might be thought to be a headline from an edition of the Daily Mail in 1940, or perhaps the title for a forgotten episode of *Dad's Army*. However, it is historically accurate and describes a period in Bexhill-on-Sea's history of which the town is justifiably proud. Over the centuries, the counties of Kent and Sussex have become familiar with being on the front line in Britain's conflicts with France and Germany. This was especially evident in 1804 when Napoleon Bonaparte was assembling his invasion fleet across the Channel, in Boulogne.

At that time soldiers had been stationed in Bexhill for several years and were building the defensive Martello towers, which remain a landmark feature of the local coastline. But it was an event in Germany which had a longer-lasting effect on the East Sussex town. In 1803 the French Army invaded and occupied the Electorate (or province) of Hanover in Germany. At the Convention of the Elbe, signed on 5 July 1803, the Electorate was formally dissolved and the Elector's army disbanded. As Hanover was then the domain of King George III of England, his seventh son, Adolfus Frederick, Duke of Cambridge, was Viceroy there. However, having been unable to obtain sufficient support to continue fighting against the French, the Duke returned to Britain.

Accompanied by several of his senior officers, he sought volunteers from his Hanoverian troops to form a separate corps in the British Army, to be known as the The King's German Regiment. Despite an initial poor response, the enthusiasm of a young Scottish army officer, later Major General Sir Colin Halkett, with assistance from Colonel Johann Friedrich von Decken, soon resulted in a steady flow of officers and other ranks of the former Hanoverian Army arriving in England. Initially this was a mixed group, mounted, infantry and artillery, and on 19 December 1803 the regiment was renamed The King's German Legion (KGL). Although it never fought autonomously, the Legion achieved the distinction of being the only German troops to fight without interruption against the French during the Napoleonic Wars.

The KGL's main infantry and artillery depot was sited at Bexhill. The cavalry was garrisoned at Weymouth in Dorset. At that time Bexhill was little more than a large village with a population of around 2,000, centred on the parish church of St Peter's high on the Downs overlooking the sea. The area is now referred to as Old Town. It is not difficult to imagine the impact several thousand German troops had on the village when they arrived in ever-increasing numbers throughout 1804. With no housing facilities for more than a handful of officers, the troops initially lived in tents, then in simple wooden huts with straw roofs.

Roger Paine

In the memoirs of Colonel Baron Christian von Ompteda, who became Commanding Officer of the Battalion, he records "October 11th 1804. Violent storm and pouring rain last night and all day today. The ground where our camp is, bad anyway, is now a morass and the present quarters are bad for the men. Beginning to build huts." By the middle of the following year the barracks stretched over twenty-five acres between Belle Hill, Chantry Lane and what is now London Road, with the parade ground running east to west. To make a firm marching surface the KGL infantrymen brought shingles and flints up from the beaches.

The infantry barracks was built on the north side of the hill, so that any French ships lurking off the coast would be unable to detect it. A further fifteen acres at the top of Bexhill Down was used for artillery and cavalry barracks. Today, although the timber- and brick-built barrack buildings—several of which were sold off and advertised in the Sussex Advertiser in 1822—are long since demolished, the military legacy remains in the names of Barrack Road, and Barrack—or Old Town—Park, on the site of the former parade ground. There was also a military cemetery in Barrack Road, where hundreds of army personnel and their dependents, including at least 152 members of the KGL, were buried. A plaque, in English and German, has been erected in their memory

When Nelson's victory at the Battle of Trafalgar in October 1805 removed the very real threat of invasion, the KGL, whose numbers in the Bexhill barracks had risen to 3,570 in the same year, began ten years of distinguished active service in other theatres of the war. These included Walcheren 1809; Mediterranean and Sicily 1808-1811; and the Peninsula and Southern France 1808-1814. By the summer of 1814 the KGL cavalry was making its way across

Ships and Sealing Wax

France to the Low Countries, whilst the KGL infantry was regrouping in Bexhill. But once Napoleon had escaped from Elba in March 1815, head-on conflict was inevitable and the Duke of Wellington, as Commander in Chief of the Army, was thankful to call upon the seasoned soldiers of the KGL, who now numbered more than 5,000. Bexhill was reported as buzzing with excitement!

Confrontation came at the Battle of Waterloo on 18 June 1815 in which the KGL, together with several other newly raised Hanoverian regiments, formed almost half the British army. The 2nd (Rifles) Light Infantry Battalion of the KGL, commanded by Major George Baring, was given the key strategic role of defending the farmhouse at La Haye Sainte, situated midway between the two opposing armies drawn up for battle. It was to be the KGL's finest hour.

A contemporary report noted: Wellington posted a detachment of the King's German Legion, who were well-known for their reliability, at La Haye Sainte where they spent an uncomfortable night in wet conditions. At 3 pm the next day, the French attacked, but this was repulsed. The KGL who were by then very short of ammunition, made repeated requests for more supplies, but to no avail. After a valiant attempt to fight off the invading French, the KGL's ammunition was exhausted and the farm had to be abandoned. The French broke in and fierce fighting took place with bayonets and rifle butts. Only 41 out of the 350 Hanoverians reached the crossroads.

Major Baring twice had horses killed under him, but despite being severely wounded managed to escape. For exemplary leadership in defence of the farmhouse he was honoured and promoted as Major-General Baron von Baring. Colonel Ompteda, in command of the 2nd KGL

Roger Paine

Brigade, attacked the French cavalry as they left La Haye Sainte, but was struck down and killed. His bravery earned special mention in Wellington's report of the battle. Napoleon, after his capture and imprisonment on St Helena, was later to swear that the stubborn resistance met at La Haye Sainte denied his troops the opportunity to break the British line and ultimately cost him victory. A plaque commemorating the KGL's heroic action, dedicated in 1998, can be seen today on the farmhouse, which was rebuilt immediately after the battle.

The Battle of Waterloo ended the KGL's time in Bexhill. It returned to Hanover with more than a few Sussex brides. Today, apart from the areas in Bexhill already mentioned, Old Town has changed little in appearance from the time when the KGL was garrisoned there. Examples of buildings that remain as they were over two hundred years ago include several substantial houses in the High Street, and, on Church Street, the weather-boarded cottages, and the former hotel The Bell Inn, a popular public house frequented by the soldiers.

St Peter's Church, founded in Saxon times, was often used by the Hanoverians, and their harmonious singing was reported as enhancing the services. Church registers for baptisms, marriages and burials between the years 1804 and 1814 record over three hundred names, highlighting the presence of the KGL. For example: Hendrich Frederich Christian Ludwig, son of Hendrich and Catherina Saltz, baptized on 7th May 1805; Henry Horsgest, infant, buried on 21st January 1808; Philip Holtzerman, married to Mary Ann Pumphrey on 6th January 1812. (The bride was the daughter of Thomas Pumphrey, a customs officer, who lived in Old Town; her new husband was killed leading reinforcements

Ships and Sealing Wax

into La Haye Sainte.);. Such intimate details of life and death amongst the German troops in Bexhill tell their own poignant stories.

The distinguished novelist Thomas Hardy often spent hours researching accounts of the Napoleonic Wars to add authenticity to his writings. In 1890 he wrote a short novel, *The Melancholy Hussar of the German Legion*, which tells the story of a young woman who falls in love with a good-looking corporal of the KGL, a tale which struck a chord with publishers at the time. In contrast to some, Hardy did not regard the stationing of foreign mercenaries on British soil as an oppressive threat to national liberty, but instead saw the KGL as a benign experiment in transnational bonding. It would appear that, in Bexhill at least, he was correct.

This remarkable episode in local history is kept alive today by the Bexhill Hanoverian Study Group, who since 1989 has researched the KGL and its unique association with the town. New members are always welcome.

Chapter 70

NELSON'S COLUMN

There are very few people, either British or from abroad, who when in London will not be aware of Nelson's Column in Trafalgar Square. The Square, a must-visit for every tourist—equivalent to St Peter's in Rome, Times Square in New York, or Tiananmen Square in Beijing—is named after the Battle of Trafalgar, which took place in 1805. Nelson's Column was built there to commemorate Admiral Lord Nelson who commanded the British fleet against the French and Spanish and was mortally wounded in the battle. But despite the column's central position in the capital, it is worth recalling its own history and other facts associated with this world-famous landmark.

It was not until 1838, a generation after the battle and two monarchs later, that a group of peers, MPs and other gentry, following much debate and controversy, formed a committee and finally decided there should be a permanent monument to Nelson, funded by public subscription, in the nation's capital. It was agreed that an appropriate site would be Trafalgar Square in front of the newly completed National Gallery. Agreement was also reached on the type of memorial

Ships and Sealing Wax

that should be erected. Several column monuments to Nelson had already been built in the United Kingdom, including the Nelson Monument on Glasgow Green, erected in 1806, a year after his death; Nelson's Pillar, erected in Dublin in 1808—destroyed by republican extremists in 1966; the Nelson Tower on Calton Hill in Edinburgh, completed in 1815; and the Britannia Monument, also called the Norfolk Naval Pillar, in Great Yarmouth, finished in 1819.

A competition for designs was held, with an estimated budget of £20,000-£30,000. The deadline for submissions was 31 January 1839. A sub-committee, headed by the Duke of Wellington, chose the winning entry, a Corinthian column surmounted by a statue of Nelson and flanked by four sculpted lions, with flights of steps leading up to the pedestal of the column, designed by William Railton. No doubt influenced by other column monuments, several entrants submitted similar schemes. However, criticism of the organisation of the competition caused it to be rerun, although Railton, having re-submitted a slightly revised design, was again declared the winner. The committee also stipulated that the statue of Nelson should be made by Edward Hodges Baily, runner-up in the first competition.

Railton's initial plan was for a gigantic column 203 feet (62m) high, including the base and the statue. But this was reduced by 33 feet in height to 170 feet (52m), with a pillar of 98 feet (30m), because of concerns over stability. Originally the base was to have been of granite and the fluted pillar made of Craigleith sandstone, but before construction began it was decided that both should be made of granite. The granite came in solid blocks quarried at Foggintor on Dartmoor.

Roger Paine

The Corinthian capital at the top, on which stands Nelson's statue, was modelled by architectural sculptor C H Smith, whose design is based on a column capital from the Temple of Mars Ultor in Rome. It was made of bronze elements from cannon salvaged from the wreck of HMS *Royal George* and cast at the Woolwich Arsenal foundry. The bronze pieces, which weigh 900 lbs (410kg), are fixed to the column by three large belts of metal lying in grooves in the stone.

The statue of Nelson, an inch over 8ft (5.5m) high, in full dress uniform with his left hand on his sword leaning against a coil of heavy mooring rope and his back to the sea, was, as stipulated by the Memorial Committee, sculpted by E H Baily, RA. It is made from three pieces of sandstone donated by the Duke of Buccleuch, former chairman of the Committee, from his own quarries.

Excavations for the brick foundations of the column began in July 1840. On 30 September, the first granite stone of the column was laid by Charles Davison Scott, Secretary of the Memorial Committee and son of Nelson's Secretary, Reverend John Scott, who had been at the Admiral's side on board HMS *Victory* at the Battle of Trafalgar. A contemporary report records that the ceremony was conducted "in a private manner, owing to the noblemen and gentlemen comprising the committee being absent from town". Construction of the monument, by contractors Grissell and Peto, progressed slowly, and the stonework, ready for installation of the statue, was not completed until three years later in November 1843. On 23rd October of that year 14 of the stonemasons who had been working on the column ate a meal on the platform just before Nelson's statue was placed on it.

Ships and Sealing Wax

The following year, as only £20,485 had been donated by public subscription, the Committee announced it had run out of money. The Government, in the form of the Department of Environment (known then as the Office of Woods and Forests) was forced to take over the project, which was too far advanced for it to fail. Echoes of the Government stepping in to take responsibility for security at the London Olympic Games in 2012 when private contractors failed to deliver on time.

Although the column and statue had been completed, work on installation of the four bronze reliefs on the base of the pedestal did not begin until 1849, six years later. The first to be put in place was the depiction of the Death of Nelson by John Edward Carew, which was installed on the south side, facing Whitehall. This was followed early the next year by Willam F Woodington's relief of the Battle of the Nile on the north face. The Bombardment of Copenhagen, by John Ternouth, on the east face of the plinth, was the next to be installed. This was followed early the following year by the Battle of Cape St Vincent, by Musgrave Watson and William F Woodington, on the west face.

Carew's relief was cast by Adams, Christie and Co of Rotherhithe. The other three were cast by Moore, Fressange and Moore, but their last relief became the subject of legal action when it was discovered the bronze used had been adulterated with iron. The partners in the company were jailed for fraud. It was finally put in place in May 1854.

The four identical sculpted bronze lions were not added until 1867, nearly a quarter of a century after the column was completed. Originally it had been intended they should be made of granite by sculptor John Graham Lough, but after a disagreement with Railton, and unwilling to work under his restrictions, Lough turned down the commission. The sculpted lions were eventually designed by Sir Edwin Landseer, one of the most celebrated and versatile artists of the Victorian Age, in collaboration with Italian-born French sculptor Baron Carlo Marochetti. It is believed the design may have been influenced by the lions which adorn the Szechenyl Chain Bridge over the River Danube in Budapest, installed there six years earlier. Landseer is known to have used a dead lion as his model, but the beast became so decomposed that it was almost impossible for him to work in his studio and neighbours called the police to investigate the cause of the stench. Landseer was paid £6,000 for his work, Marochetti £11,000.

The column was refurbished in 2006, during which time it was covered in scaffolding from top to bottom. Steam cleaning was used, together with mild abrasives, to avoid harm to the bronze and stone work. The work was funded by Zurich Financial Services who advertised on the scaffolding for the duration of the work. The column has also been climbed and used for publicity purposes. In 1979 it was climbed by Ed Drummond to draw attention to the Anti-Apartheid Movement and in May 2003 stuntman Gary Connery parachuted from the top of the column to publicise repressive Chinese policies in Tibet.

But probably the most remarkable story in the column's history was the scheme revealed in official German correspondence after World War II, dating from when Adolf Hitler was poised to invade England in 1940: "As Nelson's Column represents for England a symbol of British naval might and world domination, it would be an impressive way of underlining the German Victory if the Nelson Column were to be transferred to Berlin." It was a statement by

Ships and Sealing Wax

Britain's enemy which underlined the iconic importance of this landmark memorial. When you next find yourself in Trafalgar Square spend a moment to look upwards and give silent thanks that Nelson's Column, erected 174 years ago, is still there.

Chapter 71

TWENTY-FIRST CENTURY PRESS GANG

In 1932, the popular comedian and ukulele player George Formby released the song "Chinese Laundry Blues":

*Now Mr Lu was a laundry man in a shop with an
    old green door,*
*He'll iron all day your linen away, he really makes
    me sore.*
*He's lost his heart to a Chinese girl and his
    laundry's all gone wrong,*
*All day he'll flirt and scorch your shirt, that's why
    I'm singing this song,*
*Oh, Mr Wu, what shall I do, I'm feeling kind of
    Limehouse Chinese Laundry Blues!*

But it was probably only a timely coincidence that Chinese laundrymen should start serving in HM ships six years later, when the Royal Navy had a large number of ships stationed in the Far East, many based in Wei-Hei-Wei, once a British concession in mainland China, as well as in the Crown Colony of Hong Kong—although this tradition has

Ships and Sealing Wax

been said to date back even further, to the turn of the century and the halcyon days of the China Fleet. What is certainly true, however, and to the surprise of many nearly eighty years later, is that Chinese laundrymen are still serving in naval ships.

For many years they were known as "Unofficials", because officially they did not exist. But it is hard to imagine now how the Royal Navy could function without them. Officially, they have nowhere to sleep, and because naval architects have never included berths for them, they usually sleep on the deck or in bunks unofficially rigged up in the ship's laundry. Some have also been known to sleep on an ironing board or table. Officially, too, they are not fed. Unofficially, they barter with the ships' cooks for pieces of chicken or bags of rice or vegetables.

These are Her Majesty's Chinese laundrymen. They do the scrubbing and boiling, the pressing, ironing and mending that makes the Royal Navy the most immaculately turned out of the British armed forces. Next time you watch a warship entering harbour, with her crew in starched white uniforms standing smartly to attention along the upper deck, you will know who has been working overtime!

The laundrymen, although unofficial, go to war too. Many served in the Korean War, and there are ships with them on board serving in the Gulf and Mediterranean today. It is not that they want to savour the thrill of battle. On the contrary, when "Action Stations" is sounded they usually prefer to be shut in the laundry until the all-clear goes. That does not always make them safe, though. Two Chinese laundrymen were killed in the Falklands conflict. Lai Chi Keung was one of the 21 crew killed in early May 1982 when an Exocet missile hit HMS *Sheffield*. Kyo Ben Kuo was among the 24 casualties when HMS *Coventry* was bombed to the bottom of the South Atlantic. But like serving RN personnel they are entitled to receive campaign medals for the conflicts in which their ships are involved.

When Hong Kong was returned to China in 1997, it was thought this could spell the end for the "Unofficials", as the majority of Chinese laundrymen traditionally have their homes there. But because of their loyalty and proven effectiveness it came as no surprise that they have now become recognised as "official" and are employees of WLS, World Laundry Services, which is a direct descendant of the old system. This firm, run by the Shao family, who were previously private contractors who made their own arrangements directly with ships' captains, now provides laundrymen to all RN ships. So whilst the arrangements have, to a certain extent, been formalised and the days of free-lance contractors are over, their working practices have not changed and business is thriving.

Smaller RN ships, such as frigates and destroyers, normally have two laundrymen. Bigger ships, like the amphibious assault ships HMS *Albion* and HMS *Bulwark*, with crews of 325 officers and men and 400 embarked Royal Marines, will probably have up to 12 laundrymen and sometimes a Chinese tailor, always known as "Sew-Sew", as well. It is not difficult to appreciate that providing rapid turnaround laundry services to ships' crews, both male and female, is a profitable occupation.

In past times, ships' captains, like colonial grandees in the heyday of the Empire, had a special relationship with their own ship's "Unofficials". They always had their washing done for free, although it was recognised that at Chinese New Year there would be a small celebration on board when the

Ships and Sealing Wax

captain would hand over little red envelopes traditionally containing crisp new banknotes, equivalent financially to the cost of the laundry he had received during the past 12 months. Each would raise a glass of brandy to toast one another with "Happy New Year" and "Kung Hei Fat Choy". It is the only day in the year when the machines and spin dryers in the ship's laundry fall silent.

In one ship, the captain was so keen to get the protocol right he commissioned a decorated cake for his laundrymen. The chef had carefully picked out in red icing on the cake the four Chinese characters printed in gold on the little red envelopes. The moment of presentation arrived. The Captain proudly pointed out to Number One Boy—as the senior laundryman, irrespective of his age, is always known—the New Year greeting on the cake. "Kung Hei Fat Choy!" he exclaimed. The Chinese laundryman couldn't hide his amusement: "Ah, no, sir," he said. "That say 'Hong Kong Shanghai Bank'."

When ships are undergoing maintenance in home ports for a short period it is not cost-effective for the Chinese laundrymen to return to Hong Kong. One officer recalled that he was eating ashore in a Chinese restaurant in Plymouth with fellow officers from his ship and was surprised to find himself being handed the menu and, at the same time, receiving a polite reminder from the waiter, "Your laundry now leady for collection, sir." It was one of the ship's laundrymen moonlighting in the "Bamboo Garden".

On another occasion, when a retired admiral was Governor of Gibraltar, an RN ship arrived in port and the governor's limousine and driver were waiting on the jetty. A crowd had collected to watch the Navy's top brass disembark. After a while, a Chinese man in t-shirt and linen jacket was seen making his way down the gangway. He walked straight up to the limo and was whisked away. It was the ship's laundry and tailoring contractor. The governor wanted to renew acquaintance with his Number One Boy from a former ship and be measured for a new suit.

Irrespective of their status, either today or in years gone by, Chinese laundrymen (some positions are now filled by ex-Gurkhas from Nepal) have a proud tradition. George Formby's "Chinese Laundry Blues" shows no sign of affecting the laundrymen who continue to serve as the Royal Navy's own twenty-first century press gang.

Chapter 72

SUNKEN GOLD

Gold in sunken ships has been the subject of legend and imagination for centuries. From the days of Spanish galleons, with their holds crammed with gold bars or silver dollars, to the first 50 years of the last century when the world witnessed the greatest movement of gold by sea ever known. The sheer value of the gold moved by sea during this period dwarfs that of all other movements of gold, either before or since. One North Atlantic convoy in early 1940 shipped more gold (in excess of 700 tons) out of Europe and across to Canada and the USA than was ever moved from Spanish America to Spain during the most productive decade, 1590 to 1600. When viewed in this light it should come as no surprise to discover gold being taken by sea to Russia at the height of World War I in 1916.

HMS *Hampshire*, a 10,850-ton armoured cruiser, had just taken part in the historic Battle of Jutland on 31 May 1916. The following day she was instructed to sail to Scapa Flow in the Orkneys, to take the British Secretary of State for War, Lord Kitchener of Khartoum, on a top secret diplomatic mission to Russia, the intention being to stiffen the Tsar's resolve and offer him support in maintaining the Anglo-Russian alliance.

Lord Kitchener left London by train on the evening of 4 June. He was accompanied by a small group of officials and servants. He arrived at Thurso and crossed to Scapa Flow the following morning. He had lunch with Admiral Sir John Jellicoe, Commander in Chief of the Grand Fleet, aboard the latter's flagship, the battleship HMS *Iron Duke*, and then transferred to the *Hampshire*. For Kitchener to reach St Petersburg it was intended the ship should sail through the waters to the north of Scotland, along the coast of Norway well inside the Arctic Circle, then south past the Kola Peninsula and through the White Sea to the port of Archangel.

A fierce gale was blowing from the north-east and HMS *Hampshire*'s captain, Captain Herbert Savill, suggested to Lord Kitchener that he might postpone his voyage for 24 hours. But Kitchener refused to accept any delay. It was then that the British naval authorities made the first of a series of fatal blunders. In view of the gale they decided to re-route the *Hampshire* up the west coast of Orkney rather than the east coast, the more usual route for warships. It was thought that the ship would be able to make better speed up the west coast, which was on the lee side of the storm and therefore safer from attack by enemy submarines. But the cruiser had hardly left the shelter of Scapa Flow before the storm swung round from the northeast to the northwest, as was often the case in that area.

HMS *Hampshire*, built in 1903, had a top speed of 22 knots but was still able to make 18 knots, even in adverse weather conditions. The two destroyers assigned as escorts,

Ships and Sealing Wax

HMS *Unity* and HMS *Victor*, soon fell behind. The Hampshire reduced speed to 15 knots and headed in closer to land. But the destroyers continued to drop back. At 6.30 pm Captain Savill signalled to the destroyers to return to port. If they could not keep up, there was little point in them continuing. It was a fateful decision.

At 7.40 pm the *Hampshire* was about one and a half miles offshore between Marwick Head and the Brough of Birsay, one of the bleakest and most remote corners of Great Britain. Even though it was summer, it was still a bitterly cold, grey evening. Suddenly, above the screaming of the gale, a massive explosion rocked the ship amidships in the vicinity of the boiler room. The ship immediately took a sharp list to starboard. Hundreds of men were trapped below decks. Within 20 minutes *Hampshire* had gone down bows first. The appalling weather and the speed of the sinking made it impossible to launch any boats except for three Carley life-floats. But they were grossly overcrowded with about 70 men on each raft. Seven hundred thirty-seven lives were lost. Only 12 crew members survived.

None of the seven members of Kitchener's mission were survivors. According to those who did survive, Kitchener was last seen standing calmly on the bridge deck in the company of Captain Savill, apparently making no effort to save himself. A fortune-teller had once told him that he would die by water. The number of fatalities made the sinking of HMS *Hampshire* one of the worst naval disasters of the war.

No distress signal was transmitted by wireless from the sinking ship, not even a rocket was fired. But an islander, Joe Angus, a gunner in the Orkney Territorial Forces, noticed a cruiser in distress from his lookout at Birsay. But unfortunately the first telegraphic message did not include the information that the *Hampshire* had sunk. This omission caused a delay of two hours, until 9.45 pm. Long-lasting bitterness was engendered among the islanders when the naval authorities forbade them to launch the island's own lifeboat to assist in the rescue. Instructions were also issued that all islanders should remain indoors, away from the cliffs in the vicinity of the disaster.

The reason for this high-handed action probably had something to do with establishing proper security for Kitchener in the event of him being rescued. Or could it have been that news had leaked out that the ship was carrying gold bullion to Russia as a "sweetener" for that country's continued support in the war against Germany? But the effect of the ban was counterproductive. Those lucky enough to reach the shore alive were deprived of help in scaling the cliffs. This belated obsession with security, for whatever reason, probably only served to increase the death toll.

Reaction to the news of Kitchener's death was one of stunned disbelief. Not least because he was identified, more than any other, as the leader of the war effort. The fact that his body was never recovered gave credence to all sorts of rumours. The idea of sabotage was later fuelled by the publication of a number of books in Germany after the end of the war. The pressure became so intense that in 1926, ten years after the sinking, the government was forced to issue a White Paper, revealing the findings of an internal enquiry. The intention was to lay the entire *Hampshire* controversy to rest. The obvious question was why, in view of the sinking of another ship only three days before the *Hampshire* sailed, the cruiser was routed through the same area without it being first swept for mines. The answer given was that the mines laid there were actually the result of a mistake by the

Ships and Sealing Wax

German minelaying submarine U-75, rather than evidence of British naval complacency. It was not a convincing argument and it did not put an end to the *Hampshire* mystery.

The next time the ill-fated cruiser made headlines was the result of an article in the *Berliner Zeitung* in 1933, which carried a report referring to the salvage of £60,000 (worth £3.7m today) of gold bars from the *Hampshire*'s strong room. Overnight the ship was transformed from a warship lost due to enemy action into a sunken treasure ship. There was such an outbreak of world interest that the Admiralty once again was obliged to issue a statement. It claimed it knew nothing of the salvage but stated that HMS *Hampshire* remained the property of HM Government and could not be touched without permission.

Some light was thrown on the mystery of the treasure by a book published in the early 1950s (*Unlocking Adventure* by Charles Courtney), which described in detail a highly secretive salvage attempt in 1933 by a group of divers working out of a ship called *KSR* from Kiel in Germany. This included the report of a strange ship in the vicinity of Marwick Head during long periods in the summer of 1933, which was corroborated by local observers on the island. However, it seems that the operation had to be aborted after a serious accident which resulted in one diver being killed and two others taken to hospital. The author of the book also believed that there was in total £2m (worth £128m today) of gold destined for Russia, and that the primary purpose of Kitchener's secret mission was to provide the Tsar with financial support.

The book included details of a group of international financiers who backed the operation. These included the German industrialist Gustav Krupp and the notorious arms dealer Sir Basil Zaharoff. The latter was well known for his interest in undersea salvage and had already been part of a syndicate which two years earlier had financed a highly successful recovery of gold from the SS *Egypt*, the P&O liner which sank off Ushant in 1922, at a similar depth of some 70 metres (230 feet). Zaharoff frequently spoke about the gold he believed was on board the *Hampshire*. He was also extremely good friends with the British Prime Minister, David Lloyd George, who had previously entrusted him with carrying out a number of quasi-diplomatic missions that were too clandestine to be entrusted to the usual channels. If anyone was in a position to know what was in *Hampshire's* strongroom it would have been Zaharoff.

Nevertheless, one of the problems with the *Hampshire* gold is that the government, the Bank of England and the Ministry of Defence have consistently denied any knowledge of gold being on board, although that is not quite the same thing as saying there is no gold. It could also be explained by the government being anxious not to disturb the wreck because of its status as a war grave.

In the 1980s a German-based underwater film maker was accused by the Ministry of Defense of illicitly removing items from the wreck. Although this operation did not reveal any gold, it did confirm that the damage to the ship's hull was consistent with the explosion of a mine. The latest undersea exploration of the wreck, which lies upside down, commenced in May 2016 as part of a collaborative project between ORCA Marine, the University of the Highlands & Islands and Seatronics. The expedition's objective, under licence from the Ministry of Defence, was to undertake a detailed survey of the wreck using stills and video photography and the latest underwater photogrammetry

Ships and Sealing Wax

techniques. This information will be used to compile a detailed written and visual survey report. There has been no mention, however, of a search for gold.

Despite the dryly scientific explanation of the current survey, rumours of gold persist. One theory is that if there was gold on board the *Hampshire* it was not British gold, but privately owned Russian gold held by the Romanov family in Britain and urgently required in Russia because of the state of emergency which surrounded the royal family as a result of the impending Bolshevik revolution.

One thing that remains certain is that gold and wrecked ships never cease to fire the imagination. One hundred years on, *Hampshire*'s gold still poses several unanswered questions and continues to exert enduring fascination.

Chapter 73

WOMEN AND CHILDREN FIRST!

HMS *Birkenhead* was one of the first iron-hulled warships built for the Royal Navy. Although laid down as the frigate HMS *Vulcan* at John Laird's shipyard on the River Mersey in 1845, she was given the name of the town where she was built soon afterwards. Two 564-horsepower (421 Kw) steam engines drove a pair of 20-foot (6-metre) paddle wheels and two masts were rigged with sails as a brig. At 210 feet (64m) long, with a beam of 38 feet (11m) she was larger than any of her class built previously. Her armament was originally intended to be two 96-pounder pivot guns, one forward and one aft, and four 68-pounder broadside guns.

Launched on 30th December 1845 by the Marchioness of Westminster, the ship achieved an average speed of 12 knots when she undertook her maiden voyage in 1846. However, the *Birkenhead* was never commissioned as a frigate for while under construction it was decided that warships would be more efficient if their main propulsion was by propellers rather than paddle wheels, so she was converted to a troop ship. In 1851, as part of her conversion, a forecastle and poop deck were added to increase accommodation. A third mast

Ships and Sealing Wax

was added to change her sail plan to that of a barquentine. Although she never served as a warship, she was faster and more comfortable than any of the wooden sail-driven troopships. It was a period of monumental change for the Royal Navy, as sail rapidly gave way to steam. The *Birkenhead*, with her enormous steam-driven paddle wheels and large area of sail, had the best of both worlds.

Under the command of Captain Robert Salmond RN, HM Troopship *Birkenhead* sailed from Portsmouth in January 1852. She was taking troops to fight in the Frontier War (also called the Kaffir War) against the Xhosa tribes in South Africa. The troops included Fusiliers, Highlanders, Lancers, Foresters, Rifles, Green Jackets and other assorted regiments of the British Army. On 5th January she picked up more troops at Queenstown in Ireland as well as several officers' wives and families. On 23rd February 1852 she docked briefly in Simonstown, near Cape Town, before sailing two days later for the last leg of the voyage to Algoa Bay. In order to make the best possible speed, Captain Salmond decided to sail close to the South African coast, setting a course that for the most part was within three miles of the shore. Using her paddle wheels the ship maintained a steady speed of nearly nine knots. As she left False Bay and headed east the sea was calm and the night clear.

In the early hours of 26th February, approaching a rocky outcrop appropriately named Danger Point, some 150 miles from Capetown, disaster struck. With the exception of the duty watch everyone was asleep. The leadsman had just called "Sounding 12 fathoms" when the *Birkenhead* rammed an uncharted rock. Twenty feet to port or starboard and she would have missed it. Her churning paddle wheels drove her on with such force that the rock sliced into the hull, ripping open the compartment between the engine room and the forepeak. Water flooded into the forward compartment of the lower troop deck, filling it instantly. Trapped in their hammocks hundreds of soldiers drowned where they slept.

Captain Salmond, awakened by the shock of the impact, rushed on deck and ordered that the anchor be dropped, the boats lowered and a turn astern be given by the engines. However, this proved to be a fatal decision for as the ship slowly went astern from the rock, the sea rushed into the large gash made by the collision so that the ship struck the rock again, buckling the plates of the forward bilge and ripping open the bulkheads. The sea poured into the engine room, flooding the boilers in a great cloud of steam and drowning most of the stokers. Her stern rose in the air and the tall smokestack came crashing down, killing the men working to free another of the boats as the bow broke away.

All the troops were ordered to muster into ranks by regiment and await their officers' orders. Lieutenant Colonel Alexander Seton of the 74th Highlanders, the senior regimental officer on board, was requested by Captain Salmond "to be kind enough to preserve order and silence among the men". Captain Salmond then gave the order to abandon ship. Only two cutters and a gig were launched into the water. The women and children were embarked in one of the cutters which lay alongside. Seton pleaded with the men to stand fast where they were. "The cutter with the women and children will be swamped. I implore you not to do this thing and I ask you to stand fast". Other officers took up the cry, urging the men to remain where they were for the sake of the women and children. And they did.

Private (later Colour Sergeant) Boyden of the 2nd Queen's Regiment recalled that during the time Colonel

Ships and Sealing Wax

Seton's orders were being carried out "one could have heard a pin drop and that he walked about the deck giving his orders with as much coolness and presence of mind as if he were on parade." As the deck tilted and the water rose the soldiers stood fast. Within minutes the *Birkenhead* had broken her back and those in the bowels of the ship died instantly. The soldiers on deck must have known what would happen. Yet still they did not move.

The ship sank barely twenty-five minutes after striking the rock. Over the next twelve hours some of the survivors managed to swim two miles to the shore, often hanging on to pieces of the wreck to stay afloat. But most drowned, or died of exposure, or were taken by sharks. A letter from Lieutenant F J Girardot, 43rd Regiment, to his father, dated 1 March 1852, told the graphic story:

> I remained on the wreck until she went down and then struck out for some pieces of wood that were on the water and started for land about two miles off. I was in the water for about five hours, as the shore was so rocky and the surf ran so high a great many were lost trying to land. Nearly all those that took to the water without their clothes were taken by sharks. Hundreds of them were all around us and I saw men taken by them close to me. But as I had on a flannel shirt and trousers they preferred the others.
>
> At the court martial into the loss of the ship, held some five months later, one of the few officers to survive, Captain Edward Wright of the 91st Argyllshire Regiment, explained:
>
> The order and regularity that prevailed on board from the moment the ship struck till she totally disappeared, far exceeded anything I had thought

could be effected by the best discipline, and it is the more to be wondered at seeing that most of the soldiers were but a short time in the service. Everyone did as he was directed and there was not a murmur or cry amongst them until the ship made her final plunge —all received their orders and carried them out as if they were embarking instead of going to the bottom.

It was this account of the heroic tragedy that was later ordered to be read aloud to every regiment in the service of Frederick William IV of Prussia.

The next morning, the schooner *Lioness* found one of the cutters and after saving the occupants made her way to the scene of the disaster. She discovered 40 people still clinging to the rigging. Of the 643 people believed to have been on board, 450 perished. The survivors included 113 soldiers, 6 Royal Marines, 54 seamen and the seven women and thirteen children. The sinking of the *Birkenhead* was the earliest maritime disaster in which the phrase "women and children first" was used. It later became standard procedure in relation to the evacuation of sinking ships.

In 1893, the poet Rudyard Kipling immortalised the action, or "the Birkenhead drill", as it became known, in "Soldier an' Sailor Too":

Their work was done when it 'adn't begun, they was
younger nor me an' you
Their choice it was plain between drownin' in 'eaps
an' bein' mopped by the screw,
So they stood an' was still to the Birken'ead drill,
soldier an' sailor too.

Chapter 74

ROCK OF AGES

The southernmost point of the European continent is on British soil. From Europa Point, Gibraltar, you look across the intervening Mediterranean to another continent, Africa. Shrouded in heavy cloud, the tops of the Rif Mountains are clearly visible and you can almost touch that vast country, with its history of Romans and Moors, a land of souks and Foreign Legion forts, and, beyond them, thousands upon thousands of miles of deserts, mountains, rivers and jungles.

Gibraltar is unique. A colonial, pink pinprick on the world map, where British traditions live on. The Union Flag flies over public buildings, there is daily changing of the guard in front of the Governor's residence, pints of best bitter are pulled in the pubs, and streets and buildings have British names—The Convent, North Bastion, Flank Battery. English is spoken everywhere and the currency is pounds and pence.

It was in 1704 that Admiral Rooke, in command of the British fleet engaged in attempting to find a foothold in the Mediterranean, to stop the French advance through Spain, landed a force of 18,000 British and Dutch marines on Gibraltar to overcome the local Spanish garrison. The significance of this still remains with the Royal Marines, who retain "Gibraltar" as their sole battle honour. The Rock of Gibraltar has remained British throughout the intervening years, and has come to symbolize strength and solidarity. Spain, however, has not relinquished its desire to take back the Rock, and to this day the British presence there remains an ongoing irritant to the Spanish government.

The last unsuccessful attempt to recapture the Rock was in 1779, when for four years the town was besieged. It was during this time that a labyrinth of interconnecting tunnels and galleries was blasted out in order to make gun emplacements. Today, many are open to the public, as are the huge caves and a further 30 miles of honeycombed tunnels, which are testimony to the Rock's geological and prehistoric heritage, although do not be tempted to stray from marked routes. The story is told of two British officers who decided to settle an argument with a duel and went into the tunnels—their bodies were never found.

Emerge from the caves blinking in the dazzling sunshine to walk, or drive, around the Rock to Catalan Bay on the eastern side, where the gentle blue waters of the Mediterranean lap sandy beaches. The chill of the tunnels, with their timeless history and colonial ghosts, is soon a memory. Now the massive limestone vastness of Gibraltar itself towers above, rising almost vertically into a cloudless sky.

The Rock is just over one and a half miles long and about three-quarters of a mile wide, so everywhere is within easy walking distance. Return westward towards the airport built on the isthmus of land which separates Gibraltar from the

Ships and Sealing Wax

Spanish mainland and the border town of La Linea. The main runway runs down the middle, and as your aircraft comes into land its wingtips seem almost to brush the Rock. It makes for a spectacular landing! A new airport terminal building, and a less-congested road system to take traffic into the town, is due to open later this year.

Main Street runs almost the length of the town and as a VAT-free shopper's paradise must rank as one of the most fascinating shopping thoroughfares in Europe. Some of the shops remain Indian-owned, a legacy of the days when "Gib" was one of the refueling ports for troopships en route to the far-flung British Empire. They retain the feeling of a huge bazaar with jewelry, glassware, leather goods, silks and cashmeres being some of the best bargains, especially if you enjoy haggling over the price, although if you take a few steps more down a side-alley very often you will find the same thing even cheaper!

No visit to Gibraltar is complete without a visit to the top of the Rock. To fully appreciate the sheer immensity of this huge geographical feature, and to understand its landmark status as it presides loftily over the narrow strait which separates the Mediterranean from the Atlantic, there is no better way than to walk. As you go higher up the zig-zagging road, a spectacular panorama slowly unfolds beneath you. Once again its garrison history is ever-present. Behind stone walls bedecked in bougainvillea and vines are solid colonial villas built for dockyard superintendents, engineer captains and surveyors of works. There is the Admiral's Residence and the Old Naval Hospital where the nurses' quarters have now been converted into residential apartments.

A compulsory stop is the Apes' Den, home to the famous Gibraltar apes. These Barbary apes are the only species of monkey in the whole of Europe which is allowed to roam entirely free. Legend says they arrived from the Atlas Mountains in North Africa by scuttling along a secret tunnel that runs beneath the sea, adding that if ever the apes leave the Rock it will cease to be British. Feeding the apes is strictly forbidden, but they are often mischievous and can retaliate to well-meaning stroking by nipping fingers or pulling hair.

The views from the top of the Rock are breathtaking. Cruise liners in the bay look like toys in the bath. Spain, shrouded in heat-haze, stretches away to the right before curving around to the Costa del Sol. Immediately beyond on the horizon is the Moroccan coast and the ancient Arab port of Tangier. Return to the noise and bustle of the town by cable car and the silence as you descend from the coolness of nearly 2,000 feet above sea-level is eerie.

Not far from the cable car terminus is the Trafalgar Cemetery, where in 1805 many of the British sailors who were killed at the Battle of Trafalgar off the Spanish coast were brought ashore. Nelson's flagship and other damaged vessels dropped anchor in nearby Rosia Bay. Not all of those buried here were killed outright in the battle as indicated by the evocative headstones to those who died later of their wounds. Beautifully tended, the cemetery is a haven of tranquillity and once again reinforces Gibraltar's quintessential Englishness.

Finally, take a trip across the bay to the ferry port of Algeciras in Spain, frontier town and Europe's stopping-off point for Africa. With open-air cafés, a harbour crowded with motor launches, globe-circling yachts and the traditional Straits' fishing boats, it has a raffish, cosmopolitan population of travellers and traders. Relax with a chilled fino

Ships and Sealing Wax

sherry outside a waterfront bodega and look across towards Gibraltar.

The top of the Rock is shrouded with the "levante", or "his hat" as the locals call it. At certain times of the year this unusual cloud formation covers Gibraltar, stretching out horizontally, blocking the sun, seemingly impaled on the pinnacles of the Rock. Although a meteorological oddity, it is also a reassuring sight. You may be in Spain with a drink from nearby Jerez in your hand but your heart is in England, just a mile or two away—a tiny corner of the British Empire on which the sun has not yet set.

About The Author

Roger Paine

Roger Paine has been writing stories, poems and plays from an early age. When sixteen years old he left school in Leicester, England, and joined the Royal Navy. Over the next twenty-eight years he rose from ordinary sailor in bell-bottom trousers to gold-laced senior officer in the rank of Commander. He served in a wide variety of ships, from aircraft carriers, various frigates and destroyers, to mine counter-measures vessels, a tank-landing ship and the navy's ice patrol ship. He visited ports in nearly every country in the world.

Now a full-time writer, he regularly contributes book reviews, theatre reviews and features to magazines, newspapers and journals on subjects ranging from maritime topics to historic village churches and well-known poets. Many of these articles are included in this his third book.

He lives in an eighteenth century cottage, crammed with books, paintings and naval memorabilia, on the edge of a medieval churchyard in rural Sussex.

If You Enjoyed This Book

Please write a review.

This is important to the author and helps to get the word out to others

Visit

PENMORE PRESS

www.penmorepress.com

All Penmore Press books are available directly through our website, amazon.com, Barnes and Noble and Nook, Sony Reader, Apple iTunes, Kobo books and via leading bookshops across the United States, Canada, the UK, Australia and Europe.

BLUE WATER
SCARLET TIDE

BY

JOHN DANIELSKI

It's the summer of 1814, and Captain Thomas Pennywhistle of the Royal Marines is fighting in a New World war that should never have started, a war where the old rules of engagement do not apply. Here, runaway slaves are your best source of intelligence, treachery is commonplace, and rough justice is the best one can hope to meet—or mete out. The Americans are fiercely determined to defend their new nation and the Great Experiment of the Republic; British Admiral George Cockburn is resolved to exact revenge for the burning of York, and so the war drags on. Thanks to Pennywhistle's ingenuity, observant mind, and military discipline, a British strike force penetrates the critically strategic region of the Chesapeake Bay. But this fight isn't just being waged by soldiers, and the collateral damage to innocents tears at Pennywhistle's heart.

As his past catches up with him, Pennywhistle must decide what is worth fighting for, and what is worth refusing to kill for —especially when he meets his opposite number on the wrong side of a pistol.

PENMORE PRESS
www.penmorepress.com

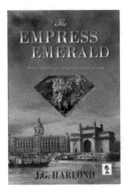

THE EMPRESS EMERALD

BY

JANE HARLOND

Stolen: A child, a priceless jewel, and an identity

Abandoned as a child in a Bombay orphanage, Leo Kazan's life takes an unanticipated turn when he becomes the protégé of Sir Lionel Pinecoffin, the city's District Political Officer in Bombay. Under Pinecoffin's tutelage, the boy, adept at learning languages and theft, is trained as a spy and becomes immersed in international espionage, revolutionary politics, and diamond smuggling. In 1918, during a visit to London, he has a brief but memorable affair with a young English woman Davina Dymond in London before leaving for Russia.

Separated, their lives take different turns. As he matures Leo begins to question his family history, seeking to uncover the truth about his parents. A pregnant Davina is married off and exiled to Spain, where she gives birth to Leo's daughter. They are fated to meet again in Gibraltar in 1936, their love rekindled. But a new war plunges Europe into crisis, the Spanish Civil War tearing them apart, leaving, Leo and Davina in a fight to reclaim their lives and their love amid the violent storms of war.

PENMORE PRESS
www.penmorepress.com

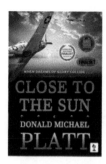

The Close to the Sun

by

Donald Michael Platt

WWII Fighter pilots, Air war over Europe. German Fighter aces, American Fighter Aces, War in Europe . Air War over Russia. German politics during WWII.

Close to the Sun follows the lives of fighter pilots during the Second World War. As a boy, Hank Milroy from Wyoming idealized the gallant exploits of WWI fighter aces. Karl, Fürst von Pfalz-Teuffelreich, aspires to surpass his father's 49 Luftsiegen. Seth Braham falls in love with flying during an air show at San Francisco's Chrissy Field.

The young men encounter friends, rivals, and exceptional women. Braxton Mobley, the hotshot, wants to outscore every man in the air force. Texas tomboy Catherine "Winty" McCabe is as good a flyer as any man. Princess Maria-Xenia, a stateless White Russian, works for the Abwehr, German Intelligence. Elfriede Wohlman is a frontline nurse with a dangerous secret. Miriam Keramopoulos is the girl from Brooklyn with a voice that will take her places.

Once the United States enter the war, Hank, Brax, and Seth experience the exhilaration of aerial combat and acedom during the unromantic reality of combat losses, tedious bomber escort, strafing runs, and the firebombing of entire cities. As one of the hated aristocrats, Karl is in as much danger from Nazis as he is from enemy fighter pilots, as he and his colleagues desperately try to stem the overwhelming tide as the war turns against Germany. Callous political decisions, disastrous mistakes, and horrific atrocities they witness at the end of WWII put a dark spin on all their dreams of glory.

PENMORE PRESS
www.penmorepress.com

Historical fiction and nonfiction
Paperback available for order on line
and as Ebook with all major distributers

Penmore Press

Challenging, Intriguing, Adventurous, Historical and Imaginative

www.penmorepress.com

Lightning Source UK Ltd.
Milton Keynes UK
UKHW02f2021130318
319351UK00001B/34/P